INSIDE THE *KAISHA*

Demystifying Japanese Business Behavior

Noboru Yoshimura
Philip Anderson

Harvard Business School Press
Boston, Massachusetts

Library of Congress Cataloging-in-Publication Data
Yoshimura, Noboru.
  Inside the Kaisha : demystifying Japanese business
behavior / Noboru Yoshimura, Philip Anderson.
    p.   cm.
  Includes index.
  ISBN 0-87584-415-4 (alk. paper)
  1. Industrial management—Japan. 2. Corporate
culture—Japan. 3. National characteristics,
Japanese.
I. Anderson, Philip. II. Title.
HD70.J3Y596 1997
302.3'5'0952—DC20   96-9274
                                                        CIP

The paper used in this publication meets the
requirements of the American National Standard for
Permanence of Paper for Printed Library Materials
Z39.49-1984

CONTENTS

PREFACE

As an undergraduate majoring in intercultural communication, Noboru Yoshimura read dozens of books on Japanese culture. He came to feel that there was something wrong with the literature, especially those works that viewed Japanese business behavior as an outgrowth of the nation's culture. Could one really explain how Japanese companies operate by focusing on the country's agricultural origins, Zen Buddhism, gardening, tea ceremonies, and the like, he wondered? With strong support from Dr. Edward Stewart, a professor at International Christian University who was Noboru's adviser, he wrote a senior thesis on Japanese corporate culture, trying to penetrate the deeper mechanisms underlying the behavior of Japanese employees and their companies.

After graduating, Noboru became a salaryman. His five-year experience at Sumitomo Bank persuaded him that only a corporate insider could tell what was really going on within a large Japanese company (a *kaisha*), because accurate information there is restricted to insiders. In fact, he learned, the possession of information is one of the keys differentiating insiders from outsiders.

Noboru liked Sumitomo Bank a great deal. He respected his colleagues and learned from them how to do business in a Japanese company and with Japanese customers. However, over time he became convinced that the deeply ingrained organizational mechanisms of Japanese companies like Sumitomo, which made them so competitive in a continuously growing economy, would keep them from adapting, should a discontinuous change slow growth dramatically. He began preparing to attend an American business school, so that he could take care of himself instead of relying on the company, and in 1991 he accepted Cornell University's offer of admission to its Johnson Graduate School of Management. When he told his boss about his decision, his superior warned him that he would lose his job security but helped Noboru make a smooth departure. Noboru was grateful, for he knew of other salarymen who had had very bad experiences once they announced they were leaving their *kaisha*.

By the time Noboru entered Cornell, Phil Anderson had been teaching MBA courses in strategy and organizational behavior for nearly five years. Determined to employ a global perspective from the start, Phil had read hundreds of books and articles on Japanese management. Drawing from mainstream organizational behavior research on Japan, he passed on to his students the canon that has become familiar to many American managers and educators. He depicted Japanese firms as "theory Z" organizations, where culture is the primary control mechanism; described the paramount importance of harmony to Japanese; and discussed the Japanese sense of obligation, the *ringi* system, and the art of *nemawashi*. He emphasized the necessity of establishing personal relationships through social interactions, working through personal networks and go-betweens, recruiting and socializing graduates of elite universities, framing loosely drawn contracts subject to mutual good-faith renegotiation, and so on.

The results surprised Phil. His Western students nodded wisely; the Japanese management literature told a coherent, if somewhat exotic, story. His Japanese students, however, reacted quite differently. Their response reminded him of the way an Englishman he once knew reacted upon hearing one American tourist trying to describe the game of cricket to another: some of the basic ideas were right, some were misconceptions or outdated, but what was missing was a feel for the spirit of the enterprise. Puzzled, Phil spent a good deal of time talking with Japanese students and continued reading more about Japan. After several years of gathering feedback and tinkering, he realized that he was simply reaching a higher state of confusion.

Consequently, in the fall of 1991, he invited all the Japanese MBAs at Cornell (over thirty at the time) to a meeting, to help him finally get the story of Japanese management right. He handed out key sections of two well-known books (*Theory Z* by William Ouchi and *The Art of Japanese Management* by Richard Tanner Pascale and Anthony Athos); described the basic outline of what he had been teaching; and asked for criticism, suggestions, and help. How, he asked them, could he best describe Japanese management and organization to non-Japanese? Each of the Japanese MBAs was an experienced white-collar employee of a Japanese corporation, and collectively their experience covered the majority of Japan's major industrial sectors. This group, Phil was sure, would show him what his intensive literature search had missed.

The result of this meeting disconcerted him even more. The Japanese students told him that, although Americans writing about Japanese management seemed to grasp a kernel of truth, much of what Western experts write about Japanese management and companies is distorted, or uncharacteristic of their generation, or somewhat correct while overlooking important exceptions. Furthermore, the students were unable to agree among themselves on a small set of accurate insights that could be conveyed to non-Japanese. When one MBA described a "rule" of Japanese business behavior, another would respond, "Sometimes, but in *my* company . . ." followed by an exception, qualification, or contradiction. Where was the famous Japanese consensus? If he couldn't get the Japanese students to agree on what lies at the core of Japanese management, how could he teach anything useful to non-Japanese, Phil wondered?

Noboru was one of the first-year students at the meeting, and afterward he stopped by Phil's office. They talked, and he gave the puzzled professor a section of his undergraduate thesis that argued that Japanese culture has no fixed ideological core, so the Japanese model of appropriate behavior depends on the context one perceives. Phil began to understand why the Japanese students could not agree on a unified description of Japanese management. Their perceptions of corporate culture were shaped by the context of what happened in their individual companies, not by the common experience of being Japanese.

So few ever worked for more than one company in a career that the company, not the country, established the context.

Phil and Noboru talked throughout the fall about the forces driving *kaisha* and salarymen. Phil concluded that, without an insider's perspective, one would never understand what is really going on inside a *kaisha*, so he asked Noboru to help conduct a session on Japanese corporate culture for the required first-year organizational behavior course in the winter. Unfortunately, the Western students were actually unsettled, not enlightened, by their classmate's presentation. Noboru explained why one couldn't reduce Japanese corporate culture to a consistent set of universal principles; this proved less palatable to non-Japanese than the standard Japanese management story. Phil felt that what Noboru had to say was very important but concluded that it could not be conveyed to a Western audience by means of a short seminar.

How, Phil wondered, did the Japanese themselves learn the right way to behave in business? Noboru explained that Japanese generally do not learn by reducing things to a framework of consistent principles. They learn by emulating a behavioral model, typically a mentor or teacher. By observing how the role model behaves and by imitating his actions,* the learner implicitly comes to an understanding of the right thing to do in a given context. Consequently, Phil became convinced that the best way to convey an understanding of Japanese business behavior to Westerners would be to put them in the shoes of a typical Japanese middle manager. A series of vignettes explained from an insider's point of view might, in Japanese fashion, help Westerners approach a more intuitive understanding of how Japanese organizations really work. And that would require a book.

The kernel of the book was Noboru's experience and insights, but we set out to interview dozens of Japanese middle managers, in order to test our ideas, generate new ones, and

---

*In Japanese business, managers are almost always men, thus "he" and "his" are used throughout.

gather illustrations. Young Japanese managers very rarely change companies, and they tend to socialize after work with their colleagues, not with contemporaries from other firms. Consequently, few realize how many similarities there are among *kaisha*.[1] Instead, what is more apparent to them are the differences between companies and industries. Our research convinced us more and more that, beneath the uniquenesses that company men perceive, there are many organizational mechanisms common to most large Japanese enterprises. We also became more firmly convinced that these organizational mechanisms, not Japan's national cultural identity, govern business behavior, largely because we observed how much the behavior of Japanese managers changes when they join Western-owned firms.

This book is addressed to non-Japanese who want to understand the Japanese business insider's point of view, but its invitation to look at the world through the eyes of Japanese middle managers must be accompanied by a warning. A foreigner who discusses any set of ideas about Japanese corporate culture with Japanese business associates is quite likely to hear that, at their companies, things work in a somewhat unique way. It is very Japanese to distrust ideologies, to focus on the exceptions when moving from abstract concepts to concrete cases. How and why this happens is a central theme of this book. Expect to be told about exceptions. Then use the intuitions developed from reading this book to analyze what mechanisms might account for them. In other words, treat this volume more like an auto repair manual than like a cookbook. The ideas presented here are not recipes for reconstructing "typical" Japanese business behavior; instead, they are tools for diagnosing why things happen in Japanese companies that consistently puzzle outsiders.

The uniqueness of this book is that it represents a collaboration between a midlevel Japanese manager and an American steeped in Western ways of thinking about organizational behavior. We believe it is the first to provide the reader with an insider's view of how Japanese managers put business behavior in context. It could not have been written without the gracious cooperation of the more than fifty Japanese executives we interviewed. Because their companies would prefer them to remain anonymous, we cannot thank them individually; however, we trust that their frankness will help Westerners achieve a deeper understanding of the way their contemporaries think. We would particularly like to thank Noboru's countrymen in the Johnson Graduate School of Management's class of 1993 for their unstinting support of his efforts.

This book would not exist without the patience, support, and advice of Carol Franco, Marjorie Williams, and Nicola Foster of the Harvard Business School Press. The tireless staff of the Amos Tuck School's Feldberg Library helped us greatly with our research, and Cindy Wiegand's careful proofreading saved us from any number of errors. Noboru thanks the many professors and lecturers at Cornell's Johnson School who strongly enhanced his academic knowledge. Phil extends special thanks to Professor James Brian Quinn for his invaluable review of the manuscript.

Above all, we are grateful to our families. Noboru's wife, Yumi, supported his decision to leave Sumitomo Bank and had their first child, Yui, in Ithaca during their years at Cornell. Phil's contribution to this book was made possible only because his wife, Rhonda, and his son, Spencer, put up with a lot of overtime. To all of them, we dedicate this work.

Why Another Book on Japanese Management?

Japan bewilders the outsider. Every foreign culture seems strange to those not raised in it, but usually one's confusion diminishes with time and experience. What is unique about Japan is the overwhelming sense of *contradiction* that non-Japanese come to feel. The Japanese seem capable of reacting in completely different ways on different occasions when faced with similar situations. The title of a famous book about Japan, Ruth Benedict's *The Chrysanthemum and the Sword,* is meant to suggest this tension of opposites.

Japan polarizes even those who know it best. Some love the country, emphasizing the courtesy, politeness, and human concern they find there. Others hate it, focusing on the rudeness, arrogance, and lack of respect Japanese can exhibit. Writer Jonathan Rauch, after his first visit to Japan in 1990, captured the feelings of both newcomers and old Japan hands when he wrote:

> Like my friend the editorial writer, who always said "I feel strongly both ways," I was divided against myself for a long time. It was, as I have mentioned, not that my picture of Japan was confused or chaotic, particularly; it was that there were two of them and they didn't fit together.[1]

What this book is about

This book is written for the reader who is frustrated because reading more and more about Japan doesn't help him or her unravel many puzzles of Japanese business behavior. Why are Japanese businessmen and their companies so difficult to peg? Why do they seem simultaneously shortsighted, yet oriented toward the long term; egalitarian, yet locked into rigid hierarchies; allies one month and competitors the next? For most Western businesspeople, lack of *information* is less of a problem than is lack of *insight* into why Japanese companies behave in ways that seem inconsistent or contradictory.

This book is not a primer on Japan. You'll find little here about national culture, history, etiquette, or industrial organization. We aren't writing about tea ceremonies, values carried down from the *samurai* warrior past, how deeply to bow when meeting a Japanese counterpart, or the alliances of interlocking ownership and trade that dominate Japan's economy. Business behavior in the large Japanese corporation is our focus. To understand it, we focus on *sarariiman,* or *salarymen,* the white-collar middle managers whose beliefs and socialization are the bedrock of large Japanese enterprises. This book's purpose is to help the reader develop a feel for the way salarymen think. By understanding the world of the salaryman, one can vastly improve one's ability to understand how Japanese organizations will behave as suppliers, customers, allies, and rivals in commerce.

The salaryman's view

In this book, you will experience Japanese business life by looking over the shoulder of a salaryman. Our aim is to help the Western reader understand why things that seem contradictory to non-Japanese make perfect sense to the prototypical Japanese middle manager. The first author of this book, Noboru Yoshimura, is a salaryman, a middle manager at Bankers Trust in Tokyo. To provide richer insight into the world of the salaryman, Noboru supplemented his experience and our archival research by conducting over fifty interviews with salarymen from a wide variety of firms and industries. Using a standard open-ended initial interview with many follow-up conversations, we have recorded hundreds of hours of conversations with middle managers throughout Japan and overseas. We believe that no other book has yet brought to Westerners the experience of salarymen *as told to one of their own*. The people we interviewed talked to us because we asked them questions that few had ever raised with them before. Salarymen tend to talk in company-specific terms with their colleagues and customers, or to share technical information with counterparts from different industries (for example, comparing quality control practices). We asked them to discuss what lies behind a specific set of behaviors that seem to puzzle non-Japanese, and many talked with us for hours simply because they found it refreshing to think about these issues.

Our pool of respondents was nothing like a random sample; to gain access, we relied on our network of contacts and on introductions arranged by friends. Our aim is not to provide the reader with a portrait of a representative Japanese manager, if one exists. We focused heavily on the kind of manager Westerners are likely to encounter in business: a white-collar male who has graduated from a prestigious university and works for one of Japan's largest manufacturing or service firms. These people do not necessarily represent their counterparts in small to medium-sized Japanese enterprises, and they do not necessarily represent ordinary workers, in either production or clerical jobs.

Why is this group so influential? Large Japanese companies provide models that other firms follow when transacting with Westerners, and these organizations operate via a system Japanese scholars have termed "middle-up-down" management.[2] An elite body of midlevel managers initiates and directs most projects in these enterprises. Virtually all senior Japanese managers in large corporations come from this pool, rising to the top only after decades of socialization in the way of the salaryman. The people we interviewed are the quintessential insiders in the Japanese system.

A number of barriers make it difficult for non-Japanese to

understand the insider's point of view. One is language: those who read about Japan or interview Japanese in English tend to lose subtle nuances. Even foreigners who speak and write Japanese fluently run up against the second barrier: Japanese are often reluctant to talk to outsiders about how they really think and feel. For example, many Japanese managers have told American writers that they are team oriented and that maintaining harmony is an absolute priority. Is this always true? Releasing little information to the outside world is characteristic of Japanese organizations. Japanese managers do not necessarily lie when they talk to outsiders. However, they strongly wish to keep "in the family" tales about the fierce power struggles that really happen inside firms.

A third, perhaps even more formidable barrier is that Japanese do not analyze themselves in a logical way, as Westerners might. The Japanese attitude toward the world is existential; being Japanese is something that is experienced, not analyzed. One learns it through years of modeling one's behavior on a series of prototypes. Being Japanese is so natural that Japanese do not consider ethnicity part of their identity, as many Americans do. Hence Japanese writers require the model of another culture with which to compare themselves. Japanese are always interested in books written about them by foreigners, and when they write books on Japan, they inevitably measure themselves against the yardstick of a foreign culture. Consequently, it is difficult to understand the mechanisms driving Japanese behavior when the rules don't fit into another culture's way of thinking.

How this book is different

What's new here? What differentiates this from other books on Japanese management and companies? Japanese writers have, of course, attempted to analyze the behavior of their countrymen. Some fine books have been written by authors such as Takeo Doi and Takie Sugiyama Lebra, who try to develop a consistent framework that explains Japanese psychology. However, such works are aimed principally at providing an alternative to Western psychological theories (such as those of Freud) and are written primarily for social scientists. Books by Westerners and Japanese that attempt to describe Japanese *business* behavior tend to fall into three categories.

The best known are *nihonjinron,* books that try to explain Japanese corporate culture by relating it to Japanese culture in general. These works introduce the reader to such distinctive features of Japanese society as its agricultural origins, gardens, methods of flower arrangement, *kabuki* theater, and so on. However, references to such nonbusiness traditions as tea ceremonies and Shinto religious rituals often confuse American readers because they have no idea what these customs actually mean. A typical conclusion of *nihonjinron* is that Japanese culture is unique, rooted in an idiosyncratic history, and hard for non-Japanese to understand.[3] Gaining insight into the mores and history of other cultures is admirably broadening, but such books do not discern why Japanese managers or corporations act as they do.

A second category is the travelogue/memoir, usually written by longtime residents or those who have just visited Japan. Such works typically relate a series of vignettes, connected by the author's attempt to make sense of the Japanese. Many books in this category offer sharp observations and important tidbits of advice on how to do business in Japan. What they lack is insight into everyday business life from an insider's perspective. Their authors often miss what insiders see as the crucial elements in their vignettes and focus too much on aspects of Japanese conduct that are unusual to them. You can learn a lot from reading a few of these works, but you will not understand how business behavior that seems puzzling to outsiders is produced.

The third type includes purely strategic or structural analyses of Japanese business. Such works analyze the operations and organizations of Japanese companies in classic business school fashion, comparing and contrasting Japanese and Western practice. These analyses provide useful facts but do not explain the real and invisible mechanisms of Japanese business. To illustrate, the large volume of writing on quality circles has described Japanese QC practice in excruciating detail without really illuminating why a concept invented and first applied in the United States has succeeded so well in Japan and so poorly in America.

Our aim, and the distinctive feature of this book, is to help the non-Japanese reader demystify Japanese business behavior. We do this by highlighting aspects of that behavior that often confuse Westerners, illustrating these puzzles, then describing from the salaryman's point of view what accounts for the conundrum Westerners perceive. We can't reduce Japanese commercial conduct to a recipe or a set of rules. However, we do highlight and apply four recurring themes that will help the reader build his or her intuition and develop useful rules of thumb for grasping the salaryman's perspective. Briefly, they are the importance of context, learning from behavioral models, the drive to avoid embarrassment, and the primacy of process over content. These recurring themes are summarized in chapter 2, and we return to them again and again to help the reader unravel a variety of puzzles in Japanese commercial behavior. Our aim is to help you develop an intuition for the salaryman's world. We have chosen to do this by emulating the way salarymen themselves develop a feeling for appropriate behavior. Like a junior salaryman learning a company's culture, you will see a limited number of motifs played out in different ways across a variety of settings throughout this book.

Why Japanese business behavior is puzzling

As we noted earlier, Japan usually strikes outsiders as more problematic with experience; familiarity with the culture seldom diminishes the perception that Japanese behavior is a study in contradictions. Outsiders usually cope with this pervasive sense of contradiction in one of three ways.

The simplest is to assume that the Japanese have no moral compass and change the rules to suit themselves whenever it is to their advantage. The sense that the Japanese are duplicitous and that their promises cannot be relied on underlies the worst of Western Japan-bashing. Yet the Japanese have one of the most highly developed senses of shame found in any culture and place an extreme emphasis on "doing the right thing." It is dysfunctional to presume that Japanese people are inherently faithless and two-faced. Reasoning from such a simplistic view does not allow one to predict what a Japanese businessman will do in a given situation.

The second way of coping starts with the presumption that Japanese society is complicated, so that to understand it one must divine all of its rules and their many exceptions. A surprising number of Western executives have stuffed their brains with an encyclopedic volume of Japanese etiquette and customs. We contend that, at best, this approach allows one to avoid the most common mistakes that foreigners make when doing business in Japan. It does not, however, provide real insight into *why* the Japanese behave as they do, because it does not reflect the way Japanese themselves learn appropriate behavior. Japanese themselves do not simply follow a set of rules that tell them what to do in a given situation; thus it is not possible to reverse-engineer the rule set into a flowchart for predicting Japanese behavior.

A third way of coping is supposedly rooted in Eastern philosophy. A number of Westerners argue that the Japanese overcome paradox by embracing contradiction and rejecting outmoded Western notions of consistency and logic. They urge non-Japanese to do the same. There is a germ of truth in this view, but it overlooks the fact that, among themselves, Japanese almost always can provide a coherent explanation of why they took a particular action. Japanese businessmen do not strive to conduct themselves in contradictory or inconsistent ways; on the contrary, few things are more important in Japan than predictable, reliable behavior.

Dichotomies are common in Japan—for example, the distinction between *uchi* and *soto* (inside and outside) or *omote* and *ura* (what appears on the surface versus what is hidden). But societies around the world also organize their social thought and their institutions in patterns of opposites.[4] An anthropologist would not call Japan a particularly dual society. For example, the Zoroastrian religion exemplifies a genuinely dualistic set of values—it holds that all things in the universe are made up of a mixture of darkness and light, the two fundamental forces that are in eternal opposition. Similarly, Chinese Taoism teaches that everything we observe is made up of both yin and yang combined. Some societies even organize themselves into two divisions so that a person from one "moiety" can only take a spouse from the other.

Taoist philosophy that insists on the coexistence of opposites is not the underpinning of Japanese business behavior, and embracing contradiction will not help outsiders understand goings-on within the *kaisha* (Japanese corporation). Japanese dualism has a different basis. The noted psychologist Takeo Doi contends that it is Japanese patterns of cognition that are dual. By this, he means that Japanese can accept two interpretations of one event as reality by adopting different perspectives.[5] What resolves the contradictions apparent to outsiders is a shift in perspective.

We contend that the fundamental reason why Japanese behavior seems contradictory is that outsiders see Japanese behaving very differently in "similar" situations, whereas Japanese view the situations as being quite different. Correct conduct depends completely on the situation. To understand what to do, a Japanese asks, "What is the context?" Behavior that seems wildly inconsistent to others is perfectly congruous to Japanese because context governs, not principles.

A book aimed at an academic audience would try to lay out a theoretical framework explaining how a Japanese manager decides what the context of an action is. We have chosen to take a different approach, because Japanese themselves have a different way of learning what they should do in a given situation. As we will describe in chapter 2, Japanese learn by studying and emulating models of behavior. Their approach is inductive, not deductive. Through proper socialization, one comes to understand appropriate behavior given a context.

Why organizational context is so important

When Westerners learn inductively from models, they often look to the behavior of particular exemplary individuals. Americans have eagerly absorbed business books by famous executives such as Andy Grove of Intel or Lee Iacocca of Chrysler, and entrepreneurs such as Donald Trump and Sam Walton. Several well-known Japanese CEOs, such as Akio Morita of Sony or Konosuke Matsushita of Matsushita Corporation, have written about their own careers, using their stories as a vehicle for reflecting on Japanese management principles. Why should a Western audience read a middle manager's book about his peers, instead of looking to Japan's business leaders to impart an insider's perspective?

One of the salarymen we interviewed expressed the thoughts of most by telling us that top management in Japan is like *mikoshi*. In Japan's Shinto religion, *mikoshi* is a decorated wooden box in which God is placed. During a traditional Japanese festival, people carry *mikoshi* throughout the town. *Mikoshi* is respected and influential; after all, it contains the essence of God. However, it does not go anywhere by itself—it goes where the townspeople carry it. So it is with Japanese top managers. To the outside world, it is imperative that they look like leaders, but they must go where the consensus of middle management wants them to go, express what middle managers want them to say, and function principally to help middle managers achieve communal goals.

To understand a *kaisha,* you must see its behavior as a function much more of organizational culture than of its top managers' will. Senior managers are far more than figureheads—most are extremely good organizational politicians or they would not have reached the top. Decades of rising through the ranks have honed their ability to sense, express, and embody the sentiment of the managerial communities they head. Some Japanese executives are strong and visionary leaders, but their very rarity heightens their profile. A Konosuke Matsushita is the exception, not the rule. Understanding the organizational context of decisions is generally far more important than understanding the views or motivations of Japan's corporate leaders.

Accordingly, we focus less on personalities here than on organizational mechanisms that drive Japanese corporate behavior. For example, if you believe that lifetime employment is a Japanese company's policy because management thinks it is the best way to maximize employee motivation, you will be surprised and upset to see the company lay off American employees just as a U.S. company would. But if you understand that lifetime employment is not a policy end in itself, but instead is the product of deeper organizational imperatives *in certain situations,* you will be able to foresee and cope with "unpredictable" Japanese actions.

When Japanese firms seemed unstoppable, it was much easier to attribute success to specific practices such as lifetime employment and to spiritual factors such as harmony and cooperation. The durability of these features in the face of very different results in the nineties suggests that they neither account for nor result from four decades of postwar economic success. For example, when a Japanese company made "patient" investments that turned out well, many experts sagely attributed the success to the long-term orientation of Japanese managers. American managers, in contrast, were lambasted as short-term thinkers pressured by their shareholders to produce rising quarterly profits and healthy cash flows. Today, virtually no Japanese analysts claim that *kaisha* executives are long-term thinkers. The country's economic slowdown in early 1990 caught most Japanese companies off guard, and an extraordinary number of them were damaged by speculative investments driven by short-term profit seeking. Had they really been blessed by extraordinary long-term vision, they would have created firms that could better have borne changes in the economy.

On the other hand, despite a few cracks in the wall, the key structural practices of large Japanese corporations have not collapsed. The media and trade associations have generated a lot of talk about Japanese corporations' abandoning the seniority system for promotion and pay, and eliminating the expectation of lifetime employment, but a sharp drop in university recruiting is the only major change that has actually been widespread. The continued existence of these institutions must depend on some organizational imperative other than economic success, because Japanese firms are unable to shake them even when top executives privately agree that they are hurting economic performance.

We would like to shift the discussion from structural practices to the behavioral mechanisms that underlie them. For instance, in our view, debating whether individual Japanese managers are long-term or short-term oriented (and whether this is good or bad in today's economic environment) is unproductive. Let us instead understand the organizational imperatives that cause individuals to appear visionary and patient, yet at the same time myopic and obsessed with immediate results. Such practices as lifetime employment and seniority-based promotion may or may not endure in an era of slow growth. They are manifestations of deeper behavioral mechanisms; understand these drivers and you have a better chance of understanding how "unpredictable" Japanese behavior will evolve in an era of change and stress.

How this book is organized

We start by describing how Japanese salarymen are socialized, beginning with their earliest educational experiences. Almost all salarymen in large corporations pass through a set of filters and experiences that lead them to one of a handful of prestigious universities. Consequently, Japanese corporations take relatively homogeneous inputs—fresh university graduates socialized in similar ways—and mold them into salarymen designed to function well in just one company's environment. Virtually all large Japanese companies manage this transformation the same way. We describe the shaping process and its consequences in chapter 1 through a composite illustration that captures the "coming of age" experiences shared by the salarymen we interviewed.

Chapter 2 is the conceptual heart of the book. Although we do not believe you can use a formula or flowchart to forecast Japanese business behavior, our interviews led us back again and again to a small number of recurring themes that help insiders make sense of a context and decide how to behave. We describe four guideposts that have helped us explain perplexing Japanese business behavior to Westerners by shedding light on the insider's perspective. We begin by introducing the critical idea of *context;* behind most apparent contradictions in Japanese business behavior lies a failure to understand the context as the Japanese see it. Next, we examine how Japanese learn appropriate behavior. Third, we explore the fundamental motivation of most Japanese: the desire to avoid social embarrassment. Fourth, we explain why to the Japanese the right process—conducting oneself with an appropriate attitude—is more important than the right outcome.

In each of the next six chapters, we focus on a particular type of puzzle that often misleads outsiders and causes them to view Japanese behavior as inconsistent and unpredictable. These include:

- Why double standards appear to apply—one for Japanese and the other for foreigners.

- Why Japanese firms appear harmonious to outsiders *despite* the widespread lack of interpersonal trust within them.

- Why Japanese firms emphasize cooperation, yet display fiercely competitive behavior.

- Why Japanese seem patient and visionary, yet extremely shortsighted at the same time.

- Why so much ambiguity coexists with fanatical attention to documentation, precision, and clear rules inside Japanese firms.

- Why Japanese firms are so egalitarian, yet so rigidly dominated by rank and hierarchy.

We conclude with a chapter that ties together these puzzles and the themes in chapter 2 by contrasting American and Japanese companies, by focusing on the experiences of a salaryman moving from a major Japanese bank to one of its principal American rivals in Tokyo. We use this illustration to convey a set of lessons that our pool of salarymen suggested we convey to Western readers. We conclude by discussing how Westerners can put some of the insights in this book to practical use in managing their relationships with Japanese enterprises.

CHAPTER ONE

The Making of a Salaryman

Freshly graduated from a top Japanese university, a fledgling salaryman is about to begin an intensive socialization process that will model for him how he is expected to behave in the company he joins. This initiation is meant to mold him into his company's man—a Toyota man or a Fuji man or a Nomura man—for life. He learns to meet the expectations of a specific company, and many of the subtle lessons he absorbs are unique to that company. For this reason, when a Westerner discusses "principles of Japanese management" with an audience of salarymen, he encounters a host of company-specific exceptions to any particular concept. Does this mean that no two Japanese managers have a comparable experience of corporate life?

Our interviews confirm that no two companies impart exactly the same lessons or ways of interpreting situations to their new middle managers. Yet the making of a salaryman is a story full of similarities that overwhelm the differences cutting across companies. Most salarymen working for large corporations absorb similar lessons and are shaped in similar ways for two reasons. First, by the time they graduate from college, they are all successful survivors of a rigid and grueling socialization process. The innate attitudes characteristic of salarymen are deeply implanted before they start their careers. Second, despite local differences, large Japanese enterprises use very similar methods to impart their values to new employees.

Consequently, this chapter will tell you the story of how a

salaryman is made by describing the experiences of a composite character we'll call "Hiro." Hiro is everyman; we have drawn snippets of his story from many individuals employed by different companies, whose tales overlap far more than they diverge. Hiro's progress through the Japanese educational system and into corporate life is meant to illustrate from an insider's perspective how a typical salaryman's mental world is shaped. Chapter 2 picks out some recurring aspects of this perspective that help explain the mechanisms that drive Hiro's behavior.

From elementary school to college

Hiro grew up in the Tokyo-Osaka corridor that contains most of Japan's population. He is the son of middle-class parents who wanted him to follow the ideal model of Japanese society, creating a context that would allow him to make a desirable life in Japan. For many years, Japanese parents have been asked in national surveys what career they wish their sons to pursue. Becoming a government official has always been their first choice; their second choice is becoming a salaryman.

Hiro's parents never sat down with him and talked about his joining a particular company. Nobody says to a child, for example, "Someday you will go to work for Mitsubishi Bank if you just do these things." His parents simply told him that he would be safe and secure if he went into a corporation. His parents knew, and Hiro picked up, that there is only one way forward, one right process to follow.

In the United States, for instance, someone can spend years pursuing his talent and interest in drawing, but during or even after college, he can change his mind and decide to go into business. There are many different paths to becoming an executive in Western societies, particularly in the United States, but this is not true of Japan. If you meet a Japanese salaryman, you know with certainty that his career did not suddenly happen; he can be a salaryman only because he has been on the right track for a long time.

The ladder starts in primary school

To join a large Japanese corporation as a junior executive, Hiro had to be a new graduate of a top-ranked Japanese college. He knew he would be disqualified immediately if he did not join a *kaisha* directly after graduation, if he attended a college outside the elite circle, or if he failed to graduate at all. To get into the right college, he had to work hard to get into a "good" high school (grades ten to twelve). A good high school is simply one with a high percentage of graduates who enter top-ranked colleges. The ticket to such a high school is a "good" junior high school (grades seven to nine), again defined as one that channels a high percentage of its graduates to good high schools.

One way to get into a good junior high school is to enter a preparatory school. Many Japanese students go to public elementary schools through the sixth grade, but some also attend private after-hours preparatory schools, which typically start in fourth grade. Admission to such preparatory schools is based on the results of an examination. In Hiro's day, the early 1970s, it was still unusual for elementary school students to attend a preparatory school. By 1985, however, 16.5 percent of them were enrolled in such schools, a figure that grew to 23.6 percent by 1993.[1] To many Japanese, it seems that the competition to enter the charmed pathway begins earlier and earlier as the years pass.

Hiro's first lesson in prep school was nonacademic. Before classes began on his first day, he remembers entering the classroom, dropping off his school bag, and leaving to run a quick errand. Upon returning, he found that his classmates had taken his bag and turned it in to a teacher, reporting that somebody they didn't know had left a bag in the room. Everyone else in the class had been together since fourth grade. Even as children, they had a strong sense of being a group, not only because they had been studying together for two years, but because they already viewed themselves as an elite, set apart from others destined to follow a different path. Hiro found himself able to keep up with them and even excel, but he never forgot the feeling that highly intelligent students who joined the race late were already treated like outsiders, even before the race officially began in junior high school.

Hiro went to extra classes four weeknights plus Saturday evenings every week for a year. Every Sunday, along with 2,000 students from different preparatory schools, he took a test, after which every student was ranked from first to last according to test score. Most children studied past midnight, believing that this was the only way to pass the extremely competitive examinations administered by elite junior high schools.

Hiro's first choice was a junior high school associated with one of the top ten high schools in Japan, ranked according to the number of students in each class admitted to Tokyo University, the apex of Japanese education. He knew exactly which schools to target because many leading Japanese magazines produce special issues ranking high schools according to the percentage of students who pass the entrance examinations of Japan's most prestigious colleges. Hiro passed the examination of his first-choice junior high school, putting him on the path to its associated high school, which spared him another grueling round of examinations after ninth grade.

Prestigious membership matters most

In his poem *Paradise Lost,* John Milton quotes Satan as saying that it is better to reign in Hell than serve in Heaven. In Japanese high schools, precisely the opposite is true. Hiro found himself near the bottom of his class of 180 throughout junior high and high school, but absorbed the important lesson that membership in a prestigious organization is everything in Japan. Constant examination and feedback told Hiro where he was ranked within his class, but the scores were not published, and he was treated no differently than other students. To outsiders, all that mattered was that he attended a very prestigious high school whose ranking was known to all. Without question, in terms of prestige and career prospects, it was better to bring up the rear at such a place than to be first at a high school that didn't get many students into Tokyo University.

Hiro found himself surrounded by very bright classmates.

Yet, for all their brightness, it seemed to Hiro that they had no clear idea how they would use their talents. Once, during open discussion in a weekly homeroom class, Hiro raised the question "Why do you want to go to Tokyo University?" Hiro's class was in the eleventh grade, a year away from selecting a college, yet very few of his peers had clear reasons for making that choice. One student told Hiro that he wanted to be a government bureaucrat, which meant that he "must" graduate from the University of Tokyo (colloquially called *"Todai"*). Others said that *Todai* was the most selective, and therefore it had to be the best. Yet these students had no idea which departments or professors had the strongest reputations and cared little what would happen after they got into the school. The answer that seemed most authentic to Hiro was "I know that Tokyo University attracts the best students from all of Japan, which shows it has the best facility and faculty, and I can also make friends with those outstanding students."

Like hundreds of thousands of other students, Hiro took a "sham" examination at the end of high school to decide which university examination to take. His score suggested that he would not get into the Tokyo University, so he entered one of the colleges in the elite tier behind *Todai*. This severely diminished his chances of becoming a high-level government bureaucrat but left him well positioned to become a salaryman at the end of four years. Like other Japanese university students, he focused more on extracurricular activities than on academic work. Japanese collegians seldom strive to achieve high academic ranking the way they did in secondary school, because they know that what they learn will seldom be tied directly to their future jobs. They do study, but not as intensively as before, because the goal is more ambiguous. Doing well in high school clearly leads to college acceptance, but university students have no clear idea how their studies may help them in their careers. Grades don't count for much in job hunting, unless one is either at the very top or very bottom of one's class. Extracurricular activities, on the other hand, show that a student is cooperative and team oriented, and making captain or vice captain of a team signals that he is accepted by the group.

The salaryman's job hunt

Hiro's job hunt started unexpectedly the June before his senior year of college. He received a telephone call at home from a friend who had graduated the year before and had gone to work for a top Japanese financial institution we will call "Ringo Bank." Hiro was unprepared for the call, because at the time, most Japanese companies had entered into a noncompulsory agreement to start the official recruiting season after October 1. The friend asked if Hiro would be interested in working for a bank. When Hiro replied yes, the two had dinner and discussed what the young banker was doing at Ringo. Hiro was encouraged to talk with a few other Ringo managers who had graduated from his university, and, one by one, appointments were set up for him.

Gradually Hiro realized that his interviewing process at Ringo had begun. Like other banks, Ringo used its alumni network to contact about a hundred potential candidates, ask each one out socially, talk about anything just to size the student up, then very informally cut down the numbers. Ringo was culling applicants without telling them they were involved in a selection process. Within a week or so after his initial contact with Ringo, Hiro received calls from several banks and security houses, asking if he might be interested in their companies. Always, the initial approach was made by an alumnus of his university, some of whom he already knew, whereas others were strangers. The point was not necessarily to tap into Hiro's circle of trusted friends; a school tie was good enough to initiate a relationship. In fact, one of Hiro's closest friends was also at Ringo, but for its own reasons, the bank chose to approach him first through a more distant acquaintance.

Today Hiro is surprised, looking back at this experience, at how casually he and his classmates went about making one of the most important decisions of their lives. Everyone fully expected to stay with his first employer for life, but no one took control of the process to ensure that he would end up with the best match. Hiro didn't really prefer the financial services industry to any other, but the year he graduated, banking and securities companies were the most aggressive recruiters. He was very interested in working outside Japan but never made up a résumé, never looked for banks active in international markets, and never initiated a contact with a recruiter. Ultimately, his choice of an employer hinged much more on whom he happened to know than on any objective comparison of the different firms pursuing him.

Hiro quickly found himself quite busy meeting many alumni of many different companies. Usually these meetings took place away from company offices, because the recruiters did not want to be obvious about ignoring the voluntary October 1 start date. After about a month of meeting with Ringo Bank managers who were alumni of his university, he was invited to meet with a manager who was not a graduate of Hiro's school. Hiro thought this signaled the beginning of the formal interview process, but, unbeknownst to him, his recruitment was almost over at that point.

After this meeting, Hiro was taken aside by a close friend who had entered college with Hiro but graduated a year earlier and taken a position with Ringo. This friend asked Hiro if he wanted to join the bank. Hiro was torn. He liked Ringo Bank, but he wanted to work overseas and had met with several managers of another bank that specialized in international business. He honestly described his feelings to his friend, who replied, "Unless you promise that you will join us, we won't be able to offer you a job." Before Ringo made a formal offer to Hiro, he was free to talk with as many potential employers as he liked, and he listened to everyone who approached him in order to avoid risk. Now, however, the game had changed. Japanese banks do not want to be compared, and only a fool would try to attract as many offers as possible before picking one, as a Westerner might. Dodging Ringo's offer would show the wrong attitude and embarrass the bank.

Hiro was given several days to make up his mind. Everyone understood that this was a decision expected to last for decades, and they didn't view his desire to think over an offer for a few days as a sign of weak commitment, as long as he did not talk with other companies while he weighed his choice. Hiro had a strong desire to work overseas and felt the other bank would give him better prospects for landing such a posting. But a fact of Japanese life is that nobody could promise Hiro a position outside Japan. Until he receives his first assignment, a new salaryman doesn't know what he will be asked to do for his new employer. In the end, Hiro chose Ringo because he had a trusted friend senior to him there, but not at the other bank. He called his friend to say he would like to join Ringo and immediately afterward received a formal job offer. Hiro's job search ended less than two months after that first telephone call in June.

Eventually, as he helped Ringo recruit at his alma mater, Hiro came to understand that personal relationships end up governing most salarymen's career choices—not only his. An alumnus acts as *senpai* (roughly, "mentor") to each job candidate. A *senpai* can be anyone senior to the person being courted, though a close, older friend from college days is preferred. The different *senpai* get together after the first casual approaches and subjectively narrow down the list of candidates to those who apparently fit the company culture best. A candidate is formally recommended by his *senpai* after he meets with many alumni and gains their informal approval. The candidate's interview with a senior who is not an alumnus of his school is usually a formality. If the *senpai* is missing something important, the formal decision maker will point this out, but usually the company's decision follows the consensus that has already been formed.

In the end, Hiro chose an employer for life based principally on his trust in a particular *senpai*. He soon learned that personal relationships also govern the career paths of most would-be salarymen. After he had been with Ringo for several years, Hiro was one of the alumni from his school asked to meet with a particular student. The young student had many personal contacts within the bank and was well liked, so Ringo extended him an informal offer. Another bank also asked him to join their firm, and there his *senpai* was a former athletic teammate. The candidate listened to both banks, tried to understand their differences, and finally told Ringo, "I will accept your offer, but please let me go back to the other bank to apologize to my *senpai*." Ringo agreed, and the man never returned. By agreement, all Japanese banks offer the same position and compensation to newly minted college graduates, so the candidate's personal relationship with his *senpai* had to be what reversed his decision. For Hiro, the moral of the story is that college seniors make one of the most momentous decisions of their life based on who they know in, not what they know about, a company.

Hiro's parents were even happier about his decision to join Ringo than he expected they would be. Graduating from a top college and joining a large, well-known corporation like Ringo brings social recognition. As we have seen, one doesn't get to be a salaryman just by being talented. It takes a long time to join this elite group, and many requirements must be met. Like most of his counterparts, Hiro felt proud of his achievement. Unlike many of his Western counterparts, he could command respect for the rest of his life for this accomplishment, regardless of whether he achieved concrete successes as an executive.

Initiation of a new salaryman

In the beginning, new salaryman trainees are never quite sure how to dress or behave. An easy solution would be to imitate one's *senpai*'s haircut and dress, but a *senpai* is, by definition, several years senior—the men in Hiro's *doki* (year group of salarymen entering the bank) had to learn how to dress like first-year trainees, not veteran Ringo men. Hiro's first lesson in the Ringo way: get a new haircut. His *senpai* had warned him beforehand that a Ringo trainee's hair should be "really, really short," so, like the others in his *doki*, he showed up for the training program prepared. Later in his career, after he had been posted to a branch bank in the Ringo system, Hiro came to understand the symbolic purpose of Ringo's code. "You are insulting our customers with that long hair!" spluttered a senior officer there, who sported a crew cut. Ringo men had to wear their hair short as a sign of respect for the bank's customers.

A new haircut was just the beginning. The company directed each trainee to master a seventy-page guide to business manners. Hiro and the others in his year group had to learn how to sit on a chair, where to place their hands while talking with others, how to bow, what posture to assume when standing, how to exchange name cards, how to get on an elevator, where to sit in a car, and where to sit in a train (a context quite different from sitting in a car). New trainees were expected to make mistakes and learn by having them corrected. For example, if a junior employee exited an elevator before a senior one, his mistake was pointed out immediately, and he was expected to feel shame. The purpose of all these rules was basically to keep the new salaryman from looking like an idiot, which would reflect badly on both him and his trainers. For example, someone who did not know where to sit when accompanying a branch manager on a business call would feel intensely embarrassed, so Ringo's minutely prescribed etiquette served to protect trainees from humiliating themselves.

Hiro later discovered that some of these rules seemed common to all *kaisha,* whereas others were peculiar to Ringo. Yet it never occurred to him or his peers to ask why they should observe rules whose violation would have gone unnoticed outside Ringo. Anyone who asked that kind of question wouldn't last long in a Japanese company. Through sharing the same rules, the employees of a *kaisha* strengthen the ties that bind them to each other. Those who do not follow the rules are outsiders, and only an insider can meet the expectations of other people, allowing him to function within the organization.

Employees don't choose job assignments

On the last day of the training program, each member of Hiro's *doki* was assigned to a branch bank. Before then, Hiro had no idea where he would go and had no chance to request a particular posting. Banks seem to be somewhat extreme in this respect; some of Hiro's contemporaries in other companies have told him that they can request specific assignments, although their wishes are often ignored.

Like many Japanese companies, Ringo manages job assignments this way for two reasons. First, a firm has to allocate limited resources to existing positions. It can't leave positions empty because nobody wants them, nor can it easily reduce the number of salarymen it hires, to match supply with demand. Were a firm to reduce its recruiting rate at a particular university, both the school and its alumni might feel insulted. Second, very few salarymen would leave a company because they are assigned jobs they don't want. The great majority of salarymen suffer through at least one posting they dislike, because they have nowhere else to go.

Although many Western managers in a similar situation would quit and find a new job, quitting over a transfer would be socially unacceptable for a salaryman. He would be seen as selfish, unwilling to sacrifice for the greater good of a group. A salaryman who quit his job would also find it nearly impossible to move to another Japanese company in midcareer. He could join a foreign company but would lose both social status and his guarantee of lifetime employment. Japanese wives, too, understand that transfers must be accepted. Even today it is common for husbands to accept a temporary separation from their families, in order to keep their children from having to change schools.

Company dormitories shape company men

Hiro's graduation from the training program into his first position was marked by his move into a twenty-square-meter dormitory room assigned to him by the company. Ringo salarymen must live in a dormitory or with their parents until they are married or turn thirty years old. Formally, Ringo told the employees that living in the dormitory was necessary for security reasons, because the salarymen were managing money and therefore needed surveillance. For the same reason, dormitory residents were not allowed to own cars. Pragmatically, the dormitory serves to keep bachelor salarymen under control and to further their education. It is customary for a young salaryman to share a room in the dormitory with a *senpai;* over the years, Hiro learned a lot about doing business from various older colleagues in the dormitory.

When Hiro arrived at the dormitory, he found that everyone had already been assigned a room and a roommate. The first evening, the dormitory manager told the new arrivals that they had the option to leave the dormitory and live with their parents. It was obvious, however, that he frowned on the idea and didn't expect anyone to take him up on the offer, because room assignments had been finalized the day before.

Hiro grew to enjoy dormitory life. Ringo sponsored vigorous sports competitions among dormitories, and the young salarymen grew close by playing together, drinking together, and learning together. One member of Hiro's *doki* quit Ringo years later to go to business school in America, eventually finding a job with a foreign bank. Hiro's friend says that he still maintains good relationships with his old comrades from the dormitory despite his departure from Ringo, because of the bonds they forged while living together.

However, dormitory life afforded Hiro very little privacy. The residents had to return to the dormitory by 11:00 P.M. unless they were working overtime; no one could stay out overnight without telling the dormitory manager where he could be found. The young salarymen were under watch all day, 365 days a year. Early in his career, Hiro was told by a senior officer of the bank that Ringo men had to be on alert twenty-four hours a day—after all, that was what it meant to work for a Japanese company. Hiro felt that, in the dormitory, this was more than just a figure of speech.

As a consequence of this lifestyle, Ringo's young salarymen found it difficult to meet women. Like about a third of his classmates, Hiro met his future wife during college. Another third of the men in Hiro's year group are still bachelors, well into their thirties, while about a third married people they met through friends or the office, because they had few opportunities to find

potential partners any other way. A significant number of Hiro's
colleagues married "office ladies" who worked for Ringo, though
such liaisons had to be kept secret from everyone except the
salaryman's boss. When such a couple married, the woman had
to leave Ringo because the bank has a rule against spouses
working in the same office.

Hiro greatly liked his *senpai* roommate, who taught him
many lessons. For example, Ringo used a formal document to
initiate new credit lines, and it turned out there was a specific
way to fill out each blank in the form. No one at Hiro's branch
showed him how to complete the form, so his *senpai* demon-
strated the way to write a correct proposal. The senior-junior
relationship between the roommates was unambiguous, even
though the two were the same age. Hiro's colleague had joined
Ringo a year earlier; in this context, seniority within the bank
is the critical factor governing who should use polite Japanese
when talking to whom. However, in an earlier time, Ringo had
recruited some employees straight from high school. Having
been with the company for some time, they naturally behaved
as *senpai* toward Hiro's year group, despite the fact that some
of these men were younger than the men in Hiro's cohort. This
caused some resentment among the college graduates, who felt
uncomfortable deferring to younger men. Generally, however,
age and seniority went hand in hand, as the great majority of
salarymen in the dormitory had joined Ringo immediately after
earning undergraduate degrees.

The salaryman's business education

The day after his training program ended, Hiro reported to his
assigned branch bank and started his career as a teller, sitting
behind a counter receiving cash from customers. After four
months, he moved to a loan department, where he reviewed
customers' credit applications. Credit analysis at Ringo was quite
formalized, virtually disregarding the customers' characteristics.
There was also a prescribed language for making comments on

the credit analysis form. When Hiro used different expressions with the same meaning, his boss returned the form for correction, so Hiro soon figured out that the most efficient way to produce acceptable work was to copy former documents, changing only the financial figures. His boss reviewed both the original document Hiro had used as a model and Hiro's analysis, and, if the two matched, with changes in the specific numbers only, the credit application was approved.

Once, while working on a credit analysis, Hiro discovered that Ringo had not done any business with the applicant for three years. He asked his boss if he could drop the analysis and was told to proceed. Hiro's manager explained that it didn't matter if the bank hadn't done any business with the customer; it would be much more trouble to terminate an unnecessary credit analysis than to copy documents that had been approved in the past. Hiro encountered similar situations many times, finding that, even if the original need for a routine had changed, it was very difficult to terminate routine processes. In the case of the credit analysis, Hiro's boss commented that Ringo might do business with the applicant again someday. There was little chance that this would happen, but even a remote possibility sufficed; flatly terminating a relationship is extremely difficult for Japanese organizations. If for some reason the credit approval had not gone through and the client had asked for some business, Hiro's section would have been criticized for dropping the credit analysis. Changing past models might be efficient, but it is also a risk most salarymen would prefer to avoid. As a result, like most of his classmates, Hiro found himself working long hours to stay ahead of routines that had piled up over the years.

After a year at the branch, Hiro was appointed a sales associate. He covered individual small or medium-sized companies within a territory, advising them on their investments, financing needs, business plans, or anything else they requested. Hiro's sales team included seven salarymen, tightly controlled by a branch manager, a deputy branch manager, and the head of the sales team. Every month, the managers assigned each sales associate targets in at least ten areas, such as opening new accounts, increasing the amount of time deposits from customers, generating new loans, and so forth.

Every Monday morning, the entire team and all the managers met, lined up in a room according to seniority. The most junior person began the meeting by reporting to all the others what he intended to do during the upcoming week. Then the next most senior sales associate made his public report, and the meeting continued in this fashion until the most senior associate had detailed his intentions for the week. The managers quizzed each associate about the details of his plan and offered advice. The meeting was equivalent to seven separate briefings for the team's management; each associate had to listen to the entire dialogue between the managers and his other six colleagues. The meeting took a great deal of time away from Hiro's main task of calling on clients, but efficiency is not the driving purpose of the *kaisha*. Hiro's job was to learn the business strategies of the other people on his team and to absorb the model of his seniors, so he would know how to behave when he was promoted to a comparable position.

Hiro's team also had a meeting every evening, at which each associate reported on his activities. The members of the team lined up in a row in front of the managers, and from most junior to most senior, each described what he had done during the day. Usually there wasn't much to report, because a sales associate could do only a limited amount of work in a day, but the purpose of the meeting really wasn't to convey information. The managers focused on what each associate had *not* accomplished during the day; the associates spent most of the meeting listening to their managers yell at them, "Why didn't you do *this* today?" Sales associates had so many targets that there was always something that had not been achieved. Evening after evening, Hiro and his teammates were lambasted for their failures and shortcomings. The evening meetings were not meant to be an adult conversation, and the salarymen were smart enough to know that one did not argue about the points raised by the managers. Most sales teams at Ringo operated the same way, and some of Hiro's peers on other teams learned how to duck the occasional ashtray thrown at them by their managers. Like it or not, this was the basic Ringo model for learning how to do business in a bank. The authority of the managers was absolute, and anyone who did not obey his boss would be out. After the daily meeting, Hiro's team—minus the managers— went out drinking together, spending the evening complaining and venting their frustrations.

It never occurred to Hiro that his bosses behaved this way out of ill will. He felt that this was how they learned about business from their superiors, and they were simply modeling the behavior of their seniors. The managers understood quite well how the salarymen felt and would take each one out for a drink from time to time to have an intimate conversation. On one of these occasions, Hiro's team leader told him, "I like you because you are quite an easy guy to yell at." Hiro felt that his superiors cared about him and wanted him to have a successful career. The evening lectures struck him as the way they showed concern for their juniors by treating them as they had been treated when they were just starting out.

The salaryman becomes a veteran

After a year as a sales associate, Hiro was transferred to Ringo's Securities Department. He had never imagined that he might be transferred out of commercial banking and was astonished when news of the transfer arrived. Hiro understood what securities were, of course, but had no idea how Ringo operated in this arena. When his deputy branch manager told Hiro about the transfer, Hiro asked, "What does the Securities Department do?" His superior answered, "I don't know!"

Hiro's amazement increased when he visited his new department for the first time. The atmosphere and culture seemed completely different. Nobody yelled at anybody else; people seemed to work in a highly professional manner. On the other hand, salarymen in the Securities Department seldom went out drinking together after work, the way Hiro and his sales team colleagues had. Hiro found that he missed the branch, even missed being yelled at nightly, because his relationships with senior people in the new department seemed much weaker, if less intimidating. He missed the familylike atmosphere he had perceived at the branch.

The end product: An insider

Hiro trained with the department for a time, then rotated through jobs there, as a market analyst and a trader. Financial markets proved to be a competitive arena quite different from the relationship-dominated world of commercial banking; as a result, the local culture of the Securities Department was vastly different from that of Ringo's branches. Hiro missed the challenge of probing relationships for weak spots and opportunities. However, he found that commercial banking and securities trading shared an important common thread: that Ringo's internal, organizational logic, not profit maximization, drove most decisions.

One February morning, the departmental controller called Hiro, whose job was trading American stocks, into his office. "What the hell did you do yesterday?" he screamed at Hiro. "I made some trades and lost some money," Hiro replied. The controller was far more irritated than the actual loss seemed to justify. It turned out that, two days previously, the controller had negotiated with the department manager a revised budget that could be achieved if the department sat tightly on its present positions. Hiro's loss had damaged the plan. The controller said to Hiro, "Meeting the budget is our top priority. The budget of each department aggregates to the budget of the bank. You'd better understand that you're ruining this process." Hiro replied, "As a trader, my job is to go into the market and try to make money. We still have almost two months before our fiscal year ends. Are you saying I shouldn't even make money because it will affect the budget?" "Yes," answered the controller, "that's exactly what I'm saying!"

On another occasion, Hiro was part of a team that was

trying to develop new products for Ringo. The team came up with a fairly simple idea that involved combining two different futures contracts to create an arbitrage position. A number of the bank's non-Japanese competitors were making money with similar strategies, and it seemed likely that the arbitrage opportunity would be profitable for Ringo. When the team presented the idea to senior managers, however, it proved impossible to implement, because the two different futures were traded by two different departments. In an arbitrage position, one typically makes money on one contract and loses money on the other. This would mean that one department would profit and one would lose, and neither department wished to risk a loss, despite the high probability that Ringo would make money overall.

Hiro is now in his early thirties. He has been with Ringo just over ten years and is due to become a manager, climbing the next rung on the salaryman's ladder. He is still assigned to the Securities Department, although he personally prefers branch banking and believes his skills would serve the bank better there. Hiro married his college sweetheart in his late twenties and moved out of the company dormitory. After ten years, he is a moderately competent salesperson, a moderately competent securities analyst, and a moderately competent trader. He is extremely competent at being a Ringo Bank insider. He understands vastly more now about Ringo's organizational imperatives than he did as a greenhorn, and his increasing command of Ringo's internal logic has helped him develop a sixth sense, an ability to predict how an idea will be received within the bank. Now more than ever before, he is locked into working for Ringo, because his most highly polished, most useful skills would be worth little in another environment.

Salarymen share certain basic behavioral imperatives because they have been molded and shaped by experiences like Hiro's. In the next chapter, we will focus on four themes that will help Western readers understand Hiro's worldview better, allowing them to grasp why behavior that seems puzzling to outsiders makes perfect sense to him and his fellow salarymen.

CHAPTER TWO

An Insider's Perspective on the *Kaisha*

Some of our Western friends who have read parts of this book have related a common experience to us. Discussing some of the stories in chapter 1 with Japanese business acquaintances, they ask, "Do they *really* yell at you every night? Do you *really* have to wear your hair that short? Do you *really* have to be back in the dormitory by eleven o'clock? Can't you *ever* tell the human resource department what kind of position you'd like to apply for?" And, of course, no salaryman shares all of the experiences of our mythical Hiro. Invariably, a salaryman will tell his Western acquaintance, "Things are not so in *my* company."

Trying to reduce the salaryman's experience to a set of universal principles can be a very frustrating experience. Quite commonly, Western managers feel comfortable with their grasp of Japanese behavior after they have asked one or two Japanese managers about their experiences. For the average salaryman is *not* full of contradictions; his story often seems unusual, but it is coherent to an outsider. Those who press further, however, and talk to five or ten salarymen become much more puzzled than those who stop after getting to know just one or two. Every rule seems to have an exception. Every exception has an exception—"There may be a lot of rules in many Japanese companies, but in *my* company . . ." "Usually Japanese bosses don't tell you directly what to do, but in *my* company . . ." "Many Japanese don't receive formal personnel evaluations, but in *my* company . . ." It's tempting for outsiders to throw up their hands and conclude either that there are no commonalties or that they exist but the Japanese won't tell anyone else what they are.

Western intellectual traditions predispose those raised within them to look for the center of a culture, a paradigm that characterizes the culture's worldview. Japanese culture, however, has no system of logical principles that creates the Japanese outlook on life. Japanese culture is more like a network. It has no center, and outcomes stem from the interaction of a loose web of elements. Consequently, one can't reduce the "rules of Japanese behavior" to a coherent, compact analytical framework. There simply isn't a cookbook or a flowchart one can use to understand the salaryman's actions as the product of a series of "if-then" rules.

However, Western readers can sharpen their feel for the salaryman's way of thinking by understanding four key themes, or mechanisms, influencing organizational behavior in the *kaisha* and seeing how they play out in different settings. By focusing on these mechanisms, one can learn to see through such myths as the imagined long-term orientation of Japanese managers or the supposed reign of egalitarian harmony inside Japanese organizations. A person cannot use these four mechanisms to predict how a Japanese manager will behave in every situation. One can, however, use them to gain insight into the salaryman's point of view.

First, this chapter will explore *the central importance of context* for Japanese behavior. Second, it discusses how the Japanese themselves learn how to behave, *emulating a model or prototype*. Third, it examines the fundamental motivation of the average Japanese: *the need to avoid embarrassment by meeting the expectations of others*. Fourth, it focuses on *the central role of process*— why, to a Japanese, doing something the right way is more important than getting the right result. Later chapters will explore how these four mechanisms often interact, linking phenomena that at first seem unrelated.

Correct action depends on the context

Western cultures are typically organized around ideologies, core sets of values. Moral guideposts, such as justice, freedom, democracy, and fairness, help the Westerner decide the right thing to do in a given situation. In contrast, Japanese culture has no cornerstones, no invariant principles that govern conduct. General rules of thumb are followed in most cases, but in others they are ignored. This is because *the correct action depends on the context of a given situation.* This difference between Japanese and Western society is reflected in differing legal systems: whereas Western judges try to apply principles and precedent to reach decisions, their Japanese counterparts take a case-by-case approach, seeking to do the right thing in each individual situation. *To unravel many of the supposed paradoxes of Japanese business behavior, one must ask how a salaryman understands the context of the situation and his relative status or position within that context.*

Here is a simple illustration. A British employee of a Japanese firm operating in England recently told a writer that he is convinced his Japanese managers are schizophrenic.[1] Graphically he described how polite, sedate, and proper they are at work, yet after a couple of drinks in a bar, they become loud, boisterous, and positively rude. To a Japanese, the behavior of these managers seems perfectly consistent. The context of an office is completely different from the context of a bar. There is no reason why behavior in one setting should resemble behavior in the other. In fact, the Japanese find it quite useful for there to be a socially approved place where one can say things that would be unforgivable in a different setting. What appear to be sudden changes in behavior are well understood by other Japanese, because they share the perception that a bar and an office are completely different settings. An American, for example, might see crude, noisy, sexist behavior as unacceptable no matter what the situation. In contrast, Japanese apply few universal rules;

what is appropriate can change dramatically if the perceived context shifts.

Different contexts provide different kinds of opportunities for salarymen. For example, virtually every salaryman learns early how to play golf, because there are things he can do on a golf course that are appropriate almost nowhere else. It's rare in a Japanese business context for a salaryman to talk one on one with a client. Discussions usually involve at least two or three people on both the customer's and the supplier's side. In this setting, it is not appropriate to talk about families or past experiences or personal issues; discussions tend to be general and focus on what is happening in a particular market. In a golfing foursome, though, it's natural over eighteen holes for pairs to become separated from time to time. In this context, executives can exchange personal information, such as where they live or how many children they have. In a Japanese business setting, it is much better for people to have some personal knowledge about those with whom they must deal, but there aren't many ways to gather such information.

In the same vein, being overseas can be a useful context for salarymen. There is a feeling of intimacy among Japanese in foreign countries that is missing in Tokyo. If a manager wants to learn something about a customer's strategy, he has a better chance of finding out what he wants to know by shifting the context. For example, suppose an executive wants to find out whether a banking customer is going to dispose of some assets. If he asks about this in Tokyo, the context is formalized, and his contacts at the customer are likely to tell him (accurately) that they haven't yet reached a decision. If he is in New York and asks his client's local managers the same question, they will likely tell him more about what kinds of problems the bank is facing and what options it has, including asset disposal.

Position relative to others is crucial

Appropriate behavior depends not only on the context everyone shares, such as a client visit, an office trip, or an after-hours soak in a communal bath; it also depends on each individual's position relative to others within the context. For example, when Western-ers are asked to attend a business meeting, they usually inquire what the subject or agenda of the meeting is. In contrast, the first thing a Japanese wants to know is who else is going to attend, for this defines the context of the meeting, regardless of its ostensible purpose. The context in turn defines correct con-duct. For example, the most junior people attending the meeting will be well prepared, show up early, and sit near the door (in the "cheap seats," as it were). The most senior person attending the meeting will arrive on time (or a little bit late), take the best seat, and forgo prior preparation, since other participants will explain whatever he wants to know. No two people will approach the meeting in exactly the same way, because no two have exactly the same status.

It is impossible for a salaryman *not* to think about what behavior is appropriate according to his relative position. This is because the Japanese language forces everybody to use a form of speech that reflects relative status. Western languages have some watered-down analogues. For example, many European languages have a formal and an informal mode; the word "you" in German can be the informal *du* or the formal *Sie*. But these can often be dodged, just as an American might manage a discus-sion with his in-laws to avoid the stark choice between "Jane and Bill" or "Mr. and Mrs. Robinson."

There is no dodging in Japanese. There are several degrees of increasing politeness in the language, and the form chosen affects both the structure of what one says and many of the words one chooses to use. When speaking to a senior person, a salaryman *must* use a polite form. Outside the setting of a company, people usually use polite forms when talking to older people, but plain forms when speaking with those their age or younger. Inside a company, things become somewhat more complicated by seniority and position, although there is usually a strong correlation between a person's age, the year he joined the firm, and his position. No matter what his position is in a company, though, a salaryman who uses plain language when speaking to older people can easily become tagged as arrogant, a cardinal sin in Japan. The rules change when salarymen talk with their customers. Businessmen always use polite forms with their customers. The customer usually follows the general rule of speaking politely to elders, plainly to younger people. Choosing the wrong form is intensely embarrassing for both parties, so Japanese are almost always conscious of their position relative to others.

Perspective supersedes fixed principles

The notion that appropriate behavior is determined by the context pervades Japanese society, not just Japanese commerce. To illustrate, in a fairly well known *Noh* play (a traditional form of Japanese theater), the audience watches a priest listening to a spirit talk about past events. The charm of the play lies in the opportunity it offers the audience to experience the same events as separate realities in different contexts. From one standpoint, the priest and the spirit are performers on a stage. Shifting perspective, the audience knows that the spirit is a figment of the priest's imagination—perhaps the ghost's interpretation of the past simply represents the priest talking to himself. But, as the audience is drawn into the play, it comes to share the priest's point of view and accept the talking spirit as reality.[2] The same idea animates one of Japan's most famous movies, Akira Kurosawa's *Rashomon,* in which a crime is viewed from the perspective of each central character in turn.

Noh theater is not a metaphor for all Japanese behavior, and one need not absorb its intricacies to grasp Japanese business conduct. Our point is that, within the *kaisha,* one's interpretation of reality and understanding of appropriate conduct depends on one's perspective, not on fixed principles of right action. This is consistent with many other aspects of Japanese society.

Let us emphasize that intentional application of a double standard is as unacceptable socially in Japan as it is in any Western country. A Japanese person cannot excuse any behavior by pleading that it is appropriate in context. On the contrary, the Japanese brand those who fail to interpret the context appropriately as unmannered fools. Japanese people do, however, set great store by one's intentions, the spirit with which one behaves in context; this often causes outsiders to think a double standard is being applied. For example, Japanese companies are extremely sensitive about their employees' social reputations. A salaryman's career can be fatally damaged if a family member commits even a minor crime. However, Japanese firms do not always strictly punish crimes. Sometimes employees violate the law as a result of their striving on behalf of the company or to maintain their power in a company. If a crime is committed in the "right spirit," not for personal gain, it can be overlooked. Criminal behavior is abhorrent to the *kaisha,* but in certain contexts it can be condoned. For example, in the early 1990s, the top two executives of Nomura, Japan's top securities firm, had to resign over a scandal that involved payments to favored clients to cover their trading losses. They returned to the firm as directors in 1995 and are still powerful because the illegal behavior was designed to cement client relationships, not for personal gain.

The idea that appropriate Japanese behavior depends on the context has two particularly important implications, to which we turn next.

Controls, not traits, account for behavior

Ignoring context is the source of the single most common error outsiders make in interpreting Japanese behavior. This mistake consists of observing an aggregate behavior and concluding that it results from an individual psychological trait. Again and again, we find Western observers presuming that the behavior of salarymen reflects certain common personality traits, overlooking the organizational control mechanisms that drive behavior inside the firm.

Western psychologists have a term for this mistake: the *fundamental attribution error.* It consists of assuming that people do things because of "the type of people they are," overlooking the way outside forces shape behavior. For example, a number of psychologists have conducted experiments in which a person being studied watches another person's actions through a one-way mirror. The watcher is perfectly aware that outside forces virtually dictate what the person they see through the mirror is doing. Even so, when asked why the person on the other side of the mirror behaved as he did, most watchers reply that he represents a certain personality type, predisposed to such behavior. If he becomes infuriated, he is "an angry personality"; if he cheats, he is "the cheating type." Most of us reach such conclusions even when it's plain to see what made a person angry or what made him cheat.

Japanese businessmen operate under a very strict set of social controls. The structure, rules, and culture of their organizations heavily influence their behavior. Yet, again and again, outside observers explain the behavior they see by referring to "typically Japanese" personality traits (such as patience and long-term thinking) or to national character. This is as great a mistake as the one we mentioned in the Introduction: assuming that a Japanese company's actions reflect the goals and directives of its top managers. The vast majority of what a salaryman does is strongly affected and sometimes positively dictated by the context, the set of social and organizational controls within a *kaisha*.

Soron-sansei, kakuron-hantai

Those who develop general recipes for understanding Japanese behavior invariably become frustrated when they encounter exceptions to what they perceive to be rules. For example, many Japanese profess an honest belief in free trade while backing import restrictions on rice. What could seem more duplicitous to the outsider? To the Japanese, it is perfectly understandable that rice should constitute a special case, because self-sufficiency in the staple of the Japanese diet is a matter of national policy. A popular Japanese phrase describes this behavior: *soron-sansei, kakuron-hantai*. *Soron* is a general case, whereas *kakuron* is a specific one. *Sansei* means "to agree," and *hantai* means "to object." Japanese may agree with an abstract principle, but in specific situations, the general idea is ignored when it contradicts what the context seems to call for. In the example above, most Japanese support free trade as an abstract principle, as one would expect of an island nation's citizens. Rice, however, may have emotional or political overtones that make it a "special case," and special cases are not supposed to be subject to general rules.

Is this a double standard? Are we simply making excuses for Japan? We're not defending rice import restrictions. Our point is that Westerners gain no insight into Japanese behavior by concluding simplistically that the Japanese favor themselves. It may be emotionally satisfying, but it doesn't help an outsider predict what the Japanese will do in a different situation.

Soron-sansei, kakuron-hantai is pervasive in Japan; it does not apply only to trade disputes. For example, in a 1995 survey by the periodical *Nihon Keizai Shimbun,*[3] 98 percent of Japanese businessmen surveyed agreed that deregulation is a good thing and Japan needs more of it. Only 25 percent felt it was necessary for their own industries.

This sort of context-bound behavior often frustrates Japanese as much as it does outsiders. For example, in a 1993 survey of section managers,[4] 43 percent of those responding agreed that the productivity of white-collar workers in their companies was low and had much room for improvement. Only 16 percent felt that way about their own sections. Many salarymen agree that there are too many middle managers in Japanese companies, but when it comes to their own circle, there are hundreds of reasons why a company needs all the salarymen it is employing. This creates a context that frustrates those who think that improving productivity is necessary in order for Japanese firms to stay competitive. It would be simple to deal with these attitudes if they were simply self-serving justifications, but we don't think they are. Salarymen are genuinely concerned about low productivity when they see the overall situation. However, each specific relationship has its own context, and each is viewed as a unique case with its own special reasons justifying its continuance.

Correct behavior is learned from models

Unfortunately, there are no rules that determine how a Japanese will apply a contextual frame to a specific situation. On the other hand, there is a certain consistency in the way Japanese define an appropriate context. Were this not so, other Japanese would have a very difficult time knowing what is expected of them, resulting in intense social embarrassment. How do the Japanese learn the right way to put a situation into context?

Outsiders are often surprised at how constricted the accepted pattern of behavior is in Japan. It seems that there is a "right way" to do everything, from hitting a baseball to bowing. In fact, a recent book by a Western expert on Japan suggests that *shikata,* or the way of doing things, constitutes the cultural programming that makes the Japanese a superior people.[5] There seems to be a *kata* (correct form) for everything—even for actions that are idiosyncratic in the West, such as eating, reading, and writing.

For example, one salaryman we know is naturally left-handed and first started to write with that hand. In Japan, some people believe that using the left hand in front of others is impolite. It isn't a universal belief, but it is sufficiently widespread that left-handedness might cause social offense on some occasions. The salaryman's parents trained him as a young child to write with his right hand. His mother, who is also left-handed, uses chopsticks with her left hand at home but switches to the right hand in front of other people. Few things are more important to the average Japanese than knowing the correct form for things, even those that may seem trivial to outsiders.

How do the Japanese absorb these lessons? Japanese schools are famous for their emphasis on rote memorization, and subjects such as mathematics and science are usually taught as an abstract set of rules to know. However, *the characteristic mode of learning correct behavior is emulating a model or prototype.*

The archetypal example is martial arts training. In the West, martial arts books and videos often break karate or judo moves into a series of steps, describing in great detail how to combine them properly. In contrast, the Japanese approach is holistic. A Japanese novice is expected to imitate the movement of the *sensei* (teacher) exactly and faithfully, though the *sensei* seldom explains in detail what he is doing. The student does not study diagrams or follow a checklist—he or she simply tries to behave exactly like the model. Eventually, through learning by doing, the pupil acquires an intuitive understanding of the skill. The *sensei* is also thought to symbolize Japanese values and virtues. He is both a physical and a spiritual model for the apprentice to copy.

This mode of learning frequently produces dysfunctional results. For example, third-rate American baseball players often star in the Japanese professional leagues. One reason is that they find Japanese hitting and pitching completely predictable and easy to defeat, if one is willing to be a little unorthodox. Japanese players learn how to throw, catch, and bat through tens of thousands of repetitions, striving faithfully to imitate the style of their coaches. More than one American player has bemusedly reported that Japanese coaches will tell a batter who is leading the team in hitting that his form is all wrong and must be changed.

Modeling starts in childhood, as young Japanese learn appropriate behavior through imitating their parents. Once they enter school, teachers become models for correct conduct, which is one reason why educators enjoy much higher status in Japan than they do elsewhere. Both Japanese teachers and parents teach their children to fit in rather than to stand out, and "the habits of intellectual submission that they learn as students follow them into adulthood."[6] As they enter the workplace, Japanese employees model their behavior on their bosses, learning the right way to do things in the context of the *kaisha*. In the case of young salarymen, as we have seen, an older *senpai* acts as a mentor. The junior member's role in this relationship is called *kohai*.

The right model is what others expect

Of course, when we say that employees model themselves on those senior to them, we do not mean that they try to imitate the boss's handwriting or go to the bathroom whenever their superiors do. The purpose of the *senpai-kohai* relationship is to teach the novice how to deal with seniors, become sensitive to human relationships inside the firm, and do business within the *kaisha*. Similarly, a child is not expected to imitate everything his or her mother does; rather, one learns from parents how to relate to other people. The emphasis on emulating a prototype allows an individual to justify behavior toward others by referring to well-recognized guides. Books, television programs, and magazines constantly relate stories about the character of great figures in Japanese history. Such tales emphasize the way a hero behaved—for example, displaying loyalty to move up the organization.

Still, emulating the behavior of models—be they mentors, parents, or famous historical personages—is not an infallible guide. One can often imagine several different models that might apply to a situation, and, just as in Western countries, every aphorism has its counterpart (for example, "He who hesitates is lost" but "Look before you leap," or "You never know until you try" but "Curiosity killed the cat"). How, then, do all Japanese behave in the same way, so that they don't stand out? *They strive to meet the expectations of other people, particularly those with power.* As a result, Japanese socialization finely hones the salaryman's ability to sense what others expect of him.

At school, for instance, Japanese students are placed in small groups with clear goals, clear individual roles, and a routinized process for reaching those goals. All these things are mutually monitored by students so that teachers can prevent the unexpected from happening.[7] This teaches students to empathize with others. The group provides a model that gives individuals their identity. Consequently, the group perspective is much more than an abstract concept or a weighted sum of individual views—

"my perspective" and "your perspective" differ from "our perspective." Because the action of others provides a model for appropriate conduct, the most popular excuse Japanese children offer when they are scolded is "All of my friends do the same thing!"—a defense that tends to be more successful in Japan than it is in the West.

Meeting expectations supersedes "authenticity"

Learning the right thing to do in a particular context leads to an important distinction. What should be done according to the model is *tatemae,* and what one really feels, which may be quite different, is *honne.* Because it is vital to do what others expect in a given context, situations arise that often strike Westerners as charades. It is very important in Japan to play them out according to what each person believes others expect to happen.

For example, one Japanese scholar relates the story of a Mr. Seward, a Western employee of a Japanese firm.[8] He joined a meeting as one of eight employees tasked with deciding where to go for a company trip. When the result of the vote was taken, it appeared that the group favored going to a place named Izu. At this point, one of the president's secretaries spoke up, saying, "The president wants to visit Suwa." In a tense atmosphere, a second vote was taken, considering the president's opinion, and it turned out that the entire group, except Seward, voted for Suwa. Mr. Seward protested the procedure, insisting that, if members were forced to follow the president's opinion, there was no point in meeting and voting, but his objections were overridden and the company trip was set for Suwa.

Why didn't the president simply send out a memo announcing the destination? For the president, having a meeting was *tatemae,* the right thing to do according to normal models for reaching this kind of decision. Going to Suwa was *honne,* what he really wanted to do. Conversely, for members, voting for Suwa was *tatemae* once the president's desires were made clear; going to Izu was *honne.*

Was the meeting a sham? Perhaps, but if symbol is substance, is this any more unusual than asking someone, "How are you?'' without really expecting a detailed answer? In Japanese society, the distinction between *honne* and *tatemae* is well accepted; *tatemae* is supposed to give a sign of *honne,* though *honne* remains ambiguous and flexible. This is bewildering only to someone who does not understand the model appropriate to the context.

Follow the model, don't ask why

Modeling also explains a common form of tension between Japanese managers and their Western subordinates or coworkers. The Japanese managers we interviewed think they express quite clearly whether they are saying yes or no, and they commonly complain that Westerners do not grasp obvious meanings. As a consequence, salarymen tend to overreact, concluding that the only way to handle Westerners is to give them very clear and simple directions, as one might instruct a child.

What lies behind this communication gap? Americans don't want clear and simple directions; they want clear and simple reasons why a particular decision was reached. Unfortunately, Japanese managers have difficulty explaining why, because they are following a model, not reasoning through a justification. Junior Japanese salarymen encounter the same problem: they never learn why a particular authorization is needed or why a document has to be prepared a particular way. In fact, in 1995, Yoshio Suzuki, president of the prestigious Nomura Research Institute, concluded that the concept of accountability in Japan is a serious defect in the system, because it means only willingness to accept blame, not providing an explanation for one's behavior.[9]

For example, one of the junior executives we interviewed recalled an occasion on which his office's paper shredder overheated. Concerned about the possibility of fire in a building full of paper, senior managers put out the word that all electrical plugs should be disconnected before the employees went home. When the salaryman's boss told him to pull the plug of his personal computer, he asked why, because PCs never overheat. Only an inexperienced salaryman would have bothered to question in the first place whether the directive applied to PCs. The junior executive reasoned that there had to be a purpose behind unplugging everything, that purpose being to avoid fires, and this clearly did not apply to personal computers. His boss, however, was conditioned to follow the model, regardless of whether the original reason for an action still applied. Once a model is established, the basis for evaluating correct behavior is simply whether or not an employee is following the model. Our junior executive still recalls the dumbfounded look his boss gave him in reply. He also recalls unplugging his PC every night thereafter.

Chapter 1 described how the prototypical salaryman, Hiro, learned to fill out credit reports a certain way, even if the original rationale no longer made sense.[10] There are many models within the *kaisha* that people must follow long after the original reason for doing things a certain way has vanished. Traditional practices aren't eliminated because they are inefficient; the only time employees can break free of existing models is when expectations change; for example, when a new manager with different ideas takes over.

Avoiding embarrassment motivates behavior

Japanese are powerfully motivated to meet the expectations of others. So deeply ingrained is this need to meet social expectations that the salaryman habitually asks himself what a person in his position is supposed to do, not what he thinks or how he feels. Just as powerfully, *Japanese seek to avoid social embarrassment*. Models are important because they provide the predictability and stability that Japanese need to avoid embarrassing themselves. By socially embarrassing behavior, we mean actions that fail to match a reference group's norms, rules, or expectations. Given a context and a group, a Japanese person should know what he or she has to do. People who behave in socially unacceptable ways are considered poorly educated, because they don't know how to act as others expect.

A prominent Japanese author who writes about embarrassment among Japanese thinks that feeling embarrassed or ashamed is the basic intangible principle guiding Japanese behavior.[11] We agree. He divides embarrassment into two categories. One kind arises when people feel ashamed of themselves because they fear being distant from the truth, goodness, and beauty for which they long. Another, far more important, emerges when a person's inferiority (weakness, wickedness, dirtiness, defectiveness, and so forth), which he wishes to hide, is revealed in public. Actually *being* weak or defective per se is *not* the source of shame. As long as one meets the expectations of other people, which depend on who he is and on the context, he is not viewed as inferior. Only socially inappropriate behavior generates deep shame. In a classroom, Japanese students are trained to meet the expectations of teachers; in a company, workers are trained to meet the expectations of their bosses.

Efforts to avoid social embarrassment lead to behaviors that non-Japanese find strange. For instance, Japanese always apologize for their lack of skill and preparation before they present something to an audience. In the West, such behavior would be viewed as evidence of a weak self-image or an attempt to seek pity. In Japan, others expect a speaker to admit his inadequacy in advance, preempting the possibility that he will fail to meet group expectations. Similarly, it is customary to apologize for the inadequacy and poorness of a gift, even one that is quite expensive. By apologizing in advance, the Japanese puts the recipient of a gift in a position in which it is impossible for him to complain that the gift did not live up to expectations. These behaviors are so pervasive in Japanese society that they are widely viewed as appropriate models. Someone who failed to observe them would risk being viewed as impolite or arrogant.

Discipline and consensus can be illusory

Japanese people conform to expectations more to avoid looking like fools than as a matter of discipline. For example, why do Japanese almost always participate in "voluntary" company activities outside working hours, such as quality circles or group outings? Does this reflect the fabled company loyalty of the Japanese worker? Hardly; although such activities are formally voluntary, everyone knows that failure to participate is socially unacceptable. Only a complete idiot would make such a blunder. Outsiders who extol the group orientation of Japanese workers are sometimes taken aback by opinion surveys that suggest that many employees participate in these affairs reluctantly. Some Japanese genuinely enjoy group activities, but it would be wrong to assume that participation is voluntary. Deviation from the appropriate model is accompanied by penalties that most Japanese are unwilling to endure.

The same applies to decision making in the *kaisha*. Business decisions are usually unanimous, but this does not necessarily mean a consensus was achieved. As many of our interviewees pointed out, it is absurd to think every Japanese person agrees on everything. Unanimity emerges because it is exactly what people expect (such as the president who wanted to go to Suwa), and because failing to achieve it is embarrassing to those who coordinate a decision-making process.

Those who conclude that Japanese psychology emphasizes cooperation miss the social dynamic that generates consensus. Consider a hypothetical case. Suppose Mr. Nakamoto makes a proposal that Mr. Suzuki doesn't like. Before committing himself to opposition, Suzuki will try to find out what other people think about Nakamoto's idea. If Suzuki finds that the majority views the proposition with favor, he will either ask Nakamoto to make some amendments or will stall for time. If Nakamoto succeeds in getting a deadline imposed or winning public approval from a powerful figure, Suzuki will vote in favor of the proposal despite his personal opposition. Suzuki will not go against the majority, because a Japanese is expected to know better and would suffer intense embarrassment and social disapproval if he did so.

Fear of embarrassment affects risk taking

The drive to avoid embarrassment can seriously hamstring Japanese firms. For example, a respondent told us how the middle managers of his company once came up with an important innovation, a strategic idea whose potential impact would be huge if it were carried out. Two departments were involved. The general manager of department A was enthusiastic about the strategic potential of the idea. The general manager of department B was more concerned about the possible risk of loss in case everything went wrong. He couldn't explicitly object to the idea, because he had to admit it had enormous potential. Given the implicit hesitation of B's manager, however, A's manager couldn't push the idea hard.

The middle managers who had initiated the idea studied its pros and cons extensively. They looked at the cost of implementing the strategy, tried to quantify the maximum possible loss, assessed its likely competitive impact—all to no avail. The general managers simply would not make a decision.

The middle managers were so frustrated that they made an unusual suggestion. Let's put this plan to the board of directors, they said, knowing that, in the company's long history, exactly one proposal brought to the board had ever been turned down. The middle managers prepared exhaustively for the board meeting, but at the last minute, the manager of department B expressed concern that the board might turn the plan down. Such an outcome was highly improbable, to say the least. But none of the middle managers could be 100 percent sure the plan would be approved, and if it were turned down, everyone involved would be extremely embarrassed. The idea was never brought to the board, and the project died.

The middle managers believed their idea would have a dramatic impact on the company. Their proposal to bring the plan before the board was politically astute; it would have created a context in which the strategy almost certainly would have been approved. Yet even the *threat* of social embarrassment was impossible to overcome. The managers simply had no model to follow telling them how to promote such a new idea. Western managers might say, "Let's give it a shot," but this kind of thinking is uncommon among salarymen, because they fear failure and because their companies aren't used to and don't appreciate unexpected behavior.

Unstructured situations create anxiety

Behavioral models protect salarymen from embarrassment. This explains why Japanese managers abhor unstructured social situations that might force them to improvise, especially with foreigners who do not know the appropriate forms of behavior. A classic example is the well-known irritation of senior Japanese executives when junior Americans speak with them frankly. There is no model for coping with outspoken juniors who ought to know better.

Additionally, Japanese people go to great lengths to avoid appearing inferior in situations in which a Westerner would readily admit ignorance. For instance, some Japanese managers are uncomfortable in the presence of foreigners because they are embarrassed about their English. One manager interviewed for this book recalled a party he attended celebrating the twentieth anniversary of his bank branch. All of the branch's important customers were invited, including an ambassador who spoke English. A group of senior executives from corporate headquarters literally hid from this important guest because they did not speak English well. A young salesperson fluent in English was available to translate, but the top managers did not know whether relying on a junior in such a situation would violate the ambassador's expectations. The only way these executives could conduct business with such a client would be to hold a formal, structured meeting, where the presence of a translator would conform to an accepted model of behavior.

An outsider might wonder how Japanese managers can act at all if everything must be arranged to avoid embarrassment. Why aren't salarymen paralyzed by the fear of doing the wrong thing in a particular context? There are simply too many ways to fail, and failure is humiliating. Japanese businessmen *would* be overwhelmed by the fear of looking foolish if they were judged solely by the results of their actions. They are saved from a crushing burden of anxiety by the society's emphasis on process instead of outcomes.

Correct process is more important than results

Doing something the right way is more important to Japanese than is achieving a favorable outcome. The methods one uses to achieve goals are more important than the results. "Process" in this case refers to the way people operate instruments or social structures. The spirit motivating a person's actions—his values, motivations, and emotions—are an important element of process. For example, most salarymen at any level don't place top priority on maximizing their company's value to its shareholders. Japanese firms are owned by their shareholders; this is *tatemae.* Serving them, the firm's employees, and society by acting with the right values, motivation, and emotion is *honne.*

Japanese businessmen set clear goals and monitor progress toward them precisely and in detail. But they focus mainly on process as they try to achieve these goals. In fact, a glorious defeat is preferable to a victory achieved without the proper spirit and attitude. Salarymen are evaluated principally on whether they followed appropriate process models and met the expectations of others in the firm. There is a strong tendency in Japanese management to believe that results are dictated by fate. A popular saying is "Do whatever I can and wait for heaven to decide." (This, roughly translated, is what *Nintendo* means in Japanese.) Given this emphasis, Japanese do not understand how you can trust or admire someone simply because he succeeded.

The point here is not that Japanese businessmen are *indifferent* to results. Processes are designed to get results, and industrial processes are often designed with the intention of optimizing results. The insight to grasp is more subtle. Japanese efforts are directed toward defining an appropriate process for a given task, and once a proper process is defined, the job is essentially completed, except for execution. As long as execution is faithful and diligent, those who carry out a process are not blamed for unexpectedly poor results. Conversely, those who get results do not automatically receive accolades.

Noble failure is better than success

A characteristically Japanese hero is the judo expert Toshihiko Koga. He won a silver medal at the 1988 Seoul Olympics but shed tears in public at his failure to win the gold. Koga is no sore loser; he cried because he felt that he had failed to meet the Japanese people's expectations. Training fanatically for four years, he won the gold medal four years later in Barcelona, despite being injured and forced to compete with the help of a legal painkiller. Koga's victory is less important than the spirit and dedication he showed; in fact, his story is a bit unusual because it has a happy ending. Being number one is extremely important in Japan, but not as important as winning the right way. In contrast, those who finish second in the West fade into obscurity. Only the victors end up posing for cereal boxes or endorsing athletic shoes.

More often than not, Japanese heroes have an aura of tragedy and noble failure.[12] Most Japanese know the story of Yoshitsune and Yoritomo, two twelfth-century brothers. Yoritomo became lord of all Japan, but Yoshitsune is more popular because he overcame a difficult childhood and separation from his family to exemplify traditional Japanese virtues. The fact that he was killed by his brother only heightens his achievements. Similarly, the great heroes of the most storied era of Japanese history, the period of warring states *(Sengoku),* are Nobunaga and Hideyoshi, both of whom fell short of their ambition to unify all of Japan. Ieyasu Tokugawa, who did unite Japan under a shogunate that lasted for centuries, is a less appealing figure, partly because his predecessors reached beyond their grasp and died nobly.

The process emphasis can backfire

The Japanese emphasis on process reflects a general conviction that everything in the universe is a part of a whole, experienced as a constant unfolding of the present. This idea is elaborated on in chapter 6, which examines the supposedly long-term orientation of Japanese managers. Japanese quality control techniques fit this model very well, because they emphasize controlling the present situation. Japanese managers collect precise data at the right moment and solve problems when they show up. Japanese workers are expected to show their ability by carrying out their assignments completely and quickly. Given a goal, a manager can take concrete actions to change the existing situation, knowing exactly what to do when there are models to follow. Process and results can be tightly linked, without the ambiguity characteristic of managing human relationships.

In business, this emphasis on managing the present as a process can turn out to be a great success or a miserable failure, depending on the environment. Faced with continuous change or crises that can be solved through continuous improvement (such as oil and yen shocks), Japanese firms adapt well because they can elaborate existing models, taking them to levels that others find difficult to match. Breaking free of existing behaviors to adapt to discontinuous change is far more difficult. Furthermore, Japanese firms are occasionally fatalistic about outside factors, which their Western rivals try to manage, if not control. For example, quite a few Japanese exporters do not employ sophisticated tools to manage currency risks. They tell bankers who try to sell them such services that they can't control these risks, because they can't control the currency markets. From their point of view, many factors affect events, and they are just a small element of a much larger process whose outcomes are unforeseeable.

Focusing on attitude or process has occasionally proven disastrous for the nation, however. For instance, a best-selling book[13] in the mid-1980s set forth a penetrating organizational analysis of the Japanese military in the second world war. The authors uncover some rather obvious mistakes and ask why they were repeated again and again. Their conclusion is that the leadership of the military evaluated the *spirit* of officers when deciding whom to promote, ignoring whether they possessed necessary skills or an objective understanding of the situation.

Although Japan had been at war with China for ten years before Pearl Harbor, there was no objective evaluation of combat performance, no mechanism to evaluate what worked and what did not. Consequently, the military failed to learn from its mistakes; if a general met defeat, what mattered was that he died well. The leadership simply sent out more generals and more soldiers with the right attitude, relying on their *samurai* spirit to prevail despite previous reverses with the same strategy and tactics. Japanese military tactics and organization in the 1940s followed the highly successful model of the Russo-Japanese War, fought at the beginning of the century. The model failed in the face of discontinuous change. More than simple inertia or traditionalism was at work here; the Japanese were innovators in many areas (such as naval aviation and using folding bicycles to enhance mobility in jungles). The point is that negative feedback in the form of poor results did not lead to readjustments, absent a perceived crisis in process.[14]

Economic efficiency isn't paramount

The importance of a process emphasis leads Japanese managers to place human relationships before economic efficiency. Getting results is subordinate to operating in a way that enhances one's ability to work with others. If Japanese want to get things done, they must make a day-by-day effort to establish firm human relationships. This means spending considerable time with their coworkers outside the work setting. It also binds Japanese workers to their employers, for changing jobs would mean sacrificing a huge investment in relationship building.

When Westerners try and fail to penetrate Japanese markets using superior technology or lower cost as levers, they wonder how the Japanese can be so illogical, why basic economic principles apparently don't apply in the Japanese market. The Japanese emphasis on process often lies at the root of such puzzles. First, as long as a process is not obviously malfunctioning in Japan, people tend to perpetuate it. If a firm's past experience with a supplier is satisfactory, it will continue the relationship even if it means temporarily accepting higher costs. Japanese who disrupt relationships, absent a clear fault or problem, can be criticized for lacking a sense of obligation.

Second, nothing is more important than a supplier's ability to meet his customer's expectations. When salarymen complain about non-Japanese companies and the products or services they provide, they usually say that consistency is missing. They want their suppliers to understand customer expectations without being told explicitly, and they want assurance that even "unreasonable" expectations, such as midnight service, will be met. They don't want their relationship manager changed frequently because of turnover; a new contact may not understand their expectations immediately. Japanese overseas subsidiaries do business with their traditional suppliers because they want to maintain continuity in relationships, even if lower-cost local firms are available. The Japanese believe that, in the long run, if both parties contribute to the relationship in good faith, results will take care of themselves.

This second chapter has laid out four important themes for the rest of the book. The approach will shift in the next six chapters. Each one takes up a particular kind of puzzle or apparent contradiction in Japanese behavior. Within a chapter, a type of puzzle will be illustrated, played out in different situations, and eventually shown to be noncontradictory from the insider's perspective.

One of the most pervasive of these puzzles is the seeming ubiquity of double standards in Japanese business. The next chapter will show that if one *expects* that insiders and outsiders *ought* to be treated differently, many apparent double standards come to appear not only natural but appropriate.

CHAPTER THREE

Insiders and Outsiders: Dual Models Mean Double Standards

Chapter 2 suggested that, to unravel many of the supposed paradoxes of Japanese business behavior, one must ask how a salaryman understands the context of the situation and his relative status or position within that context. An important aspect of context, which lies at the root of much puzzling behavior, is whether other parties are perceived as insiders or outsiders. Appropriate Japanese behavior toward insiders is quite different from that appropriate for outsiders.

In some contexts, Japanese are insiders and foreigners are outsiders. The different treatment of the two naturally infuriates foreigners. Without condoning or rationalizing such discrimination, it is important to realize that this behavior is endemic in Japanese business, explains much commercial behavior in contexts that have nothing to do with foreigners, and creates some interesting opportunities for outsiders—along with some obvious problems.

An insider is always an insider with respect to a *reference group*. Asking what the reference group is in a given situation is a very handy mental habit to develop in order to understand Japanese behavior. This chapter begins by discussing how reference groups are defined inside the *kaisha*, determining who is an insider and who is an outsider in a particular situation. Then the unit of analysis changes from people to companies, to the way organizations are slotted into reference groups (for example, "our industry"), dictating which companies are insiders in a particular situation. Next, the level of analysis moves still higher, to cases where the insider-outsider distinction separates Japanese from foreigners. At this level, the insider-outsider distinction explains a puzzle that perplexes many Westerners who develop friendships or working relationships with Japanese: How can Japanese people seem so caring and place so much emphasis on humanity and warmth in some settings, while appearing cold and even frightening in others? The chapter concludes by examining how insider-outsider distinctions explain the pervasive sense among foreigners that the Japanese operate according to a double standard. This discussion leads to the conclusion that being an outsider can sometimes operate to one's advantage.

Insider status depends on reference groups

Many societies outside Japan have insiders and outsiders. Western bureaucratic culture, which separates a person from his office, is a recent development. In much of the world, favors reign, and people are expected to look out for their families and their clans. Nepotism and tribalism are frowned on in Japan and are not the basis of the insider-outsider distinction. In many societies, being "in" or "out" is more or less permanent—either you have a powerful friend in the government or you don't; either you are part of an elite social set or you aren't. Japan puzzles nonnatives because people or companies that are insiders in one context are outsiders in another. It is naive to say that a particular person or company "is an insider" all the time. The insider-outsider distinction depends on the situation.

A reference group shares an identity

A *reference group* is a closed circle whose members mutually define themselves as insiders. Those within the circle share important information, follow common models, and make decisions with the aim of maintaining harmony among the members. The sociologist Alvin Gouldner defines it as a group with which individuals identify and to which they refer when making judgments about their own effectiveness.[1] In this book, the term is used in more encompassing fashion, because a reference group can, for example, be a group of competitors. As discussed in a later chapter, a firm never tries to eliminate competitors in a reference group and sometimes finds it appropriate to cooperate with such rivals. However, outside such a group, driving a competitor out of business is perfectly permissible.

Different context, different reference group

A person's generation may serve as his reference group in some contexts; in other situations that stretch beyond domestic affairs, Japanese society is the salaryman's reference group. For this reason, Japanese people love to read books about how different their society is from others. In an American bookstore, there are few books on the uniqueness of American culture; in a Japanese bookstore, there are dozens. The Japanese avidly devour books on Japan that highlight differences more than similarities in order to strengthen their identification with their society as a reference group.

Many groups, not just generations and societies, can serve as reference groups depending on the setting. The relevant reference group changes according to the context, even as it helps define the context. For example, when a Japanese businessman introduces himself, he usually identifies himself as part of the largest reference group dictated by the context. Speaking with an employee of another company, he will use his company to introduce himself. Within the firm, he will identify the section to which he belongs. Speaking with a non-Japanese, his primary identification is as a Japanese citizen; if another Japanese is present, he may emphasize the part of Japan where he lives. Once the Japanese selects a reference group, he knows who is an insider and who is an outsider. What this really means is that he knows whose expectations he must meet to avoid social embarrassment.

Language forces a choice of reference group

A salaryman can hardly say a word to another person without implicitly defining the reference groups to which he thinks both of them belong. As noted earlier, failing to use proper language is socially embarrassing, and the correct form of Japanese to use with someone else depends not only on the relationship between the two people, but also on the relationship between their reference groups. Juniors defer to seniors in Japan, but even this relationship is complicated when the junior person works for a much more prestigious organization (for example, a government bureau) than the senior. It is likely that both will use the polite form to avoid social embarrassment.

The Japanese believe that their language is hard to master, and this is often a point of pride—so much so that even relatively cosmopolitan Japanese are often startled when they encounter *gaijin* (non-Japanese) fluent in the Japanese tongue. Why do Japanese think their language is especially difficult to learn? It is not so much a matter of grammar, syntax, or even the challenge of mastering Chinese characters. To use the language effectively, a foreigner must understand much more about reference groups and Japanese social structure than Japanese imagine they can absorb.

Insiders gain allies, information, and status

A reference group sets forth models and expectations for its members. To be an insider, the salaryman has to conform to them. As long as he understands the reference group's models, he will not fail to meet the expectations of others in the group. His behavior becomes predictable, and this predictability lets others trust him, as discussed in more detail in the next chapter. Being capable means knowing how to write a report the right way, knowing who should be consulted and when in any situation, and knowing when and whom to inform as events progress. It means mastering the right processes.

Why is it so important for Japanese people to identify reference groups, conform to their models, and meet the expectations of their members? Why does the group's way of behaving become so deeply ingrained? Three different reasons help account for the paramount importance of reference groups. First, there is a *social exchange*. Group members commit to meeting one another's expectations, hiding conflicts from outsiders, and caring about and devoting time and energy to one another. In return, they are treated as insiders. It's impossible to win insider status unless one buys into the Japanese group concept, which we have contrasted with the American team concept.

Second, insiders gain access to *information* that never reaches outsiders. Information is power in an organization where process is more important than structure, and power matters a great deal to salarymen. Someone who doesn't know what is going on behind the formal structure cannot get anything done in a *kaisha*. One harmony-reinforcing rule of a reference group is that, if a salaryman fails to provide information about a decision to even one person who should have received it, that person can veto the decision. Lacking critical information, outsiders cannot be an effective part of a decision-making process. In fact, they usually are the last to realize that a decision has been made. Japanese managers are very deliberate in choosing to disclose information; insiders get it, and outsiders do not. That provides a powerful incentive for protecting one's standing as an insider.

In the West, it is also true that information is power, but in a different sense. The information that confers power in a *kaisha* is knowing who thinks what. A salaryman isn't powerful because he possesses unusual market information, or because he has advance knowledge about a competitor's new product. He is powerful because he knows the *honne* behind the *tatemae* of other insiders.

For example, a salaryman who works for a very well known company that many salarymen view as "classically Japanese" described during our interview the politics of a recent presidential succession there. There were two logical competitors, and the winner had to emerge as the consensus choice of several dozen senior managers. Only one division manager publicly committed to supporting one of the candidates. Yet each insider had to know who favored whom, and whether one candidate therefore had a decisive edge yet. In the West, it often happens that those who lose such power struggles move on to other companies, but salarymen do not have that option. Thus they must know when such a decision will be finalized and how it will turn out, to ensure that they end up on the winning team. It is in this sense that information is power inside the *kaisha*. An insider must know above all what other insiders are really thinking when that information is not public.

Third, *social status* in Japan stems much more from a person's reference group membership than from his individual accomplishments. As seen in Hiro's case in chapter 1, it is far better to be the (unobserved) lowest-ranking member of a prestigious group than the highest-ranking member of a lesser-known group. For example, it is often the case that firms transfer salarymen who cannot be promoted but whose seniority precludes them from remaining where they are. These salarymen are typically reassigned to a subsidiary *(shukko)*. Some salarymen, faced with this prospect, have asked their employers to postpone the inevitable until their children are married, because their social status will drop once they leave the parent firm.

Profit centers are the basic reference groups

Outsiders see Japanese managers as the quintessential company men. The Japanese are renowned for being loyal to their employers, but the notion that all employees of a company behave like a family should be taken with a grain of salt. When a businessman competes against another company, his employer *is* the reference group; from the outside, a company may appear totally united. Internally, however, it is very common for sales departments to fight with plant managers, for regional departments to clash, or for staff and line executives to quarrel. The company as a whole is not a salaryman's only reference group, or in many cases even his primary reference group. He changes his definition of the appropriate reference group according to the context.

Our interviews suggest that salarymen identify most strongly with a smaller basic unit: the "division," which is roughly equivalent to a business unit. The primary membership for the average Japanese white-collar employee is his division, not his company. Why is this the basic reference group?

The division isn't necessarily the lowest level of management within the *kaisha*. In some companies, a salaryman starts out after five to ten years at the "management level" despite the fact that few subordinates actually report to him. This level is a distinct personnel category in the firm, with a unique set of responsibilities and authority. At other companies, the lowest level of management is a *kakari-cho*. A *cho* is a supervisor, and *kakari* means "job" or "role." For example, a *kakari-cho* in a typing pool may have responsibility for approving the work of a typist. To illustrate further, a firm that has a group exporting videotape recorders might have a group head in charge of the U.S. market and a *kakari-cho* in charge of advertising for that market.

The main level of manager actually in charge of subordinates is the *kacho*. *Kacho* is the lowest managerial title that is recognized with respect in the society. Although such managers supervise people, they are not usually responsible for profit centers. Above the *kacho* is a *bucho* (division[2] head) or *shitencho* (branch manager). (The two are virtually equivalent, so *bucho* will be used for both from now on.) He is usually the lowest-level manager with profit-and-loss responsibility for his division. This is why the division is typically the smallest reference group with which a salaryman identifies; because it is a profit center, all members share the same goal. As a result, the division maintains unity with respect to the outside world and doesn't permit overt competition, so that its members may cooperate toward the common objective. In a typical firm, a division might range in size from 30 to perhaps 150 people, but the size of the unit has nothing to do with its status as the primary reference group. The orientation toward a shared profit goal makes all the difference.

Kyocera, a diversified ceramics manufacturer that is consistently one of Japan's most widely admired firms, has succeeded in part because it makes intelligent use of profit centers. It habitually breaks the divisions of Kyocera and its affiliates into "amoebas," the smallest possible business units capable of acting as profit-and-loss centers. Top management then carefully tracks three performance measures for each unit: net production per work hour, the income:expense ratio, and value added per hour worked. Each amoeba behaves as if it were a small company, and each is given its own clear set of goals.[3] Such a form of organization suits the salaryman's mentality very well, leveraging the fact that the welfare of the profit center is more directly relevant to most workers than is the welfare of the company as a whole.

Insiders share responsibility and embarrassment

The Japanese firm's budgeting process sharply focuses responsibility and potential embarrassment at the division level. Within the *kaisha,* budgeting starts with the divisions. Each division *(bu)* is asked to forecast how much money it will make. To construct the forecast, a *bucho* will ask each *kacho* under him for estimates and will add them up to determine the divisional total. But the president of the company—and other division heads—hold the *bucho* alone responsible for making the targets. Managers outside the division will not be publicly aware which *kacho* did or did not make his target. The *bucho* is typically responsible for attending monthly meetings at which the division's performance against targets is made public, holding the group accountable for results. Because the division as a whole would share in the social embarrassment of failing to meet expectations, the budgeting process welds the section within a division into a reference group.

Fellow employees can be outsiders

The respondents interviewed for this book unanimously reported that there is little overt competition within a division, at least none that outsiders would recognize. If conflict were visible to outsiders, everyone would think the division had lost its integrity, its morale would crash, and eventually the *bucho*'s management ability would come into question. It would be naive nonetheless to think that there are no conflicts inside the division. A typical division is organized into sections of about ten people, each responsible for a different function or region. Conflicts between sections are a natural consequence of the division of labor, but they must be kept within the division, because the reference group defines who the insiders are and provides a model for their conduct. Emotionally, some employees feel a stronger sense of belonging to the section than to the division. Section members often drink together after hours; there are too many people in a division for all its members to go to a bar together. But the section is not usually a reference group, because it is too small to have its own clear goals or behavioral models.

Competition across divisions is often quite intense, and clashes are common. The Westerner who assumes that every employee of a particular *kaisha* is committed to maintaining harmony with every other employee draws the wrong conclusion because he fails to understand the insider's reference group. Those in other divisions may be considered outsiders for many purposes.

To illustrate, return to Ringo Bank, Hiro's employer in chapter 1, for a moment. At this bank, as in many others, competition among branches is fierce. Often, branch managers are more concerned with beating other branches than with beating other banks, because that's how the group is measured. At Matsushita, divisions are ranked monthly according to their financial performance, publicly shaming units that do not perform comparatively well. This reinforces the division's standing as a reference group, because its members share the embarrassment of feeling inferior—but it also intensifies interdivisional conflict.

Similarly, competition among divisions *(kyoku)* of government ministries such as the Ministry of International Trade and Industry (MITI) or the Ministry of Finance (MOF) can be ferocious. A popular phrase suggests that, for bureaucrats, "there is a ministry but not a country; there is a division but not a ministry." Bureaucrats don't necessarily make decisions in the best interests of the Japanese nation. To understand what a bureaucrat will do, one must understand which reference group's expectations he is trying to meet. If his reference group is a division, he is probably motivated by his need to meet the division's goals and prevail in infighting with other divisions.

Inside the firm, a salaryman seldom identifies with a reference group smaller than the division, but he often expands his perception of the relevant reference group to larger units, depending on the context. In a recruiting context, for example, the company or ministry becomes the reference group, and partisan politics among divisions is put aside—now outsiders are other companies, not other divisions or branches. When a company belongs to a *keiretsu* (Japanese industrial grouping characterized by long-term relationships and interlocking ownership), its most senior people may in some contexts consider the *keiretsu* to be the reference group. The presidents of *keiretsu* affiliates usually meet every month, solidifying the bond and forging a group identity. However, the average salaryman has no relationship to others working within a particular *keiretsu* and does not always view the employees of *keiretsu* affiliates as insiders. A Westerner should not take it for granted that an employee of, say, Mitsubishi Bank and an employee of Mitsubishi Heavy Industries will view each other as part of the same reference group. It depends on the context.[4]

One special reference group cuts across divisional lines within a firm. All college graduates who join an organization in the same year belong to a reference group called a *doki* (*do* means "same," and *ki* means "period," in this case almost always a year). This affiliation is particularly strong for graduates of the most prestigious Japanese universities, such as Tokyo, Keio, Hitotsubashi, and Waseda. One can almost guarantee, for example, that all Tokyo University graduates in a particular year group will view each other as insiders for most purposes. In fact, salarymen count on the universal acceptance of the *doki* as a reference group to smooth over the conflicts that arise naturally between divisions. If the heads of two competing departments are from the same *doki,* everyone would expect them to cooperate and reach some resolution when conflicts arise. Of course the "old school tie" is a common bond in the West as well. However, one would not expect all of the 1994 Stanford graduates working at Citicorp or all the 1993 Harvard alumni at General Motors to meet periodically, know one another well, or look out for one another, as members of a *doki* will.

"Warm" and "cold" behavior coexist naturally

This book has emphasized that, to predict what a salaryman will do, one needs to understand how he defines his reference group in a given situation. The insider-outsider distinction also helps to unravel one of the most frustrating communication gaps between American and Japanese businessmen. Quite commonly, American and Japanese managers find that getting to know each other doesn't necessarily lead to trust, friendship, and a sense of penetrating the barriers separating insiders from outsiders. When Japanese who have spent time with Americans are asked to describe them, they often use phrases such as "cold" or "difficult to get to know well." Remarkably, Americans use almost exactly the same words to describe Japanese. In American graduate schools, for example, Japanese students as a group are often perceived as quiet, distant people who mostly keep to themselves.

The insider-outsider distinction, especially as it affects Japanese attitudes toward disclosing information, provides insight into the confusion. Japanese and American cultures have different thresholds of intimacy, points at which one feels free to disclose personal information.

Americans seem too open toward outsiders

The relationship between disclosure and intimacy for Americans is a gentle slope that starts out high and remains high. It appears to Japanese that Americans disclose a remarkable amount about themselves to people they do not know well and are only a bit more forthcoming with their closest friends. For instance, one respondent recalled his surprise when he first arrived at a U.S. business school and attended a beginning-of-the-year party. He was introduced to a female American classmate, and within a few minutes of conversation, she began talking about her boyfriend in Japan and how difficult it was to conduct a long distance relationship. It amazed the salaryman that someone he had just met would talk so frankly about her romantic relationships. However, what seemed to him a high level of disclosure meant little to the woman; Americans are frequently open with relative strangers. For the next two years after this conversation, the two said hello to each other in the hallways but never became particularly close friends.

Japanese wonder why Americans talk freely about themselves on a first or second meeting. Americans seem quite willing to discuss their goals, careers, and ambitions, which Japanese view as quite personal. On the other hand, this openness interferes with the salaryman's ability to achieve intimacy with Americans. Once a Japanese person starts thinking of an American friend as part of "our group," he begins to feel some frustration that the American doesn't disclose as much as he expects a group member should. At that point the Japanese feels a sense of isolation, and the American's behavior begins to seem cold.

One respondent recounted a case in which an American colleague quit the firm after working with him for two years, but did not tell the salaryman he was leaving until his last day. To the salaryman, it was extremely disconcerting that he, a close coworker, found out about the resignation at the same time any stranger or the public could learn the news. Recall that access to information one wouldn't receive otherwise is a valuable reason to be an insider. The salaryman expected such major news would be shared, with insiders only, at the earliest possible moment. The incident lessened his confidence in treating any American as if he were an insider.

Test, then cross the threshold of intimacy

Japanese usually strike Americans as reserved and difficult to get to know. This is because, at low levels of intimacy (reflecting how much time one spends with another person and how close one feels to him or her), it is not part of the Japanese behavioral model for a person to disclose much about himself. To do so would be "pushing too hard," and that is the most common complaint Japanese express about Americans—they expect too much forthrightness in the early stages of an acquaintance, when disclosure should be kept low. Many Japanese are thrown off by the common American practice of calling a person by his first name before the threshold of intimacy has been crossed. In contrast, when a Japanese has trouble assessing the degree of intimacy he has with another person, he tends to err on the side of conservatism, avoiding any subjects that might be deemed private.

Among Japanese themselves, relationships begin with a fairly long period during which two people feel each other out. Eventually, one person begins testing whether the other is ready to cross the threshold of intimacy. One sign that a person is ready to cross the threshold is that he occasionally drops the use of polite forms of language in favor of more casual forms of address commonly employed with friends. The shift is not abrupt. Expectations dictate a transition period during which each person might use a mixture of informal and formal speech to see how the other responds. The easiest way to cross the threshold is to go out drinking. In a bar, two people can pat shoulders and playfully punch one another to see how the other person reacts. If the other party doesn't respond in kind, it is socially acceptable to cover up by attributing one's actions to alcohol, minimizing the possibility of embarrassment.

Most Westerners don't understand this probing and testing process, especially if they don't speak Japanese, because the cue that the salaryman is ready to move toward friendship is intermittent use of casual language. Some of those interviewed for this book were nonplussed that, when they invited an American to go out to a bar, the American would suggest coffee instead. The purpose of going to a bar is to provide cultural cover during the exploratory phase of forming a friendship. A salaryman can blame alcohol if he makes a move toward intimacy that the other is not ready to reciprocate. "It must be the coffee" doesn't count as an excuse in case of a mistake.

There is a point at which a Japanese decides that someone he is getting to know has become part of his primary group and is now an insider who can be trusted. Then, suddenly, the level of communication changes sharply. Now both people can talk about more personal things, such as whom they like and don't like, their hopes and aspirations, and so forth. For example, one respondent described the evolution of one of his closest friendships. He was transferred to a new department at the same time as another salaryman, and the two did not hit it off at first. The probing period was marked by frequent conflicts and fierce discussions. Despite the occasional argument, they began to respect each other. They proceeded to go out drinking, exchanged thoughts about family and career, and discovered that they shared many common ideas about business and their jobs. Suddenly, the line was crossed, and they became good friends. When our respondent decided to leave their *kaisha* to work overseas, he told this comrade before he told anyone else. Their relationship continued during our respondent's years away in the United States, and they still exchange business information they would not discuss with outsiders.

Caring behavior depends on the context

The warmth of this relationship typifies the caring that insiders extend to one another. Outsiders do sometimes remark about gestures made by Japanese that strike them as extraordinarily humane by Western standards. Often this heightens their confusion: How can the Japanese seem so cold, yet occasionally make such warm gestures? For example, one American who had worked in Japan for a U.S. company for three years told us a story about how his boss had paid a hospital visit on the wife of a company employee, after she had suffered an accident. "I think Japanese management shows great concern for the well-being of individual workers," he said. He is correct, but one should not interpret such actions as personal courtesies. The behavioral model Japanese managers must follow demands that they display caring for colleagues and their families. If the executive had not gone to the hospital, he would have been viewed by subordinates as a cold person. This is quite different from the genuine warmth that salarymen feel for those with whom they have crossed the threshold of intimacy. Japan's custom of semiannual gift exchanges falls into the same category. Most Japanese observe this rite because gift giving is a model to be followed, not because they want to show their appreciation through giving presents to other people.

The other side of the coin is that Japanese are often deeply touched when Americans show them unexpected kindness. Japanese generally think Americans are cold, because they seem unable to share true intimacy with their friends. They are amazed when Americans they don't know at all treat them very courteously. One salaryman told us what a deep impression it made on him when he received numerous offers of help from complete strangers while he was trying to juggle a baby and some packages on a shopping trip. The probability of getting that kind of help seemed to him much higher in the United States than in Japan, because Americans appeared more willing to assist someone they didn't know.[5] Another salaryman attending a U.S. graduate school described to us how he sent letters to several well-known American professors and executives, asking for help with his research for a paper. He was pleasantly surprised at how much assistance he received. The Japanese counterparts of those who helped him would be very unlikely to respond to requests from people they did not know. What Americans might regard as typical American hospitality strikes the Japanese as unusually warm and caring behavior.

This section has examined in some detail why Americans and Japanese see each other as unpredictably warm and cold, because this perception gap can have serious consequences. It is difficult for a Japanese to treat an American as an insider when he can't predict how an American will behave. Many Americans seem unaware that there is a process by which one is admitted to a reference group. The warmth-coldness puzzle is thus best understood as a symptom of a more fundamental mechanism with wider-reaching effects—the ubiquity of reference group influences on Japanese behavior.

Industry reference groups exist as well

The insider-outsider distinction is also important at the level of organizations, not just at the level of their employees. Westerners often perceive that they are competing against a monolithic "Japan, Incorporated," where all firms work with the government to defeat non-Japanese companies. Typically, Japanese counter that such an idea is hardly imaginable, because their firms compete ferociously in the domestic market. Contradictory points of view characterize Western analyses of Japan's economic success. Some attribute Japanese strength to the economy's ability to foster cooperation and suggest changing antitrust laws to make it easier for Western rivals to work together in the face of Japanese competition. Others argue that Japanese firms are strong because those who sell overseas are the hardy survivors of Japan's extremely competitive environment. Typically, those who hold this view stress the importance to Western firms of competing in Japan, even if they lose money, so that they may harden themselves as the Japanese do.

Both perspectives contain some truth. In the usual context, all companies in the domestic market are tough competitors. On the other hand, especially in a foreign market, Japanese tend to see other Japanese as part of a large group welded together by social ties. For example, one respondent, employed by the U.S. subsidiary of a large Japanese firm, told us that he had an intimate relationship with his counterparts in the U.S. subsidiary of his company's biggest Japanese rival. "We share a lot of information because we can understand intuitively what they think," he said. "This can't happen with an American company, and anyway the American competitors in this market are much bigger." Domestically, both companies are big players, so they compete tooth and nail. This sort of information exchange between their domestic employees would hardly be imaginable. However, in the United States, each thinks of itself as a smaller player, so their salarymen feel comfortable helping each other. As before, context and perspective govern who is an insider and who is an outsider. It is often quite difficult for non-Japanese to tell which firms are insiders and which are outsiders in the corporate world of Japan.

For example, Japanese banks scrap mightily for every point of market share. Yet recently, when Japanese banks were allowed for the first time to open branches in a Southeast Asian country, only six applied. "Coincidentally," that was the number established by Japan's government as the limit. Nearly all of Japan's banks were interested in this market, so why did exactly six apply? Domestically, banks see each other as outsiders, but in a case such as this, the *kaisha*'s reference group is Japanese banks as a whole. To prevent confusion, the Ministry of Finance will guide the situation and communicate what group members should expect. What is remarkable is how well the banks understood the ministry's expectations and accepted its decision—so much so that every bank knew exactly which six should throw their hats into the ring.

Rival firms are insiders under outside pressure

Generally speaking, Japanese firms view their direct rivals as insiders only when operating overseas or when coordinated by a government ministry. A good example of the latter case is a scandal that recently broke concerning government construction contracts. Such jobs are awarded through competitive bidding. Although there are many construction companies in Japan, the Ministry of Construction decides who can participate in the bid. Naturally, once a reference group is created, social expectations take hold and firms are anxious to model their behavior on what they think others expect. Within the chosen circle of bidders, they talk among themselves and agree who will bid what amount. The winning bid is pegged to the sponsoring ministry's budget for the project.

In the West, if bids always exactly equaled government expectations, watchdog groups would suspect corruption. In Japan, minimizing the possibility of embarrassment is paramount. Recall that such embarrassment stems from failing to meet the expectations of a reference group. A bid below the budgeted amount would embarrass the bureaucrat who estimated the project cost, by signaling that he had made a mistake. Consequently, government officials communicate what they have budgeted for a project and discourage companies from bidding below this figure. The winner subcontracts out parts of the job to its rivals, sharing part of the profit.

The Japanese steel industry provides another example of a closed circle. The focus of competition is not rivalry among Japanese companies, but rivalry between the closed circle and outsiders. Within the closed circle, the most cost-competitive firm doesn't win all the bids; instead, the firms take turns. For instance, starting in the mid-1980s, the Japanese steel industry faced intense competitive pressure from foreign rivals, especially Koreans. Interestingly, Korean companies were on occasion treated as insiders, but it was almost impossible for the steel industry to include British or American companies in the reference group. A salaryman who works for a steelmaker explained in his interview, "Koreans have a good sense of what we Japanese want to do and how we want to do it." Western norms simply don't fit with the rules of the game as insiders understand them. The reference group sets social expectations, and failing to meet the reference group's expectations is both upsetting and embarrassing. Consequently, a firm cannot be included in the closed circle if it is not prepared to meet the expectations of its peer companies.

The necessity for outside pressure to weld together a reference group is clearly illustrated in the microprocessor market.[6] From 1988 to 1993, Japan's top ten semiconductor manufacturers grew at only half the rate of the world industry as a whole, and the Japanese industry was not profitable. The principal culprit was Japan's reliance on memory chips. Large-scale entry by Korean manufacturers drove prices below the levels needed to recoup the huge capital investments characteristic of this segment. Meanwhile, companies such as Intel increased their worldwide share of the more lucrative market for microprocessor chips. To attack Intel, Japan's major computer manufacturers backed a high-profile project called TRON, intended to pioneer an alternative to the Intel standard. The TRON project failed, partly because it was not compatible with the huge base of software written for Intel processors. Just as importantly, however, NEC refused to participate in the TRON project. Because NEC's share of the Japanese personal computer market exceeded 50 percent, the TRON effort was probably doomed from the start. NEC did not perceive a crisis, as it was not losing market share to foreigners. In this case, NEC did not acknowledge its rivals as fellow insiders and did not strive to meet their cooperative expectations, because it did not feel subjected to significant outside pressures.

Size and tradition define industry insiders

When an industry reference group does form, how does a firm become defined as an insider? A combination of size and prestige is essential, and tradition plays a major role. In Japan, each firm strives to be one of the leading companies in its industry so that it will be treated as part of the inner circle. Government ministries ask leading firms, particularly the largest company in an industry, to help them determine rules, set prices, and make other important decisions. These insiders also share important information. For example, Toyota and Nippon Steel jointly decide the price of steel for the auto industry, and the leaders in the hotel industry not only set prices but also determine how much all companies will discount during the off-season. This looks like a cartel to outsiders, but it is not a cartel in the Western sense. The reference group leader sets prices, and insiders follow; prices are not the outcome of a negotiation among cartel members. The leader's prices have to be acceptable to all the members of a reference group; if they aren't, the company won't be accepted as the leader. Those who do not follow the model are excluded from the circle of information exchange, and if they fail, insiders will make no effort to save them.

Size is extremely important, but tradition and prestige matter, too, as illustrated by the recent upheaval in Japanese banking. It was long the custom that everything was decided by Japan's five largest banks, which exchanged numbers at a monthly meeting called the *gokokai. Go* means "five," so the very name of the meeting implied that it involved the "big five." However, when

Mitsui Bank merged with Taiyo Kobe to form Sakura Bank, Japan's sixth largest, the Ministry of Finance directed the five leaders to enlarge the circle and include Sakura. Why?

Mitsui used to be a very prestigious bank before it fell on hard times. Because of its reliance on a shrinking market for corporate financing, it gradually dropped in the rankings, becoming Japan's seventh-largest bank. Such a shift was considered unthinkable because the Ministry of Finance regulates the asset size of Japanese banks, but it turned out the ministry was only committed to preserving the order of the top five banks, and Tokai Bank was allowed to pass Mitsui, taking over sixth place. What would have happened if Tokai and Taiyo Kobe had merged? This, too, would have produced the sixth-largest bank in Japan. Would this combination have been admitted to the closed circle? Such a move might well have set off a scramble among the big five to acquire regional banks, as each tried to become the largest bank in Japan. The five were able to admit Mitsui without inaugurating a merger wave, because of Mitsui's traditional standing and the fact that it used to be one of the largest banks in Japan.

The strength of the insider circle varies from industry to industry. In some cases, the reference group is very strong and insiders control nearly everything, whereas in others the reference group is nearly nonexistent. The stronger the reference group, the more difficult it is for newcomers to penetrate the inner circle. Insiders must continue meeting the expectations of others in the reference group, just as salarymen do. As long as they do so, they will be involved in the decision-making process and included in the information exchange network. The needs of firms that behave in accordance with the reference group's model will be taken into account by the industry leader, so they won't be driven from the industry.

Foreigners are almost always outsiders

Westerners are well aware of the fundamental distinction between "we Japanese" and foreigners (*gaijin*). Clearly Japanese firms feel quite comfortable applying one standard of conduct to foreign employees, suppliers, and rivals, and another to their domestic counterparts, when the reference group is "we Japanese."

Employment security clearly illustrates how conduct depends on perceived context. Despite Japan's present economic troubles, laying off Japanese workers from the largest companies still violates Japanese social expectations.[7] For instance, in January 1993, Pioneer told 35 employees, all over the age of fifty, that they needed to leave the firm.[8] All belonged to the large class of salarymen known as "window gazers" *(madogiwazoku),* executives with no subordinates and no responsibilities whose days are spent "sitting at a window." Pioneer offered terms that would be considered generous in the United States: two years of salary as severance pay. The storm that Pioneer's action caused badly damaged its image in Japan and forced management to apologize.

No such outcry occurs when firms terminate the employment of their foreign workers, however. For example, in the spring of 1993, the New York subsidiary of Japan's largest advertising agency, Dentsu, fired 26 of its 125 employees, explaining that the reductions were necessary due to cutbacks in client spending.[9] Although a significant proportion of the office's employees— including 40 percent of the managers—were Japanese, all but one of those let go were American, and the lone Japanese manager had expressed a desire to retire early. Similarly, when the Tokyo stock market's slide caused Japanese brokerages to rein in their push overseas, firms such as Daiwa Securities America did not terminate any Japanese executives, but did let go the 3 American executives it had brought in at senior levels in 1990.[10] Because of low profits, in August 1992, Fujitsu Microelectronics closed a twelve-year-old factory in San Diego, putting 260 people out of work.[11] The *kaisha* offered these employees sixty days' severance pay and promised to pay San Diego employers $2,000 per laid-off Fujitsu worker they hired. The model applied to foreign employees permits layoffs, although they should be administered with compassion. In Japan itself, for instance, recent budget squeezes on universities resulted in the firing of many long-secure non-Japanese faculty, leading even experienced Japan hands among the professors to accuse the Ministry of Education, Science, and Culture of "academic apartheid."[12]

When the U.S. Public Broadcasting System's documentary show "Frontline" profiled Matsushita's closing of its Quasar factory in Illinois a few years ago,[13] the Japanese interviewed for the program were astonished at the bitterness exhibited by American employees. The Americans thought that a huge *kaisha* would guarantee them job security; after all, this was the "Japanese way" at the largest companies. In return, they tried very hard to acquire Japanese business manners, make friends with Japanese colleagues, and become members of the Matsushita family. These employees hardly realized that, from Matsushita's point of view, they were neither insiders nor a part of the Matsushita family. One manager told "Frontline" that he accepted as a fact of life that businesses sometimes have to shut down, but that he was terribly disappointed by the way the company had fired him. On the morning he was terminated, his boss asked him to pack his belongings and vacate his office no later than noon the same day. This treatment was the opposite of what he expected from a caring, Japanese-run enterprise. Matsushita's managers, however, saw nothing inconsistent about shuttering an unprofitable plant and letting employees go, because it adopted the course of action it thought appropriate for the situation.

On a more personal level, a number of articles have surfaced documenting the frustration Western executives who work for Japanese firms feel when they are shut out of decision making.[14] Several of the respondents in this book work for the U.S. subsidiaries of Japanese companies. One told us, "My direct boss is an American. He usually leaves the office at five o'clock. The Japanese employees usually have meetings after five o'clock, because we need to communicate with headquarters in Tokyo. I report to him the next morning what happened in these meetings, but he doesn't seem to like it." Many non-Japanese managers have concluded that the real decisions in a Japanese-owned firm are made after five o'clock in closed meetings where only Japanese is spoken. Regardless of what the organization chart says, junior Japanese salarymen assigned overseas are part of the decision-making circle, whereas their nominally senior American colleagues are outside of it.

Treating outsiders differently is accepted

Kaisha obviously treat foreign and Japanese employees differently in these examples. Such behavior can be interpreted in one of two ways. One interpretation is that Japanese managers live by a double standard. Americans who believe this often argue that Japanese companies have to be forced to change these practices. Another interpretation is that salarymen always predicate their behavior on reference group expectations, and in these cases, foreign employees are outsiders.

A person who wishes to understand why salarymen behave the way they do must not become so focused on the Japanese-versus-*gaijin* distinction that he overlooks a deeper mechanism governing Japanese business behavior. Even among themselves, the Japanese carefully distinguish outsiders and insiders and have very different models appropriate for each. Japanese people do apply different standards to insiders and outsiders, but from their perspective no duplicity is involved—why should one treat apples and oranges the same? To predict Japanese behavior, try to understand who in a given situation will be framed as an insider and who will be considered an outsider. It is all-important to grasp what reference group the Japanese is using to distinguish insiders from outsiders. When the reference group is all Japanese, then non-Japanese are outsiders. But when the reference group is a company, all those outside the company are outsiders. When a division in a company is a reference group, those in other divisions are outsiders even though they work for the same company.

Some foreigners gain deeper acceptance

It is extremely difficult for a *gaijin* to become a true insider, even though members of his section may regard him as one for limited purposes in pursuit of a common goal. This is so because Japanese fear that no one from a different background without similar experiences inside the firm can have or meet the uniform expectations that reference groups impose. Nonetheless, some foreigners are accepted at a much deeper level than are others. A person's command of Japanese makes a significant difference. When we asked respondents what American coworkers could do to become closer to them, many emphasized the importance of learning the language. Practically, the language plays a vital role in the subtle process by which Japanese get closer to one another. Symbolically, the Japanese esteem the attitude of a foreigner who struggles to learn Japanese. He is following a model they can appreciate. An implication for Westerners employed by Japanese firms or working closely with Japanese partners and customers is that investing time in language courses may be more important than immersing oneself in Japanese culture or even matching the typical long hours of the salarymen. For example, respondents suggested that few Japanese would resent a colleague who left work at five o'clock in order to take a Japanese language class.

The outsider who takes up the language challenge will benefit from the Japanese emphasis on process over results. A novice Japanese speaker risks giving offense by using improper forms of the language, but if he has good human relationships with his Japanese colleagues, they will help him out. Many non-Japanese speak the language well but are not accepted, whereas others with poorer language skills are accepted. Skill is not as important as human feeling, character, and attitude.

One respondent, for example, told of a program for non-Japanese managers which brought two trainees, an Asian and an American, into the company. The Asian was well liked because he impressed everyone with his serious efforts to learn Japanese. The American was not appreciated because he made no attempt to learn Japanese. Unfortunately for the American, no one would tell him outright what the problem was. The salarymen felt that, because he didn't have the proper attitude and wasn't striving to communicate better, he was unlikely to last more than a year, so why should someone bother to point out his error and perhaps anger him?

The salaryman never mentioned whether the Asian trainee ever spoke Japanese well. That was beside the point. Salarymen understand that it takes a long time for a foreigner to acquire the skill needed for daily conversation, much less business. But they expect someone working for a Japanese company at least to *try* learning the language. Those who study Japanese not only display the right attitude, but also show that they understand and wish to meet their colleagues' expectations. Some Westerners working for *kaisha* seem to be satisfied when they learn some Japanese. Whether they "know enough" yet is not important; to meet expectations, they must continue to learn more. Expertise is a secondary consideration. The person who understands and tries to meet various expectations is the one who earns trust from others and can move forward within the *kaisha*.

This chapter has emphasized that reference groups are held together by a combination of fear and need. At the level where one could be embarrassed by failure to meet expectations (within firms, the smallest profit center), identity is strongest. Moving up to the level of firms themselves, reference groups are strong only when rivals feel themselves driven by outside pressure. It is not some distinctively Japanese clannishness or drive to cooperate that binds insiders together. A corollary is that trust need not be what binds Japanese groups together either. The achievement of harmony without trust is very Japanese and is the subject of the next chapter.

CHAPTER FOUR

Harmony Prevails, but Trust Is Rare

The puzzle discussed in chapter 3, the seeming prevalence of double standards, perplexes people who are just starting to acquaint themselves with Japanese management. The puzzle discussed in this chapter, harmony without trust, doesn't even strike most outsiders as a puzzle until they get to know Japanese companies better. People looking in from outside the reference group see Japanese companies as models of harmony. Many Western writers have characterized the *kaisha* as a tightly knit clan permeated by mechanisms for generating trust among employees and along supply chains. Western scholars have picked up on this theme and are starting to build organizational models in which trust affects the outcomes of competitive games. Western firms have hired consultants to help them manufacture internal trust, so that they can compete successfully with the harmonious Japanese. Western journalists have heaped scorn on managers who have been unable to duplicate the warm, nurturing atmosphere that supposedly characterizes Japanese organizations.

Interpersonal and interorganizational trust does create positive and important economic effects. We support efforts to forge more trusting bonds between people and between companies. However, we question the notion that Japanese firms are harmonious because people there generally trust one another more than they do in the West. Harmony in the *kaisha* is mostly a product of organizational control mechanisms. We think that Western managers who focus principally on winning hearts and minds through better interpersonal skills are likely to become frustrated when these efforts don't transform their enterprises into Japanese-style companies.

Polls frequently show that Japanese workers are *less* committed to their companies and *less* satisfied with their jobs than American workers are. One survey in the late 1980s, for instance, reported that 15 percent of Japanese employees described themselves as satisfied with their current employment situation, compared to 53 percent of American employees.[1] A good deal of academic research finds that workplace commitment is lower in Japan than it is in the United States.[2] How can this be, if trust and harmony are bedrock Japanese values? This chapter explores how salarymen think about trust and harmony, using the concepts developed in chapter 2 to explain how organizational mechanisms produce the appearance of concord, even absent genuine interpersonal trust.

The central thesis of much Western writing on Japanese organizations is that the *kaisha* resembles a clan, depending primarily on subtle social controls to create trust and harmony.[3] The original writers who drew this analogy emphasized that harmony is a product of social control. That message may have been drowned out by others, which emphasize harmony at the individual level and suggest that widespread trust allows Japanese companies to operate with few overt controls. Taken to extremes, this idea has led some companies to invest large sums of money trying to reshape Western employees into more harmonious people, who can be trusted to do the right thing because they have internalized the company's goals. In some cases, form has been confused with substance. For example, because Japanese firms emphasize slogans and vision statements, some Western executives have put great effort into crafting similar devices.

Those who believe that trust and consensus make the Japanese *kaisha* work mistake an effect for a cause. Japanese behaviors harmonize because individuals follow well-understood behavioral models. Once a particular interpretation of the context is accepted, everyone falls into line. Deviant behavior is severely punished in a system that depends on avoiding social embarrassment. Consistency and the need to conform to an accepted model underlie the harmony and subtle controls that the outsider observes. At the individual level, salarymen are seldom more trusting or harmonious than their Western counterparts who are asked to be "more Japanese." And, given the right context, Japanese managers can behave in ways that would shock those conditioned to believe that preserving harmony and maintaining trust are the essence of the Japanese style.

Harmony is often just a surface appearance

A person who talks with Japanese managers *will* hear them emphasize harmony a great deal. But harmony is an outcome, not a fundamental axiom of Japanese behavior. Some Western writers suggest that harmony (which they usually translate as *wa*) is the central value in Japanese society because of Japan's agrarian past. But, beneath the surface of the Japanese firm, hidden from outsiders, trust gives way to interdepartmental conflict that is at least as bitter as that found in Western organizations.

For example, a respondent from a well-known Japanese company told the inside story of how his firm had withdrawn from one of its business lines in the United States. Stiff price competition and continuing losses had finally convinced the company that its position was untenable. Because the largest market for the product was in the United States, corporate headquarters asked the U.S. subsidiary's Japanese managers to draw up a plan that would allow the firm to exit the business with minimal losses.

Back in Tokyo, a different team crafted its own plan for exiting the business. Did a compromise emerge to protect harmony? It did not; the Tokyo team successfully politicked to have its plan executed. The foreign subsidiary team was far away, and the Tokyo group was able to position the overseas salarymen as quasi-outsiders, who were perhaps too close to the American market to achieve an objective understanding of the situation.

The process of exiting the industry turned into a disaster. The salarymen in the American subsidiary had been right after all, and the Tokyo plan caused the *kaisha* to absorb huge losses. The head of the Tokyo group blandly placed all the blame on the American team. His attempt to scapegoat the U.S. subsidiary worked; to this day, the salaryman interviewed for this book worries about whether there is a black mark on his record that will eventually short-circuit his career, because he was part of the group that was blamed for the debacle.

Why did the salarymen from the U.S. subsidiary take this miscarriage of justice lying down? Not one of the U.S.-based managers chose to tell the truth to the president of the company, even though being painted as scapegoats may limit their future opportunities. Understanding why requires penetrating the facade of harmony that surrounds the *kaisha*.

The American managers could have told top management what had really happened and fought to assign the responsibility to Tokyo, where it belonged. They were too experienced to try. They knew they couldn't avoid the blame, for two reasons. First, all decisions are at least superficially unanimous, so whether or not they opposed the Tokyo plan, they shared responsibility for it. The president would simply have told them it was their fault for failing to object to the plan when the decision was made. Second, the foreign-based managers would have been blamed for disturbing harmony inside the *kaisha*. However right a Japanese manager may be, he cannot start a dispute without seeming disruptive. Once the expatriates were maneuvered into a position in which they couldn't speak up without appearing to start an argument, they had nothing to gain by presenting the truth. The best outcome they could have hoped for would have been to bring down the careers of the Tokyo salarymen, surely destroying their own.

Why did the Tokyo team try to place the blame on the American team instead of accepting responsibility and apologizing? The answer is that they could get away with it, because the

U.S. managers were too far from headquarters to intervene. Had another Tokyo-based team crafted the alternative exit plan, it would not have been as easy for the culprits to dodge the blame. But once they persuaded the president that the losses were someone else's fault, they were protected by the old Japanese adage that, if two people fight, both should be punished. The way to avoid responsibility is to manipulate the context, because, once an appropriate interpretation is established, it is very resistant to change. Harmony may be preserved this way, but trust has nothing to do with it.

Harmony is an outcome, not a behavioral driver

Because context is everything, it is not surprising that the organizational mechanism at work in the previous example wouldn't apply in a different setting. One respondent related a different incident that illustrates this. He works for a large Japanese financial institution which does a lot of business with a smaller American partner. The U.S. managers once made an urgent request to their Tokyo-based liaison and were dismayed when the response took longer than they wanted. Furious, the Americans demanded that the bank fire its "ineffective" representative. Should one expect the Japanese to preserve harmony by switching liaisons?

The Japanese were appalled. Salarymen are not fired, and in any case, the bank's representative took longer than the Americans wished because he had to follow proper procedure for pushing the customer's request through channels. The delay may have cost the partnership economically, but for the Japanese, process is more important than results. Each party accused the other of arrogance. For instance, the salaryman we interviewed told us that he believes strongly that Americans always insist business should be done by their criteria, which they consider superior to Japanese practice. Japanese firms are passionately devoted to their customers, and it is true that serving the customer is of paramount importance, but not at the expense of appropriate process. The partner's demand that a bank fire a salaryman grossly violated Japanese norms and shattered the partnership's harmony.

Why did the Americans fail to understand how inappropriate their request was in context? Is this simply a case of cultural ignorance that could have been fixed had someone sat down and explained the concept of lifetime employment to them? More likely, a deeper phenomenon operates here. Americans generally seem less concerned with process because they don't have to worry about losing membership as insiders of a reference group. The salarymen in our earlier example had to consider their future careers in a company they could not leave, and they knew that they would probably have to work with some of the members of the Tokyo team in the future. This is why they couldn't destroy the appearance of harmony once a model had been established that would have framed dissent as an assault on unity. The Americans in our second example faced a different set of social constraints.

Where conflicts arise, the *kaisha* must perform a delicate balancing act. If two people are promoted to top management from one group and only one from another group, the power imbalance will result in conflict. For similar reasons, banks that have formed from mergers (such as Sakura Bank and Dai-Ichi Kangyo Bank) have been careful for many years after the union to maintain a balance between the number of people in top management from each side of the merger. Following a model that does not threaten the alumni of either side preserves harmony; again, harmony is an effect, not a cause.

Maintaining harmony is not a central principle

The lack of harmony and the prevalence of conflict beneath the surface of Japanese firms is especially puzzling to those who have absorbed the idea from some books about Japan that maintaining *wa* (harmony) at all costs is the fundamental value in Japanese society.[4] Too many Westerners writing about Japan convey the impression that *wa* underlies all things Japanese. Chapter 2 suggested that you question the notion that there is *any* fundamental value underpinning Japanese behavior. To determine whether harmony is a core cultural value, the salarymen interviewed for this book were asked, "What is *wa*?"

About a third responded, "I don't understand what that means exactly." Another third answered that it is a harmonious state deriving from people sharing things in everyday life, a definition fairly close to that employed by Westerners who write about the concept. Another third expressed a different opinion, suggesting that harmony is something that they are *forced* to maintain.

When a group of Japanese MBA students was asked during this study whether maintaining harmony should be the primary goal of a group, only a small minority said yes. Maintaining harmony is desirable, but the Japanese focus much more on maintaining a smooth continuation of process. For example, consider the following story that a respondent related during this research. When he was a Japanese student attending a U.S. business school, he joined a project group that included both Americans and Japanese. "In the first meeting, we didn't specifically tell each member what he had to do before the next meeting," he noted. "In the next meeting, I found that the Americans hadn't done anything. Each Japanese had independently carried out a background study of the assigned problem, because it seemed necessary given the deadline." Salarymen have absorbed a model that tells them to think about the process and prepare for the next step without being told to do so. Any other behavior might disrupt the continuity of the process.

In general, many Japanese MBA students said that working with Americans in group project situations is difficult. They felt that Americans assumed that the goal of the group is a concrete objective, something to get done. Americans seemed to place far less emphasis on compromising to further an appropriate group process. For instance, whenever Americans had an objection, they expressed it, without regard for the effect of their action on the group's process. The disruptive impact of such behavior on group harmony isn't really what irritates the salarymen. The Japanese were bothered because such conduct departs from their accepted models of group process. In their world, a group's chief task is to carry out its job the right way. Meeting a deadline or producing the highest-quality output are secondary outcomes.

Harmony stems from social controls

Usually, salarymen act to preserve harmony because they have to preserve their membership in a group. In many situations, Westerners can abandon a group if serious conflicts arise, but this is simply not an option for a salaryman.

For example, a banker interviewed for this book discovered soon after joining his firm out of college that practically everyone in the bank belonged to an informal clique, typically composed of seven to ten members. Those who stood outside any clique were almost completely isolated and ineffective. He ended up becoming part of an informal group bound together by the members' shared interest in playing tennis. After a few years, he was selected to go to the United States for MBA training. As his two years in America drew to a close, one of the senior members of his tennis-playing group called and asked if he would be interested in joining the senior executive's department.

He accepted the offer, although there were many other jobs inside the firm that he would have preferred. An outsider might interpret his action as an attempt to retain good relations and harmony with a mentor. In fact, the newly minted MBA was not particularly close to his prospective new boss. He accepted the invitation because he feared that, if he declined, he would be excluded from the tennis-playing clique. Deprived of group membership, he would be unable to function in the bank.

Why, then, do some Western analysts place so much emphasis on *wa* as a central Japanese value? In school, Japanese children learn about Shotokutaishi, an eighth-century prince who served a female emperor. Shotokutaishi is one of Japan's most familiar historical figures; his visage formerly appeared on the 10,000-yen bill. He produced a famous text that set forth seven principles, similar in spirit to the Bible's ten commandments. One of these strongly emphasizes *wa*. Even so, *wa* is a difficult concept for many salarymen to pin down. It is more about maintaining an absence of conflict than a positive reign of harmony.

Shotokutaishi's maxim is a model that calls for curbing conflict within a reference group. Of course, the reference group can change with the context. Overt internal conflicts occur within the firm when the reference group is a smaller unit. For the salaryman, maintaining *wa* means getting along with his working colleagues. Within a reference group, contention is curbed, process is respected, membership is maintained.

Harmony in a Japanese firm, such as it is, stems from social controls. Therefore, it could exist without widespread individual-level feelings of interpersonal trust. The next section examines what trust is and how it is generated in Japanese business, to explain why harmony without trust seems perfectly natural to a salaryman.

Real trust exists within a very small circle

Some Western writers have suggested that Japanese firms do not need control systems that are as extensive as those of Western companies, because trust replaces hierarchy as the primary way to coordinate departments. Loose, informal controls give Japanese firms competitive advantages over more bureaucratic rivals, according to this view. The Japanese managers who contributed to this research are quite skeptical about this notion. In their view, real trust is limited to a small group of people. Consequently, external coordination must be called upon to resolve interdepartmental conflicts.

For example, one junior executive in a telecommunications firm described a classic interdepartmental conflict, which might arise in any Western organization. One department in his company is a profit center providing a certain fee-based service. Another is a profit center selling machines. The hardware unit decided to offer the service without charge to those who bought a machine. A huge internal battle resulted, which dragged on and on because no single coordinator was directly responsible for both units. If trust and harmony prevail within the *kaisha,* why couldn't the units work out a resolution themselves? Because each is a profit center, each is concerned with its own bottom line, not with maintaining harmony. Japanese firms are organized hierarchically, and Japanese managers spend so much time coordinating precisely because departments cannot be relied on to resolve differences by themselves.

Trust is based on predictability

There are two principal translations of the word *trust* in Japanese, and they are quite different. When salarymen say that genuine trust is rare in the *kaisha* and is limited to a small group of colleagues, they have a specific meaning of "trust" in mind.

The salarymen in this study more characteristically think about *shinrai*. *Shinrai* has more to do with reliability and predictability than with an emotional bond between trusted people. One can *shinrai* that a machine won't break down; one can *shinrai* that a person will do something exactly the way someone asks to have it done. When asked how many people they felt *shinrai* in, most respondents ticked off five or at most ten very close friends. Even in this mechanical sense, the salaryman does not trust in all the employees of his company, nor even all the colleagues in his reference group, the division. *Shinrai* depends on the context. In strong contexts, a salaryman can *shinrai* that others will follow appropriate models to avoid social embarrassment. Where shared interpretations are weaker, models may not be clear, and people may violate them without necessarily suffering a penalty.

The other translation of "trust," *shinyo,* has a strong emotional content. If a person has *shinyo* in another, he believes that the other will not take advantage of him. A salaryman would disclose confidential or personal information only to those they *shinyo.* Even this meaning has a different emotional basis than the English word *trust* implies. In the West, the foundation of trust is caring, whereas in Japan the foundation of *shinyo* is duty. A man can *shinyo* another person because he believes the person is a "man of honor." Like the movie stereotype of a Mafioso, such a person knows the score and can be counted on to do the right thing (keep confidential information away from outsiders) as a matter of obligation.

Shinyo is even more rare in the *kaisha* than *shinrai* is. The typical respondent shares such emotional bonds with only one or two other people. If *shinyo* and *shinrai* extend to such small groups, it is hard to see how the foundation of harmony can be interpersonal feelings of trust. True harmony—the glorious atmosphere of helping, caring, and cherishing one another—is found only within a very small circle.

Trust extends vertically, not horizontally

The surveyed salarymen were asked, "What leads to feelings of *shinrai?*" They replied that the most important factors are shared value orientations and shared experiences. Salarymen share these with superiors much more than they do with peers or juniors. Accordingly, the salaryman's circle of trust extends mostly to his superiors, who are seen as role models and therefore persons to be trusted. Trust builds up because the junior models his behavior on the senior. Because a junior tries to internalize the way a senior handles a situation, the kinds of experiences seniors and juniors share are particularly intense. In this modeling relationship, the senior's role is to know exactly what the junior is doing, not just how it turns out. The Japanese emphasis on process creates downward trust. The senior spends a tremendous amount of time ensuring that the junior does things the right way, almost regardless of success or failure. He comes to trust the junior because he understands how the junior goes about his business.

A vertical chain of trust results. For example, one manager interviewed for this book said that, when he joined his company fresh out of college, his first boss said to him, "I will take responsibility for anything you do, as long as you report everything to me." That supervisor in turn kept his boss informed about what his subordinates were doing for, if he didn't, he would have to take responsibility for their mistakes. Information keeps flowing because managers at all levels know they will be taken care of as long as they report everything to their supervisors.

Think back to the education of the archetypal salaryman Hiro, described in chapter 1. Ringo Bank's training program is designed to mold subordinates who follow a process that their superiors can trust. If outcomes were all that mattered, Japanese firms would simply hire the most capable people. Instead, they use social networks based on school ties to identify people with "appropriate attitudes," paying more attention to extracurricular activities than academic performance. Then they pass down a company way to do things—exchange business cards, talk over the telephone, conduct business with customers, and so forth. (This emphasis on doing everything the company way often seems Orwellian to Westerners.[5])

The purpose of training is to provide models of right behavior. Modeling creates a bond of trust between trainer and trainee, which is why salarymen tend to trust superiors more than they trust members of their *doki,* or juniors. If a salaryman chose whom to trust on a purely human basis, we might expect him to rely most on the peers in his year group *(doki)*. However, his peers are almost never role models. We asked the salarymen we interviewed what common thread characterized the people they trust. Again and again, we heard two answers: the people they trust taught them many things in business, or the salarymen respected these people's *way of doing business* (the process, not the outcome).

Trust is built between seniors and juniors because the subordinates need such a bond to get anything done. Through day-to-day observation, a senior eventually concludes that his subordinate is predictable. Before this happens, if it takes ten decisions to accomplish something, the senior will make all ten. Gradually, he will let the junior make one or two or three of the ten himself. If the junior person makes the decisions the senior would have made, his latitude is expanded, to the point where the subordinate might be allowed to make nine of the ten decisions by himself. This is why salarymen emphasize that they trust people who teach them things or whose way of doing business commands their respect. They earn trust by absorbing a particular individual's style and methods.

Trust is situational

Junior salarymen do *not* trust all those who are senior to them. There aren't many *global* expectations about senior-junior relationships. For instance, some bosses expect immediate responses to their requests; others are willing to wait for a day. A salaryman trusts *his* boss—not bosses in general—because he learns his particular supervisor's way of doing things.

The members of our panel were also asked why some individuals earned their respect. Almost all the salarymen emphasized one key area of conduct: they respect people who don't lie or hide, who take responsibility, who do what they say. Again and again, respondents said something like this: "He understands me; that's why I trust him." The salaryman trusts people who know and accept their character and way of operating. That sort of empathy is limited to people whose behavioral models map very closely onto one another. It characterizes only a very few of the many relationships a salaryman must form to get work done in a Japanese organization.

The *senpai-kohai* relationship and the boss-subordinate relationship are the linchpins of trust within the *kaisha*. Salarymen feel constrained to be indirect with most people to avoid social embarrassment, but they can be frank within the context of junior-senior relationships. The salaryman expects his supervisors and subordinates to be honest with him and vice versa. He does not expect senior and junior managers in other reporting chains to be frank with him, because that's not the model. These expectations stem partially from the fact that goal alignment between two individuals is seldom more perfect than in the superior-subordinate relationship. The junior executive has a personal interest in helping his boss get ahead because the boss will carry his trusted subordinates with him. The senior executive worries little about being leapfrogged by the junior, because promotion depends on seniority, and he wants his subordinate to get ahead so that his apprentice can provide useful contacts and opportunities in the future. Goal alignment creates the right context for trust.

Insiders understand that real trust is limited and hinges on bonds between seniors and their subordinates. Why, then, do Japanese organizations look like clans, substituting informal coordination for formal rules? Japanese control mechanisms produce the appearance of clanlike bonds, but they are based on predictability, not trust. Customers rely on their suppliers to keep time schedules and deliver goods of appropriate quality. Salarymen generally behave toward one another in predictable ways, because they know that both parties share common models of right conduct reinforced by the firm's training regime. They also know that senior managers emphasize doing things the right way, not results. They may feel neither *shinyo* nor *shinrai* toward salarymen outside their tight circles of trust, but they are assured that anyone who fails to meet the expectations of other insiders will feel intense shame.

Trust is situational for many Japanese because it depends on predictability and not personal feeling. As one banker said when interviewed, the set of people he trusts changes as his position within the firm changes. Some Western writers argue that features of Japanese corporate life such as frequent rotations and consensus building exist to help young salarymen build up personal networks of ties. Although it is quite true that one gets things done in the *kaisha* through relationships, very few of the salaryman's ties are bonds of genuine interpersonal loyalty. If a person is one's subordinate, he can generally rely on their mutual expectations to ensure that the junior person can be trusted. However, if a subordinate moves to a competing department, he can no longer be trusted in the same way, for he must cope with a different set of social expectations. The *kaisha* is designed so that, by the time an executive reaches high rank, he has developed personal ties and exchanged favors with every other high-ranking executive.

Trust a *kaisha* only within limits

Thus far, this chapter has focused on trust within the firm, but many Western managers are trying to build relationships of trust between their organizations and Japanese customers or suppliers or partners. What are the potential pitfalls? For example, many Western organizations admire the nonadversarial relationships that seem characteristic of Japanese supply chains. Yet there is a stream of Western writing on Japan warning, for instance, that Japanese firms will drain all the know-how they can out of joint venture partners, then violate the partners' expectations by dissolving the partnership. Should interorganizational relations with Japanese firms hinge on mutual trust?

Depending on the context, Japanese organizations can take actions that run counter to the *shinrai* that others place in them. The key to understanding when one may trust a *kaisha* and when one may not lies in understanding the context and knowing what would cause the firm social embarrassment. When the context shifts, a company or government ministry is perfectly capable of behaving in ways that Westerners would consider perfidious.

To take one illustration, before the 1973 oil shock, the Ministry of International Trade and Industry (MITI) guided oil industry pricing. The ministry provided an estimate of production, which became a target. Individual oil companies were supposed to prorate their output according to MITI's forecast. MITI encouraged the oil companies to form a cartel, without asking directly, forging a formal agreement, or documenting its actions. The entire system eventually became public, and a scandal erupted when Japan's Fair Trade Commission indicted oil companies for price fixing. Members of the oil industry were deeply upset because they felt they had only been carrying out MITI's wishes. MITI refused to accept responsibility and denied that it had done anything wrong—certainly a violation of *shinrai*.[6]

The lesson for outsiders is that a company can work hand in hand with a government ministry on the basis of trust, informal guidance, and human relationships, yet be left holding the bag if the environment changes. From MITI's point of view, the model of appropriate conduct when things were *sub rosa* differed from the model of appropriate conduct once a public scandal emerged. Protecting the ministry is more important than protecting the industry in such cases. MITI didn't dodge responsibility because things went wrong. As long as matters were private, MITI's reference group was the industry as a whole, so the oil firms were treated as insiders and harmony had to be maintained. Once the arrangement became public, it was necessary for the section of MITI responsible for oil to change its definition of "reference group" and ensure that the ministry as a whole was not damaged.

Such violations of trust and tacit understanding affect Japanese firms as well as foreign oil majors. For many years, Nomura, the world's largest brokerage firm, was a favorite of the Ministry of Finance. When it was difficult to sell government bonds to Japanese companies because of the high public deficit in Japan, Nomura helped the Ministry of Finance place the necessary bonds with its corporate customers. This aid cemented the relationship between the ministry and the firm. Nomura also took a leading role in the 1985 public stock listing of Nippon Telephone and Telegraph, weathering criticism from many quarters that NTT's stock price was manipulated by the government and the securities industry. In return for its favor, Nomura was able to influence administrative policy and use the ministry's information-gathering resources to gain a vital edge on its rivals.[7]

When the Tokyo Stock Exchange dropped in the early 1990s, Nomura found itself losing money for its key clients, other Japanese companies. Among other things, these important customers had accepted the government bonds Nomura needed to place. In consultation with the Ministry of Finance, Nomura and other major Japanese securities dealers decided to make up their largest customers' losses. The ministry worried that, if these losses were not made good, Japan's largest firms might liquidate their holdings and drive the market down further. When the policy became public knowledge, a scandal ensued because the losses of smaller customers were not covered. The scandal was compounded because one of the large customers helped out in this way was clearly controlled by the *yakuza* (Japanese criminal societies resembling the Mafia). When the context shifted from a private arrangement to a public debacle, the Ministry of Finance redefined its reference group, looked to its longer-term interests, and denied having a role in the scheme. For the ministry, preserving its power and reputation in the constant jockeying among the major government bureaucracies was far more important than preserving the industry-government alliance.

Nomura paid a heavy price. Its chairman and president

were forced to resign, and the firm, Japan's most profitable in
1987, made only 10 percent as much in 1991 as it had four
years earlier.[8] Nomura's bitter conclusion: "We can depend only
on the law."[9] The fallout continued for years. Nomura lobbied to
eliminate the Ministry of Finance's key source of power over the
industry: its ability to license securities firms.

Don't rely on a sense of obligation

Western policy makers who admire the government-industry
nexus that they see as "Japan, Inc." have often called for more
trust and closer relationships between the private and public
sectors. Recent events, however, suggest that "tit for tat," not
genuine trust, underpins the relationship.[10] For many years, *Keidanren,* the association of Japan's largest and most prestigious
enterprises, was the biggest contributor to Japan's ruling party,
the Liberal Democrats. *Keidanren* backed the Liberal Democratic
party because the alternative was a communist-socialist opposition, and because it needed the government to stimulate the
economy during downturns. The disappearance of the commu-
nist threat opened public cracks in what always was a love-hate
relationship, contributing to the party's defeat in the early 1990s
after unbroken decades of rule. *Keidanren* complained that the
compulsory political contributions it imposed on members did
not buy the influence it expected. Many causes it supported went
nowhere in the government, and now both parties have dropped
attempts to maintain a public facade of harmony. The basis on
which they occasionally cooperate is the "classically Western"
what-have-you-done-for-me-lately, not trust built up through long
years of mutual dependence.

Violations of trust occur outside the government-industry
connection as well. Several prominent incidents have struck at
the heart of the supposed relationship of mutual trust and understanding that characterizes Japan's main banks, their customers,
and the banks' *keiretsu* allies. For example, during the early
1980s, Daishowa Seishi (a paper manufacturer) fell into deep
financial trouble. In classic Japanese fashion, Daishowa's main
bank, Sumitomo, sent executives to help the ailing client and

bailed the company out by providing full financial support. Sumitomo tried to reduce the top executive's power, so, once the crisis had passed, a conflict emerged between the two firms, and Daishowa terminated its main banking relationship with Sumitomo. From Sumitomo's perspective, this was unthinkable. Most banks don't even bother trying to develop new business by replacing a prospective client's main bank. Daishowa was supposed to feel a sense of obligation for Sumitomo's aid, and in any event, terminating such a relationship would be an unacceptable model of behavior in almost any context. Sumitomo's president at the time, Mr. Komatsu, said that a main bank relationship is established on a continuous process of trust between the top management of the two firms and that Daishowa had completely destroyed this trust.[11]

Sumitomo is the central bank of one of Japan's largest *keiretsu*. Why, then, didn't the members of the Sumitomo group punish Daishowa by cutting off business relations? The complex interlocking of relationships between a firm and various *keiretsu* members makes it difficult to tell who is a supplier and who is a customer. It would have been easy for companies in the Sumitomo group to retaliate had they all been Daishowa's customers. However, Daishowa is almost certainly an important customer for some members of the group (such as Sumitomo Chemical). Instead of retaliating directly, Sumitomo Bank can only hope that, if Daishowa gets into trouble again, other banks will be less willing to help. Relying on a party's need to protect its reputation, not interpersonal bonds of trust, seems like a very Western approach to relationship management.

In a similar vein, the real estate firm Azabu Building fell into such straits that, by 1992, it generated a negative cash flow of $42 million per month. The chairman, Kitaro Watanabe, was a former used car dealer, so, with many parking lots in the middle of Tokyo, Azabu had a huge asset base. Mitsui Trust loaned Azabu money against these assets, which Watanabe squandered. Following the usual Japanese model, when trouble surfaced, Mitsui sent a team of five executives to restructure Azabu and injected fresh money into the beleaguered client. In March 1993, however, Watanabe and his board of directors threw out Mitsui's team, essentially daring Mitsui to foreclose on him. Watanabe gambled that Mitsui could not afford to let Azabu go bankrupt. Watanabe's various companies owed 700 billion yen to seventy different creditors, who would not appreciate Mitsui pushing him over the edge.[12] In this context, Watanabe believed he could take actions that in normal times would be considered unthinkable. Once again, trust alone failed to discipline opportunistic behavior.

Westerners generally seem to expect that Japanese firms root their interorganizational ties in trusting relationships. The Japanese do, of course, value relationships, but not under any circumstance. Japanese can very flexibly change their definition of the context, reference groups, partners, enemies, and friends. Trust and harmony are the product of social constraints and controls, not drives inbred into every individual Japanese. The best way to preserve them is to create obligations that can be broken only at the cost of great social embarrassment.

Families trust, kaisha follow models

At the beginning of this chapter, it was suggested that the existence of harmony without trust doesn't even strike most outsiders as a puzzle until they get to know Japanese companies better. However, many Westerners who work for Japanese companies painfully discover how inappropriate the metaphors used to describe Japanese firms ("family," "team") are. Shock and fury often result.

Japanese companies do use these metaphors a great deal; for example, emphasizing that each employee is part of the "Nissan family" or the "Toyota family." Those who take the family metaphor too far are bound to be disappointed. The salarymen who contributed to this book were asked whether they felt like part of a family of people who work for the same company, and whether this was similar to being with their real families. Two-thirds saw some truth in the metaphor of the firm as a family, but more than half reported that they feel less comfort with their firms than they feel with their kin. Some, especially those who do not feel that their firms resemble a family, believe that the metaphor is a useful fiction employed by top management to encourage employees to work hard.

What do Westerners mean when they say that a company feels like a family? A family atmosphere means that the individual is cared for, that people can be relied on to look out for one another, and that it is less necessary to guard against being taken advantage of by one's kin. To a salaryman, the company feels like a family because it provides strong membership, which confers identity and keeps him from being an outsider. The salaryman relies on remaining a member in good standing as long as he behaves appropriately. However, caring for the individual is not a central value of the "company family," adhered to through thick and thin. When a company does look out for its members, it does so to follow a model of employer-employee conduct, which can change when the environment shifts.

Joseph and Suzy Fucini's penetrating examination of life inside Mazda's Flat Rock, Michigan, automobile assembly plant clearly illustrates the limitations of the family metaphor.[13] In accordance with the Japanese emphasis on process, Mazda rigorously screened candidates to select employees with the proper spirit. It ended up with a very young workforce, full of people who had little experience making automobiles. Throughout the recruiting process, the company portrayed itself as a caring employer, concerned with the "whole person" who joined the Mazda family. It emphasized the company's lifetime employment policy in Japan; its investment in building a safe, comfortable plant; ongoing training and development programs that employees could apply to their social lives; and its employee fitness center, built next to the plant. Mazda's recruiting interviews and tests emphasized job candidates' ability to work in teams and solve interpersonal problems. As part of the assessment process, interviewers explored how job applicants applied problem-solving principles in their homes. The American manager put in charge of the plant was chosen in part because he served as a father figure to the novice workforce.

The reality of life at Flat Rock differed sharply from what many workers thought they had been led to expect. Employees who asked for flexibility to handle family demands received little sympathy. Although Mazda paid attention to the "whole person," its models didn't allow for family business to interfere with work. In Japan, most of Mazda's employees were either bachelors, or married men whose wives handled such details. Injuries exceeded the norm for similar plants, although Mazda had engineered safety into the plant design. In Mazda's model, employees were expected to take risks in order to keep the line moving. The Mazda "family" embraced not only permanent employees, but also a growing pool of "temporary" workers, paid 15 percent less than regular employees for the same work and subject to dismissal at any time. Employees were very closely monitored by supervisors instead of being trusted to do their jobs. During the summer, as temperatures on the plant floor soared to over 100 degrees, the company consistently refused to install fans or allow supervisors to bring cold drinks to workers on the line.

The Flat Rock workforce discovered through experience what Japanese take for granted. Japanese companies genuinely do engage in a number of humanistic practices that can make the company seem like a family. However, the Japanese system is designed above all to make sure employees work hard and produce results. In the world of the *kaisha,* employees are not supposed to let personal considerations interfere with production. Japanese management is humanistic and personal when the context calls for it, but not at the expense of meeting production goals.

Trust is a by-product of social controls

As related in chapter 3, the *gaijin* employees of Matsushita and Fujitsu discovered that even membership is not guaranteed in many contexts. Those who expect the Japanese firm to be a warm and fuzzy place are in for a rude awakening. Relationships in the *kaisha* can superficially resemble those in families, because employees feel pressure to adhere to group norms and to get along with others whose approval they need in order to maintain group membership. When reference group pressures do not apply, however, conflict erupts just as it would in the West. Within the firm, trust holds together only very small groups, and loyalty is created principally by the context that junior-senior relationships supply. Between firms, trust and harmony prevail only under special conditions in which an industry or the largest firms in the industry are socially defined as a closed circle.

Some Western economists have created models in which cooperative behavior dominates competitive behavior even if individuals are looking out for themselves. These models don't rely on feelings of trust or altruism. The individuals in them forgo some chances to take advantage of others because they don't want to damage their reputations, or because they want others to develop certain expectations about them. In short, cooperation flows from their need to be reliable. These models in fact capture a basic truth about the *kaisha,* although they usually misspecify what motivates the salaryman. The appearance of trust and harmony arises as a by-product of the need to meet others' expectations, which in turn depend on the context.

Those who behave as if trusting is an emotional value instead of a by-product of social controls usually end up feeling violated by the Japanese. For example, one salaryman related the following story about an incident within his *kaisha.* An Australian employee working in his section came up with a good idea and proposed it to the section manager. The section manager liked the idea and promoted it to his superiors as the section's idea. The Australian thought the section manager had stolen his idea and became quite angry. He had trusted the section manager to credit his subordinates when they came up with good ideas, and he felt that trust had been betrayed.

Many Westerners would have felt the same way. This sort of story is one of the most common examples people use when they describe "backstabbing" in Western corporations, and, of course, a person can only be stabbed in the back by someone he trusts. However, the great majority of salarymen would judge the section manager's behavior to have been appropriate. They understand that promoting an idea is the role of a section manager, not an employee. Had the Australian promoted the plan himself, he would have violated everyone's expectations, and no one would have listened to his idea. On the other hand, once an idea proved successful, his section would have recognized the Australian as its originator. This is how trust is built within a reference group. From a salaryman's point of view, the section manager's action reflects caring, not theft. He tried to help one of his juniors enhance his reputation within the section by pushing the subordinate's idea to higher-level managers. However, absent shared mutual expectations, one man's honorable behavior is another's perfidy.

Commenting on the way expectations diverge, a salaryman remarked during his interview that he thinks American team spirit depends on shared goals, defined roles, and clear individual responsibilities. Harmony breaks down when any of these becomes fuzzy. In contrast, Japanese groups maintain the appearance of harmony even when nothing is clear, because insiders will conform to behavioral models shared within a reference group. *Wa* has to be maintained (through social controls) within groups where there is no job description for each employee, or jobs can't get done. Westerners become frustrated when they don't understand why people have to take a certain course of action, but salarymen don't need logical reasons for doing things a certain way. It matters much more that they fulfill mutual expectations.

If trust and harmony are not overriding cultural values in Japan, there is no reason to assume that cooperation is an overriding value either. Depending on the context, Japanese managers and organizations can be ruthlessly competitive or can cooperate with one another effectively. The odd tension between cooperation and competition in Japanese business is the subject of chapter 5.

CHAPTER FIVE

Cooperation Serves to Curb "Matching" Competition

Japan's industrial system has been called a new form of capitalism, combining competition with cooperation. On the one hand, many Westerners attribute Japan's success to the intense competition that characterizes most Japanese industries. On the other hand, they contrast the presumed Japanese spirit of cooperation with Western individualism. Within the firm, internecine warfare is supposedly subordinated to teamwork, as workers strive to do well as a group. Despite seniority-based promotion and emphasis on group rather than individual performance, however, Japanese workers compete to outdo one another in devotion and contribution to the firm. Are Japanese cooperating or competing?

Pundits tell Western workers and executives that, to compete with Japan, they must share more, undertake more joint activities, and curb their individualistic, out-for-yourself competitiveness. The "cooperative nature" of Japanese is a myth, though. For example, one large-scale survey showed that almost 30 percent of young Japanese workers viewed their colleagues (of the same age) as competitors, whereas only 13.7 percent of American workers felt that way.[1] How can this be so if Japan's "new capitalism" hinges on cooperation?

Asking whether salarymen and their firms are basically cooperative or basically competitive will always lead to contradictions and puzzles, because neither is a central value in Japan. Both competition and restraint follow from the same underlying drivers: context, expectations, social embarrassment, and models. These factors lead to intense competition in some arenas, but strictly curbed competition in other contexts.

This chapter examines how competition and cooperation intertwine predictably in Japanese business. Four key ideas underpin the salaryman's concept:

- Competition centers on preserving market share, not on seeking profitability, and on avoiding loss rather than seeking gain.

- Rivalry is driven by *yokonarabi,* the pressure to match competitors move for move.

- Cooperation arises because such fierce rivalry must be curbed by third parties.

- Forbearance, not mutual aid, is the basis of Japanese cooperation.

Success is preserving domestic market share

The salarymen interviewed for this book were asked what criteria they use to measure competitive success. Overwhelmingly, they rely on market share—specifically, domestic market share.[2] It is not necessary to gain market share everywhere in the world, but losing share in Japan is anathema. The firm's Japanese sales must grow at least as fast as the market is growing or the firm is losing, whatever else happens. For instance, were Hino, Japan's largest truckmaker, to lose 5 percent of the Japanese market to a European rival such as Magirus, it would be a stinging defeat, even if Hino simultaneously gained 5 percent of the much larger European Community market. For years, Honda was the most successful Japanese automobile manufacturer in the United States; nonetheless, many Japanese used to consider it a troubled firm when its Japanese market share occasionally slipped. The firm with the largest domestic sales is number one in the industry, regardless of what the global share of rivals might be.[3]

There is a fundamental difference between Western and Japanese thought on this issue. Of course, Western companies pay attention to market share, and it has been suggested that, in practice, large Western firms try to maximize their size or growth rate, because larger firms provide more perks and power to their executives. Western societies generally sanction the pursuit of profit, because orthodox Western economics promises that the "invisible hand" will guide profit-seeking firms to make socially desirable choices. Sometimes this doesn't happen, so governments should intervene, but by and large it is accepted that firms ought to maximize profits. Most Japanese economists accept this orthodoxy, at least in their writings, but Japanese society as a whole sanctions the pursuit of market share. Virtually all of the salarymen in this study, across all industries, agreed that the basic benchmark of success is a firm's share of the Japanese market relative to others in its industry.

Competition that centers on defending market share is quite different from competition that centers on increasing profits. Market share (as opposed to gross sales) is definitionally a zero-sum game—no firm can gain share unless another loses it. Profitability is not a zero-sum game; it is possible for all firms to increase profits, by increasing revenues, cutting costs, or improving efficiency. This is why many salarymen feel that domestic competition is very hard. It is not possible for all firms in the industry to achieve their goals unless market shares stay absolutely stable from one year to the next. Furthermore, Japanese firms can't pursue their goals as adaptively as Western companies can. For example, Western companies can flexibly divest business units to improve profits. In Japan, shrinking the business is seldom an option because such a move will surely cost the firm market share.

Share confers status and power

Sometimes, market share competition is artificially restricted in Japan, and in such cases, the basis of competition does shift to profitability. For instance, the market share of Japanese banks is regulated by the Ministry of Finance, so the main banks care very much about which is the most profitable. In general, however, the *kaisha* emphasizes market share for two reasons.

First, Japanese society is more aware of this measure than any other. Most Japanese can name from memory the largest firms in the country's principal industries. Usually this includes about five companies per industry. A salaryman who works for a firm most Japanese know about enjoys *much* more social prestige than one who works for a company most Japanese have not heard of.

For example, one respondent in this study, who works for a smaller firm, stated that his company's goal was to become one of Japan's top five companies in his industry. Contrast this with General Electric in the United States, whose CEO demands that all the firm's business units be either first or second in market share. GE's aim is profitability through industry leadership. The *kaisha* doesn't aim to become number one or number two for similar reasons. It strives to achieve or maintain membership in the magic circle of insiders, which usually means being one of the top five firms. (The leading firm in the industry often enjoys special privileges, but being second or third is normally not significantly better than being fourth or fifth.)

The second, more practical reason why firms emphasize market share is that members of the inner circle (defined by market share) gain access to the organs that work with the government to establish policy for an industry. Respondents working in many industries indicated that, in their sectors, the ministry responsible for the industry asks the leading firms to help it set policy for the industry—for example, by setting prices. One salaryman, who works for the largest company in his industry, told us that his company planned and wrote government guidance for the ministry that oversees the industry. His employer did this after talking with the other "major" companies in the industry, a reference group whose membership was well known to all. Another salaryman, who works for a major company that is not the industry leader, confirmed that the government's production guidelines for the industry were written by the company with the largest market share, in consultation with its principal industry rivals.

Market share determines who is in that inner circle of firms that help shape policy and share advance information about policy. Many industry leaders are losing money under today's slow-growth regime, but profitability has nothing to do with the definition of who belongs to the industry's inner circle. There are very practical reasons why a firm strives to remain part of the group of insiders, even at the cost of profitability; their membership puts them in a proprietary position to know what the government wants to do next and to help the government set the rules.

At its root, the defense of market share is about power. In a society that values process more than results, whose people are motivated to avoid social embarrassment above all, power is far more important than profit. Power stems from belonging to a highly recognized and respected reference group. Membership provides unique access to information about what other powerful insiders think, and outsiders often don't even realize a decision is being made, so they can't influence what will happen. The art of Japanese politics will be examined closely in a later chapter, but at this juncture it should be emphasized that market share–driven competition is another aspect of Japan's power orientation, not a separate, idiosyncratic feature of Japanese business life.

Winning is less important than not losing

The basic benchmark of Japanese competitive success is market share, but there is a big difference between gaining market share and losing it. We have argued that avoiding social embarrassment is the salaryman's most important incentive. A corollary is that the most important definition of winning is *"not losing."* A firm that loses a percentage point of market share has suffered a huge defeat. Avoiding this fate is far more important than gaining a percentage point. Inevitably, this means that Japanese market shares are fairly stable, as each firm's primary goal is to defend what it has. A salaryman won't have his bonus doubled for successfully increasing his *kaisha's* market share. On the other hand, if the firm loses market share on his watch, it can adversely affect his career. There is no good reason for such a loss to happen, so losing share is embarrassing both for him and for the reference group to which he belongs. A division manager would be held responsible for such a result in the *kaisha,* and no salaryman would want his boss to bear such a humiliation.

Because "not losing" is of paramount importance, Japanese firms tend to imitate each other. For example, Sumitomo Bank for a number of years topped Japan's banks in terms of profitability. It became clear in January 1993 that Sumitomo would not be able to hold onto this position. As a result, the bank wrote off all of its bad debts, on the theory that, if it was going to slip from the top position, it hardly mattered whether it fell to second or seventh place, especially if it could point to the write-off as justification for the reversal. Losing is losing, and by taking all the write-offs in one year, it at least positioned itself for a rapid return to the top. Naturally, the other banks could not permit this to happen, so all of them fell in line and did the same thing.

The emphasis on "not losing" also explains why it is rare in Japan to see a firm attack companies with larger market share. Those who initiate a price war run the risk of failure and consequent market share loss. Salarymen place far more weight on avoiding that fate than they place on the prospective gains from winning share. The managers of Japanese firms care most about maintaining their size *ranking,* which is of course relative to competitors'. Those who would upset the established size rankings—at least among the top five or six firms—would be accused of trying to destroy the market, and fear of violating group expectations blocks most firms from even contemplating such a move.

One respondent, for instance, said, "Our company is the second in the industry. It is not advantageous for us to attack the leading company. If we make that kind of move, many companies behind us will attack us. There is only one company above us, but there are so many behind. Although we are number two, it is best for us to maintain the current order." The second-largest firm is an insider under the present regime, and it reaps significant informational advantages from this status. A leading company would not risk such a position simply to gain sales.

New entrants confront fierce defense of shares

The emphasis on protecting share and rankings helps explain why Japanese firms are so reluctant to let foreign firms enter established Japanese markets. The only way new firms can enter is by taking some of the jealously defended share of an existing firm. For instance, in 1992, as part of its global drive to become one of the world's largest automobile makers, Volkswagen announced to its Japanese importer, Yanase and Company, that it wished to double its sales volume in Japan. Not wanting to destroy the market, Yanase's head, Jiro Yanase, refused Volkswagen's request, even when Volkswagen threatened to terminate a thirty-eight-year relationship. Yanase's action cost him Volkswagen's business, which accounted for 60 percent of the firm's unit sales volume and 33 percent of its revenues. Jiro Yanase is well known for his strong views on how to sell cars in Japan, but even if he felt differently, it is hard to imagine what else he could do. Yanase's third-largest shareholder is largely owned by Toyota, and its sixth-largest shareholder is the main bank that backs both the Mitsubishi and Honda auto manufacturers.[4]

As a result, there are only two ways for newcomers to crack the Japanese market. One way is to get a government ministry to reserve part of the market for the new entrants, as has been the case in semiconductors. The ministry can guide an orderly process by which existing firms give up shares precisely in proportion to their present market position, preserving relative rankings within an industry. The other way is to destroy the whole system. Toys "R" Us, for example, was barred from opening stores by a law protecting small retailers. MITI took advantage of pressure brought by Toys "R" Us to change the law regulating big stores. In retaliation, wholesalers refused to sell toys to Toys "R" Us. So the American retailer went directly to the manufacturers, attempting to eliminate the middleman. Wholesalers responded by threatening to boycott any toymaker selling to Toys

"R" Us. At this moment, the Americans do not have access to all the toys available in Japan. But many manufacturers are selling to Toys "R" Us, and the giant retailer may succeed in bringing down the long-established structure. Its stores are now packed with Japanese customers, and ultimately the toymakers must satisfy customer expectations or suffer social embarrassment.[5]

Foreign firms are not the only targets of defensive tactics such as those employed against Toys "R" Us. Japanese firms that try to overthrow an existing system face similar competitive reactions. For example, Daiei became the largest supermarket chain by pioneering discounting as practiced in the West.[6] Quite a few distributors refused to sell to Daiei because they knew that, if Daiei succeeded, they would have to discount their wholesale prices. Daiei prevailed by using scale economies to overpower small-sized grocers, and gradually its triumph was accepted as fate. Discounting became viewed as something that would eventually have happened anyway. Daiei destroyed the old market share order, and because it succeeded, some firms that wouldn't supply it have failed.

Revolutionary change shifts share positions

Another well-known example illustrates how a marketing revolution can end up moving market shares only by revolutionizing the existing order. Stability in the Japanese beer market was long maintained not by the brewers but by the distributors. Each wholesaler purchased beer from four major suppliers: Suntory, Asahi, Sapporo, and Kirin. In the late 1980s, Asahi Beer elevated to its presidency an executive who was originally from its main bank. This newcomer, who did not have strong relationships with the heads of the other major firms in the beer industry, approved the introduction of a new product: dry beer. When Asahi introduced the new beer, demand was so strong that the wholesalers were simply unable to hold the line. The entire system by which they managed market share was destroyed by the unexpected success of an amateur, and Asahi scored major sales gains in a very short period of time.

An outsider might think that, to preserve industry order,

Asahi would limit production and generate artificial shortages until rivals caught up. However, the new president had approved the new beverage in response to Asahi's long-term, gradual loss of position in the beer market. For quite a long time, Asahi had been the second-largest brewer behind Kirin, but at the time dry beer was introduced, it had fallen to third place behind Sapporo. From Asahi's point of view, the firm was simply regaining its rightful position. Asahi was careful not to project the image of trying to overtake Kirin as the industry leader. In the end, Asahi's rivals came up with their own dry beers (and a spate of other new products) before the entire industry was overturned. Asahi's conduct did change the industry's customs completely. Before dry beer appeared, the number of beers in Japan was fairly limited. Asahi's breakthrough changed the rules, and for years thereafter, the four leaders have introduced beer after beer after beer.

Share defense leads to matching competition

One might expect that competition aimed at avoiding the loss of market share would produce stagnation, not fierce rivalry. Competition in Japan is, however, quite intense, because it is driven by the fear of falling behind competitors. As discussed in chapter 2, Japanese people are much more motivated by the fear of appearing inferior than they are by the desire to succeed. As a consequence, Japanese firms engage in a practice called *yokonarabi,* which is the engine of much that is competitive in Japan. *Yoko* means "horizontal," and *narabi* means "side by side." Each of the major rivals in a market mirrors one or two others, matching their every move and trying to do the same thing. If Fujitsu enters supercomputers, its electronics rival NEC will, too. If NEC announces a multimedia system, Fujitsu must have one as well, because customers who have good relationships with Fujitsu may go to NEC if their customary supplier can't offer a competitive product.

Of course, this matching competition doesn't necessarily

occur in every business line. If Fujitsu doesn't perceive NEC as a competitor in a certain business area, it may choose not to follow NEC, but in most cases, rivals compete across the board. Furthermore, such competition need not be symmetrical. A relatively weak number two firm may benchmark the leader of its industry without being benchmarked by the leader in return. A firm can shift its focus depending on the context. For example, one of Japan's leading banks used to compare itself most closely with the rival nearest it in profitability. Recently, it began matching another industry leader, because that rival dedicated itself to beating the bank in its regional home base.

Often such rivalry becomes myopic, as firms strive so hard to achieve slight superiority that they disregard the drivers of customer purchase decisions. For instance, during the "bubble economy" era that ended in 1990, many manufacturers producing goods such as cars or appliances kept adding new functions to their products to differentiate themselves from rivals. Prices increased accordingly, and as the economy entered a recession, these products didn't sell well. It turned out that customers didn't really value all of these features. The recession laid bare the extent to which these firms simply tried to match or surpass their rivals' new features, without listening closely to customer needs.

Yokonarabi exists in part because "not losing" is more important than winning. If Sony introduces a product with a new feature, it may fail, but then again it may succeed, cutting into Matsushita's market share. Since losing market share is abhorrent, Matsushita will match Sony's new feature. In this way, Japanese firms are perfectly capable of following one another off a cliff, all of them introducing a doomed product as a hedge against the off chance that it might succeed.

For example, an American working for a U.S. firm in Tokyo mentioned that he went to Akihabara, the Tokyo district known for consumer electronics, to buy a coffeemaker. He was initially bewildered by the variety of choices available to him—every major Japanese firm sold several models, so there were hundreds to choose from. Three months later, he broke the coffeemaker's pot, so he returned to the store where he had purchased the device, to buy a new pot. He had to wait several days while a replacement was special-ordered, because every one of the coffeemakers the store had carried ninety days earlier had been replaced by new models. To a Westerner, such variety and rapid model turnover makes no economic sense. Yet Japan's manufacturers continue to proliferate models, because they cannot bear to think that a rival might steal the march on them by introducing a hit coffeemaker that has no counterpart.

Yokonarabi is so pervasive that it even influences the budgeting process in many *kaisha*. Most Japanese firms arrive at an annual budget the same way. Top management asks each division how much they can improve next year's sales or profits over this year's and aggregates the divisions' estimates. Usually, top management wants more and returns to the divisions, "asking" whether they can meet a higher, specific budget target. In such cases, salarymen in budgeting departments check indirectly with their counterparts at benchmarked firms, to get an idea of whether their forecasts are similar. They use a number of ways to find out what others think, typically employing a third party or an analyst (from a securities firm or the government). They don't want to be embarrassed by being too far behind the others. Were company A to forecast 10 percent growth and company B, 5 percent, it would be highly embarrassing for company B's top management. The senior executives would ask the divisions whether they were serious about their business. So salarymen tend to base major efforts, such as a new factory or a new product, on expectations about what others will do. If companies A and B do the same thing and fail, everything is offset and no one is embarrassed. But if a salaryman's firm is the only one to try something new and it fails, it will certainly be humiliated.

Each firm benchmarks few rivals

A firm does not practice *yokonarabi* against all the companies in the same industry. It chooses one, possibly two highly visible rivals, as a benchmark, and every salaryman knows who the benchmarked competitors are. (There are very few exceptions to this rule in Japanese business; for example, Nippon Life is number one in insurance by such a large margin that it reportedly does not use any of its rivals as a benchmark.) This form of competition resembles a marathon race. Most top marathoners pay attention to only a couple of other runners, not the entire pack. They know that, at the end of the race, some rivals can't win, so they pay little attention if such competitors break out front. However, they never allow the runners they are tracking to get out in front by more than a certain distance.

Choosing the wrong benchmark can lead to disaster. For example, Nissan suffered terribly from its attempt to benchmark Toyota, matching the larger firm in every category of car. Nissan held a strong position with customers who bought small, inexpensive vehicles. Because of *yokonarabi*, Nissan stretched past its limits trying to match Toyota. Toyota brought out the Lexus model, so Nissan introduced the Infiniti. Toyota introduced sporty cars, so Nissan strove to match them; although the "Z" line did quite well in the United States, it fared poorly in Japan, where it counted. In the end, Nissan had to close its passenger car factory in Zama—a crushing defeat for any Japanese manufacturer and a severe blow to Nissan's suppliers, who invested huge amounts to locate near that plant and provide just-in-time service.

Usually, a firm that selects an inappropriate benchmark realizes this earlier than Nissan did, and it gives up, typically by making a public announcement that the strategy was wrong. For example, with the blessing of its main bank, Mazda undertook a significant spending program in the late 1980s, aimed at making it Japan's third-largest automaker behind Toyota and Nissan. The bank reasoned that Mazda needed to break into the top three in its industry to assure its survival, especially because its rivals for the third position were backed by other banks. The 1992 slump in automobile sales forced Mazda to abandon its plans to market, through an exclusive sales network, a luxury car (the Amati) to compete with Lexus and Infiniti.[7] Mazda had already invested over $3 billion over three years to build a new assembly line, develop the Amati, and undertake a significant expansion of its distribution channels.[8]

Benchmarking is usually strongest between the first and second-largest firms in an industry, but this varies from sector to sector. Thus Toray tracks Asahi Kasei in textiles, Canon benchmarks Minolta in optical equipment, Asahi Glass matches Nippon Glass in glass products, and Hitachi benchmarks Toshiba in electronics. Most firms in third place or those that don't belong to a "major league" don't expect to beat the first two. They know that, if they initiate competition, a long battle will likely result, which will predictably pit them against bigger rivals in a price war. The risk of being caught from behind while the firm is distracted is not worth the potential gain. If a firm is in the insiders' circle, it has much less to gain by moving up within that domain than it has to lose by falling out of the circle.

Benchmarking is not against "best practice"

Benchmarking has become quite popular in the West, where companies usually try to compare individual business processes or units to "best-in-the-world" operations, which often are found in different industries. Japanese firms, however, benchmark themselves against other firms as a whole, not "best-in-class" individual business units, as long as companies are socially recognized in this way (which can vary depending on the industry and the context). For example, Japan's top six city banks benchmark the best in this group. The Bank of Tokyo used to be number one in foreign business, but other city banks won't benchmark it in that business alone because it did not belong to their benchmarking group before its merger with Mitsubishi Bank.

On the other hand, a department-by-department comparison of benchmarked firms can affect a bank's strategy. The major banks exchange enough numbers with one another that they can calculate where differences arise. Suppose bank A reports a 100-billion-yen profit, and bank B makes 80 billion yen this year. Different areas produce those profits: trading, securities, lending, foreign bonds, and so forth. The banks' reports include a breakdown of balances by category. If bank A finds that it is winning in lending by 50 billion yen, then it must be 30 billion yen behind bank B in other areas. Through analysis, bank A learns where it is losing. If, for example, it turns out that bank B made 20 billion yen more in foreign bonds than did bank A, top management will order bank A to match bank B in this area. It is clear that the Bank of Tokyo is the dominant player in foreign bonds, but this is irrelevant. The basis of competition is an area-by-area comparison of bank A with bank B, regardless of whether either is the dominant player in a particular line of business.

A Western observer might ask whether it makes economic sense for a department of bank A to benchmark itself against its counterpart in bank B, instead of against the best comparable operation in Japanese banking as a whole. It is important to remember that *yokonarabi* is not a rational strategy. Where *yokonarabi* is strong in an industry, what matters is understanding the context and the rules of benchmarking. A firm that didn't understand which insiders were benchmarking which other insiders would soon find itself locked in a fierce and destructive competitive spiral against opponents whose motives and logic it failed to understand.

Japanese firms that understand *yokonarabi* are sometimes able to take advantage of their second-rank status to steal the march on competitors that are not benchmarking them. Suzuki Motors, for example, has long accepted that it cannot compete with Japan's automotive giants. Its strategy is to target developing countries with large populations and serve them through local partners, which help make and market inexpensive minicars and subcompacts from knock-down kits. In major markets, Suzuki is strong in four-by-four sport utility vehicles (such as the Samurai). Until recently, this was an overlooked category because such vehicles were not popular in Japan. Precisely because Suzuki has no large overseas factories and competes in overlooked countries and market segments, it has enjoyed better results than most of its larger rivals during Japan's economic downturn.[9]

Competition by matching pervades the Japanese business world at the individual level as well as between *kaisha*. Consider the behavior of researchers in a laboratory. Studies suggest that British technicians abhor competition, whereas Americans try to compete by inventing something unique. In contrast, Japanese researchers do the same thing their peers are doing, with slight variations, striving to stay just ahead of others whose work closely resembles their own. They become uncomfortable if no one else is researching in their areas, fearing that, if they deviate too much, their work may not be recognized as competitive.[10]

Why are researchers—and salarymen in general—so competitive with their peers? Because evaluations are based on meeting behavioral models, there aren't many ways for them to differentiate themselves from other people. Since seniority governs a person's role in the *kaisha*, salarymen do not compete with their seniors or juniors. But, given that inferiority can be socially embarrassing, Japanese compete hard with those on the same level. It is too difficult to find an unoccupied niche, and too painful to fall behind others who are doing practically identical work.

Cooperation emerges to curb competition

Cooperation of a sort arises within and between *kaisha* precisely because the Japanese employ matching competition to play a zero-sum game, in which no one can win unless someone loses. The only way to excel is to do the same thing as others, in a slightly better way. Left to their own devices, Japanese individuals and firms might compete with one another to the death. Among first-tier companies, this is unacceptable because company membership provides salarymen with social identity. Consequently, formal structures have emerged to curb competition. This is perhaps the unique feature of Japanese capitalism—not because it taps the intrinsic cooperative nature of Japanese but because it embodies mechanisms to control the bloodletting that many fear would occur without restraints on competition.

Many salarymen say with all sincerity that, in Japan, domestic competition is war. Like medieval knights, however, warring Japanese firms bash and crash at each other, drawing blood without much actual killing. Among first-tier firms in major markets, domestic rivalry *is* quite tough, but companies seldom withdraw from those markets or businesses. Japanese companies don't care if they destroy non-Japanese companies, but they do avoid driving Japanese competitors out of existence. Behind fierce competition lies a fundamental level of cooperation that rests on an agreement to allow competition to proceed only so far and no farther.

Why? Like any reference group, a circle of competing firms is bound to preserve the existence and membership of insiders. For example, one salaryman commented during an interview, "One of our rivals made some competitive strides and began to threaten the leading position of my company in a particular market. We put price pressure on this rival, but eventually we had to stop because our affiliated companies and other, smaller firms suffered most from the war. As the leading company in our industry, we had to take care of these small companies." The salaryman believed that beating a competitor to death would break the unspoken rule that no one should destroy the order of the industry. Concurred another salaryman, "If you kill your competitor, it will hurt your reputation, and other companies will decide they can kill you as well. In the long run, it wouldn't pay." However, driving firms *outside* the reference group into exiting the industry is perfectly appropriate under the model. As usual, the Japanese perceive no double standard when insiders and outsiders are treated differently.

Japanese firms do occasionally go into bankruptcy. How is this possible? Expectations for first-tier companies in major industries differ from expectations for companies that compete in niche markets. Niche markets come and go, so meaningful reference groups do not form around them as they do around industries that are expected to endure for decades. Bankruptcies can occur outside of first-tier reference groups but are very rare in first-tier companies, occurring only when such a company has somehow violated expectations and lost its legitimacy.

Illegal or socially unacceptable conduct can create a context within which the bankruptcy of a big company becomes acceptable. For example, Itoman was long one of the largest *sogo shosha* (general trading firms) in the Kansai area (around Kyoto and

Osaka) and was a Sumitomo affiliate. The president of Itoman became involved in illegal business, damaging the company and its main bank, Sumitomo Bank. Although Itoman staggered under heavy debts, Sumitomo Bank wouldn't let the trading company go bankrupt in violation of society's expectations. Gradually, over a period of two and a half years, a consensus emerged that Itoman should vanish because of its crimes, not because of its financial troubles. One of the Sumitomo affiliate trading companies merged with Itoman, eliminating it from the scene. This is one of the very few ways a big company can die in Japanese society. In a normal context, the Japanese business world expects a main bank to help its affiliates no matter how deeply it gets into financial trouble. In the context of illegal activity or political scandal, a solution such as an acquisition becomes acceptable.

Third parties curb the carnage

As one might expect, there are Japanese models for curbing competition that threatens to get out of hand. A third party often intervenes to limit the carnage—usually the government, but occasionally a coalition such as a group of banks. Where competition is excessive, all the participants wait for a third party to step in. The model for such situations is that an arbiter emerges and finds some cooperative solution.

Because the *kaisha*'s model depends on the context, the arbiter need not worry that bitter rivals will hold grudges or prolong blood feuds. A company's relationship to other firms depends on the situation, so treating yesterday's rival as tomorrow's partner is perfectly acceptable. The simultaneous prevalence of brutal competition and extensive cooperation in Japanese businesses does not reflect any uniquely Japanese emphasis on teamwork and getting along. The Japanese emphasize conformity and have developed a model for dealing with the predictable consequences of conformity.

The government's role as third party is illustrated in the Japanese chemical industry. At the time of the second "oil shock" in 1979, the chemical industry overinvested, leaving it with huge excess capacity. By ordinary market logic, someone should have gone bankrupt. However, MITI stepped in and allocated capacity among the firms. The chemical manufacturers simply depreciated the excess capacity. Every company had to write down investments, taking huge losses. Because all other competitors were doing the same thing and the losses were not fatal for any company, this was acceptable. Interestingly, the same thing happened in the 1990s, when there was once again overcapacity in chemical production. This time MITI said publicly that it wouldn't fix the problem. MITI believed that it couldn't fix the chemical industry forever because it is not a strong industry in Japan, and it worried that foreigners would complain if they saw MITI stepping in. Eventually MITI might well rescue the industry again, but with much more resistance than the model ordinarily calls for.

Usually, the government is not so reluctant to act as a third party, because the ministries want to avoid social embarrassment as much as anyone else does and because acting as referee gives them tremendous power over an industry. For example, in the liquor industry, formally, all companies can set prices freely. In practice, one interviewee noted, Suntory sets whiskey prices, whereas Kirin sets beer prices. The Ministry of Finance wants all other companies to follow these market share leaders. Why? Bureaucrats in the ministry forecast alcohol tax revenues, and they would be embarrassed if these estimates were either too high or too low. Note that maximizing tax revenues is not necessarily the ministry's primary goal. If alcohol demand in Japan is elastic—and there is some evidence that this is the case—theory suggests that the government would increase its tax revenues by letting firms set prices below the levels that market leaders such as Suntory and Kirin would prefer. However, the potential gain is not worth the risk that tax revenues might go down. For the ministry, the optimal outcome is for the industry to charge a known price, at which sales can be estimated with some precision, producing tax revenues that fulfill the bureaucrats' projections.

Cartels are meant to limit bloodshed

Because calling in a third party to regulate competition when it becomes too intense is a well-accepted model, occasionally firms will create their own third party in the form of a cartel. In the 1970s, for example, competition among paint manufacturers became so intense that the entire industry was worn out by price wars. Competitors began meeting and forming a reference group, and the ten largest started meeting to fix the price of paint. Similarly, competition in the VCR market heated up when retailers began discounting. The major manufacturers—Matsushita, Sony, Toshiba, and Hitachi—took unified action, requiring retailers to adhere to the sticker price or face a supply cutoff. Japan's Federal Trade Commission indicted the paint manufacturers for price fixing but merely told the electronics firms to end their arrangement.

In classic economic theory, cartels are formed to push profits higher, but academic studies suggest that cartels organized by the Japanese government have no impact on a sector's profit margins.[11] In Japan, the need for certainty may be more important. For instance, one salaryman talked to us about the structure of his industry, in which trading companies buy a product from its manufacturers and resell it to their customers. Because the trading companies vie for market share, they have established an unwritten custom that a single representative company from the group buys the product from the manufacturers and distributes it to the other insiders, at a negotiated price that is the same for all. When outside competition arises, the firms in the industry talk with one another about how to cope with the threat.

Once, a firm in this reference group violated the model and underbid the agreed-upon industry representative. (Who knows why? Perhaps a new *bucho* took over and made a mistake.) The insiders punished the firm the next year by excluding it from the redistribution agreement, costing the renegade its entire business for a year. This behavior is quite cartel-like, except that members are forced to remain in the circle because they fear being punished, not because they want to extract extraordinary profits.

One obvious question is why manufacturers support the buyers' practice. If the manufacturers rewarded defectors, this arrangement would collapse quickly. The circle of insiders here includes both the manufacturers and the trading companies that buy from them. The buyers give the manufacturers predictability, placing bids even if they cannot find enough customers for the product. The price is firmly set only after resale. If the trading companies can find buyers, prices will be set to divide the profits; if not, prices will be set to split the losses. In this case, the manufacturers valued predictability enough to help the buyers punish the defector, even though the defector's "crime" was to offer the manufacturers a higher price.

Other devices also curb competition

Third parties are not the only device for curbing competition. Consider, for example, how rivalry among salarymen is restrained. Each employee is evaluated based on the performance of his group, not just for his individual contribution to the group. Senior managers rely on such subjective performance measures as degree of cooperation, creativity, and reputation. This way they ensure that correct attitudes and ways of doing business outweigh one-time achievements, transforming peer rivalry from a short-term battle into a long-term race.

Models also serve to regulate rivalry. The ritual of competition informally prohibits firms from surprising the market leader in an industry, but conversely, the leader cannot eliminate an upstart competitor if doing so would upset the industry's balance. For instance, in the early 1990s, Tokyo Steel, a highly profitable minimill, built a new factory. The president was directed to come to Nippon Steel's headquarters to explain what products the company would make. The notoriously independent president of Tokyo Steel, Masanari Iketani, balked at the visit (although he eventually did go), and Nippon Steel tried to drive the smaller firm out of business. Iketani may have appeared to be an easy target, because he has steadfastly refused to join an industrial group. However, Tokyo's very size and independence worked to its advantage. Nippon Steel has enough customer control that it can discipline its integrated rivals, but it had no such control over the client base of a minimill. As a consequence, Nippon Steel had little choice but to initiate a price war, which it ultimately had to give up because other steel companies couldn't take the pressure. By 1993 Tokyo Steel enjoyed the highest margins and return on assets in the industry, and, with one-tenth the sales of Nippon Steel, it reported slightly higher earnings than its mammoth rival.[12]

Cooperation is really forbearance

The salarymen interviewed for this study were asked what cooperation between competitors means in Japanese business. Their answers suggested that, in Japan, cooperation more often than not implies forbearance, not active sharing and mutual aid. For example, one said, "You don't want to kill your competitor. If you do that, it will hurt your reputation and cost a lot, both in money and in public standing." Added another, "We try to protect the interests of the industry. The market leader is afraid of disturbing the market order by killing competitors, and this is the understanding in the industry." Said a third, "Your company has to be accepted in Japanese society. You can't kill your competitor, and you have to observe commercial customs in business." In this, as in all aspects of Japanese behavior, however, the reference group defines who cannot be destroyed. If an American or British firm were to go out of business, for example, that would indicate that they were not efficient. The *kaisha* only stops short of destroying other Japanese firms in its reference group.

Those who must follow the lead of the largest firm view this mandated behavior as cooperative. One respondent pointed out that there is not much competition in his firm's home base, the mature basic materials industry, so cooperation consists of eschewing price wars or discounting. The largest firm in the industry sets the price, and no one else undersells it. Instead, all compete on getting costs down or providing superior service.

Information sharing is also a common form of cooperation,

especially among Japanese firms in foreign countries. Said one salaryman, "We trade information to assure that we do not get left behind." Another noted that all salesmen in his *kaisha* know their counterparts who call on the same customer accounts for rival firms. In such cases it is common for each salaryman to tell the other what he is doing to avoid excessive competition. The basis of the relationship is tit for tat; the salesmen swap information because there is no way to get information without giving it up. A third salaryman told us that his firm exchanges market information with Japanese competitors overseas because it knows that this would not be possible with U.S. rivals. Overseas, an atmosphere of friendly competition among Japanese companies prevails, and information is pooled that might be kept confidential domestically.

By including their rivals in deals, companies form social ties that curb competition. When a salesperson closes a deal, he brings his *bucho* to the signing. If it is a multiparty arrangement, the *bucho* will meet his counterparts from other firms (if he does not already know them). Later, if the salesman has problems with a competitor, he will ask his *bucho* to talk with his opposite-number *bucho* at the rival organization. Said a salaryman working for a telecommunications firm, "We always wish that we could take all the orders. However, it often happens that our boss and the boss of our competitor are acquaintances, and we simply can't bump them out. Also, certain competitors are our customers as well as our rivals."

When rivals do not restrain themselves as expected, the typical Japanese response is one of shock, anger, and determination to retaliate. In early 1992, for example, an American jury found Minolta guilty of using technology in its highly successful autofocus cameras that violated two Honeywell patents. According to Minolta's model of behavior, this sort of dispute should be worked out through personal relationships. Unfortunately, because Honeywell abandoned its efforts to build autofocus cameras twenty years ago, Minolta has not built up the kind of relationships there that it enjoys with most of its rivals. There is no Honeywell camera *bucho* to see in order to sort things out.

Minolta has publicly charged Honeywell with waging an "unfair attack." To a Westerner, Minolta's stance may seem bizarre and duplicitous. Why should a firm that infringed on another company's patents assume the stance of injured party? From Minolta's point of view, Honeywell is failing to cooperate the Japanese way, working things out informally. Minolta isn't upset that Honeywell stood up for its patent rights. It sees as unfair the *process* by which Honeywell attacked it. Minolta has been unable to find a third party to curb competition from a firm that cannot be restrained by Japanese behavioral models it does not understand. Consequently, Minolta has taken the only option it sees open to it—threatening to unite Japanese firms in ostracizing Yamatake-Honeywell, the "offender's" joint venture in Japan. The alternative, simply paying the fine and negotiating a royalty with Honeywell, doesn't fit Minolta's model of how to treat a firm that doesn't behave in the prescribed cooperative way toward a camera industry leader.

Just as Western managers and enterprises have been criticized for relying on rules or incentives instead of trust, just as they have been scored for failing to cooperate as effectively as the Japanese do, they have been chastised for short-term thinking, which is contrasted with Japanese patience and vision. By now, the reader will suspect that, once again, a product of social controls is being mistaken for a personality disposition or a stable behavioral trait. In the next chapter, many of the same mechanisms that produce harmony without trust and forbearance within the sum of a matching, zero-sum game will also be seen to produce the illusion of long-term vision.

CHAPTER SIX

Stop Bashing the West for Short-Term Thinking

Westerners, particularly Americans, are obsessed with short-term results. They can hardly think past the next quarterly earnings statement. In contrast, the Japanese are very long-term thinkers. Their CEOs lay out plans for the next ten or twenty or even a hundred years, not the next quarter. They are willing to invest for years and take losses to build the basis for a big payoff. On a national level, they undertake national efforts that no Western nation has the patience to tackle. If you're going to compete with the Japanese, you have to adopt their time horizon.

Many executives and academics have heard this lecture in various guises many times, from Western experts on Japanese management, from Japanese senior executives, and from both nations' politicians. They have seen it lead to arguments about the two countries' interest rates and capital markets. And they have seen it lead to similar arguments about whether Western countries and companies are willing to take the kinds of risks that future-oriented Japanese seem ready to shoulder. One manifestation seems to be a gnawing anxiety in the West that Japan will own the twenty-first century because it is willing to make investments in pioneering technologies that won't have an immediate payoff.

There are at least two puzzles at work here. First, how do we reconcile the supposed long-term orientation of Japanese with the kind of short-term, speculative behavior so prevalent in Japanese markets during the 1980s? Second, how do we reconcile the notion of Japan as a risk-taking technological threat with the widely held view that the Japanese are imitators, not creators?

This chapter shows how the fundamental attribution error (assuming that outcomes result from traits or personal dispositions) once again underlies some of these conundrums. Individual salarymen are frequently very shortsighted, but social controls sometimes produce what appears to be extraordinarily farsighted behavior in the *kaisha*. This section of the book will highlight some genuine differences in strategic planning processes, which separate Japanese from Western firms, and will then explore why the Japanese seem ultraconservative in some situations, yet in other settings prone to taking risks few Westerners would accept. Finally, it will examine innovation in Japan, asking whether a long-term vision really drives the nation's major science and engineering projects.

Individually, salarymen are short term–oriented

Both Westerners and Japanese frequently claim that Japanese companies invest for the long term at the cost of short-term profit. Western enterprises are scored for short-term myopia and urged to "think long term like the Japanese." Yet Japanese psychologists and sociologists have documented that the individual Japanese typically uses a very short time horizon. There are plenty of examples of Japanese firms that operate for the short term, and the speculative Japanese markets for land and stocks in the late 1980s are very difficult to explain as long-term investment arenas. The confusion over Japanese time horizons is driven by the fundamental attribution error, the mistake of inferring that, if one sees a certain type of behavior, it must be produced by an individual personality disposition or trait.

As with anything else, salarymen have absorbed a certain view of time by emulating a model. Most Japanese in the course of their education are conditioned to focus on the here and now.

When a Japanese worker is given an assignment, he shows his ability by accomplishing it quickly and completely. Problems are solved as they occur, "just in time," and through continuous improvement, Japanese get to the future in small steps, each with a short time horizon. They emphasize grasping the present situation and working to improve it as a continuous process, progressing bit by bit.

One Japanese scholar summarizes this model by suggesting that Japanese perceive the future as an inseparable continuation of the present.[1] He uses traditional picture scrolls as a metaphor for the Japanese point of view. Such scrolls are not placed on a wall as are Western pictures. A Western painting is hung so the viewer can take it in at a glance, perceive it as a whole before focusing on the details. In contrast, a picture scroll is viewed as it is unrolled from right to left. The scene evolves as it is unrolled, and unexpected perceptions are part of the experience; what appeared to be one thing often turns out to be another as the unrolling progresses. To view such a scroll, you must continuously adapt your perception to what you are seeing right now, giving yourself over to the experience of letting the picture unfold from moment to moment. The idea is to enjoy fully what the picture shows now, not to anticipate what will come next. The picture scroll does not tell a story in a sequence as it is unrolled. For example, a typical scroll might gradually expose the life of a whole town, starting at one end and progressing to the other. All the things that are happening in the town occur at the same time; your progress through the scroll is not to be interpreted as a succession of events.

There are Japanese scholars who argue that Japanese managers prefer short-term, very clear goals, such as catching up with others.[2] Japan's best and brightest bureaucrats often pursue very short-term industrial policy goals.[3] However, a strong body of literature suggests that Westerners also perform better when they have clear, short-term goals to pursue.[4] It may be more useful to think about the way Japanese follow models than it is to think about the way they pursue objectives, because modeling helps explain both short-term and long-term goal pursuit.

Occasionally, both salarymen and their firms seem amazingly shortsighted. At other times, both appear fantastically patient. At both levels, organizational mechanisms are responsible for the behavior we observe, so it is not worthwhile to debate whether the individual Japanese is psychologically predisposed toward a long-term or a short-term orientation. By examining how the salaryman frames different kinds of problems, an outsider can gain insight into what type of time horizon the Japanese manager will adopt in a given context.

Short-termism is a response to social pressure

In the appropriate context, Japanese businessmen are as focused on near-term results as are any of their Western colleagues. Westerners are often chided for making short-term compromises in order to enhance the results of the current fiscal year or quarter. Japanese managers do exactly the same thing, when they think they must in order to meet social expectations.

For example, many firms artificially enhance their balance sheets at the end of the year by cross-selling stocks. Suppose a firm has 1 million shares of Nippon Steel on the books at 200 yen, and the stock is currently trading at 400 yen. The company can arrange with its broker to sell the shares and buy them right back, creating an illusory 200-million-yen profit. This sort of thing happens frequently enough that the Ministry of Finance has asked companies to refrain from the practice lest it affect the stock market adversely. No good analyst would be fooled by the transaction, but Japanese managers are as concerned with making this year's results look good on paper as managers anywhere else are.

A much more dangerous short-term game cost Showa Shell a loss equal to 82 percent of its capital base.[5] When markets are difficult to understand, fund managers under pressure to make quick money may take both long and short futures positions. If the market goes up, they sell the long position to report profits; if it goes down, they close out their short holdings to create paper profits. Of course, they are stuck with the other position, but it can be rolled over and kept off the balance sheet, where it doesn't have to be reported. The same thing can happen with currency exchange market positions. Several *kaisha* held a huge number of long-yen, short-dollar positions at around 120 yen, rolling them over for four years. Finally, the Ministry of Finance asked companies to report their position marked-to-market in early 1993, when the dollar was worth much less than 120 yen. Showa Shell, which kept shorting the yen the entire time it appreciated, was compelled to report a loss of 125 billion yen. In the end, the firm's traders had purchased $6.4 billion worth of dollar contracts for a company with an annual oil import bill well under $1 billion.

Two aspects of this incident cannot be explained if we suppose that Japanese people are long term–oriented by nature. First, why did the company seek quick profits by speculating in the currency market? Showa Shell is not unusual; many of the salarymen we interviewed said that their companies frequently apply pressure on managers to show immediate profits. Second, why didn't the firm decide to close out its position before the loss mounted so high? Salarymen have very strong incentives to avoid social embarrassment by not disclosing such losses. In a game like currency speculation, there is always a chance they might recover their losses if the market moves in their favor. A short-term thinker tends to wait until the trend reverses, whereas a long-term trader focuses on the way the market is really moving, disposing of or changing his position. Showa Shell's managers blinded themselves to the yen's long-term trend, hoping the market would change drastically and spare them deep social embarrassment.

Showa Shell's behavior is unexceptional. Between 1994 and 1996, a series of trading debacles shook a number of Japanese firms.[6] Kashima Oil lost $1.4 billion trading foreign exchange contracts. Tokyo Securities Company shed $296 million trading U.S. treasuries. Nippon Sanso, an oxygen equipment maker, was hit with $110 million in losses from interest rate swaps. Kane-matsu, a trading company, traded futures on crude oil into a $83 million loss. Daiwa Bank suffered $1.1 billion in losses trading U.S. Treasury bills, shaking the bank to its foundations. Sumitomo's trading arm topped the list by logging $2.6 billion in losses from trading copper. In each case, an individual or small group of traders overreached, striving for short-term gains, and their firms lacked the control mechanisms needed to stem the losses before they mounted too high. Even the most skeptical Japanese observers agreed by the time of Sumitomo's debacle in mid-1996 that there had been too many incidents to explain away on a case-by-case basis.

The great Japanese stock market bubble of the late 1980s provides another classic example of the way social pressures can create pressures to act for short-term gain. As land prices boomed and stocks soared, most Japanese firms feared being left behind more than they feared speculating. Consequently, a number plunged into risky bets that came back to haunt them in the 1990s. A fair number of manufacturing and service firms (for example, the steel trader Hanwa Corporation and the gift-item manufacturer Sanrio) made almost all their profits in the late 1980s by playing the stock market instead of sticking to their core businesses. This practice was so common it was given a name: *zaitech*.[7] It was quite clear to everyone that these firms were neglecting their core businesses, but many joined them in the hunt for short-term stock market gains lest they appear inferior. This proved very damaging when, after peaking in late 1989, the Nikkei average fell more than 50 percent in three years. Some supposedly blue chip stocks fell even more than that (Nippon Telephone and Telegraph, for example, lost $7/8$ of its value in the plunge). Were Japanese companies really long term–oriented, they would have left stock picking to professionals and avoided the losses they suffered as the markets tumbled.

Long-termism is a response to different pressures

On other occasions, Japanese managers strike outsiders as remarkably farsighted and patient. Foreigners cite the willingness of *kaisha* to invest for future profit at the cost of immediate earnings and marvel at their vision, including their expectation of discontinuous change. The source of such farsightedness is exactly the same as the source of the shortsighted episodes described above. When the context and a firm's models demand long-term thinking, the *kaisha* delivers it.

The apparently longer horizon of Japanese firms does not stem from a uniquely Japanese propensity to plan for the long term. Japanese firms are as driven by short-term considerations as any others, but five organizational mechanisms, discussed in the sections that follow, constrain commercial behavior so that it appears to be focused on the future, not the present.

Enduring relationships, books that never balance

Westerners who write about Japan have rightly emphasized the paramount importance of human relationships to Japanese. Relationships enforce long-term commitment and account for many actions that appear to be driven by long-term thinking. In business relationships, the important thing is just to start the ball rolling. For example, a Japanese corporation might ask a foreign bank to look at the impact of an accounting rule change overseas, or make a presentation about new financing ideas. Salarymen respond to such requests knowing that it would be a great success for them to get business from the prospect after five years of providing such services. The salaryman doesn't have a five-year plan; he simply knows that, in Japan, you can't do favors for a customer today and expect results to flow tomorrow.

Japanese firms usually compete in domestic markets by matching the competition on price and new products while striving to gain a tiny edge in service and relationship management. Consequently, salarymen constantly look for opportunities to give favors to customers. That is why Japanese businesspeople sometimes try to arrange marriages for their customers; such a favor can be a starting point for an enduring relationship. Receiving a favor from a customer is almost as useful, for it doesn't really matter who owes whom first; a relationship will last as long as exchanges of favors continue.

In the United States, people often feel uncomfortable if they owe someone a favor. Someone who receives a favor without trying to "balance the books" is considered boorish, except perhaps if the debt is to his closest friends. In Japan, the books never balance, and the salaryman wouldn't want them to. Certainly the Japanese who receives a favor is obliged to return it. In fact, someone who ignored a favor, violating society's expectations, would experience more severe social punishment in Japan than in the West, but the point of returning favors is not to "get even."

Once two people enter into a relationship, their relative sense of obligation also depends on social criteria, not just some calculus of favors. People who are older than a salaryman generally think that, on balance, he owes them. If a salaryman felt on balance that he owed a junior colleague more than the junior owed him, both would view the situation as volatile and potentially dangerous. People of the same age generally feel that they owe each other a great deal.

Yokonarabi

The Japanese competitive benchmarking system, *yokonarabi*, also contributes to the appearance of individual long-term thinking. Writes Kiyoshi Yamauchi of NEC:

> An executive at a large Japanese electronics manufacturer once confided to me that he personally did not believe that the management decisions at Japanese companies were the result of mature deliberations based on a long-term perspective. When investing in plant and equipment, some consideration may be given to earnings and expenditures, but the most important factors in a company's decision-making process are keeping up with other companies in the same area and the absolute determination not to be beaten by another firm. . . . As long as a company keeps up with its rivals, even if it fails, management or those directly responsible will not be called to account. Thus, the desire on the part of Japanese management to keep pace with the competition can be said to have a rational basis.[8]

For instance, Sony took over Columbia Pictures in 1989 for $3.4 billion. A year later, Matsushita paid $6.1 billion for MCA, owner of Universal Studios. Many Westerners praised Sony and Matsushita for purchasing American movie studios some years before multimedia and interactive entertainment began to receive the attention they enjoy now. Sony publicly put forth a long-term vision of marrying hardware and software to create the systems of the future, and many American observers bemoaned the lack of a strong U.S. consumer electronics firm that could copy Sony's and Matsushita's integration strategy.

Sony had a much more immediate motive for acquiring CBS Records and Columbia Pictures. In the late 1970s, Sony pioneered home videocassette recording, only to see its archrival Matsushita wrest away market dominance, and Sony is still scarred from this defeat. Its engineers remain convinced that its Betamax format was superior to the VHS standard that prevailed. However, Matsushita won when consumers became convinced that the VHS section of a video store would always be larger than the Betamax section. Sony wanted to ensure that it could build "software momentum" behind the consumer electronics products it rolled out in the future. The movie studio provides a film library, which Sony can use to promote new high-density video disk formats, high-definition television, and new video game players, whereas the music company provides recordings for Sony's new MiniDisc audio players.

Because of *yokonarabi,* once Sony purchased a movie studio, Matsushita was bound to follow at virtually any price. After it acquired MCA, Matsushita laid out a long-term vision of hardware-software integration resembling Sony's. It is much more likely, however, that Matsushita simply feared that Sony might leave it behind. Matsushita had no strategic plan for leveraging its investment in a studio, and it relied on MCA President Sidney Sheinberg and Chairman Lew Wasserman to run the company much as they had before Matsushita bought it. By 1995, when it sold 80 percent of MCA to Seagram, Matsushita had made very little use of the subsidiary's huge library of entertainment properties. Seagram paid $5.7 billion for its stake, so Matsushita's investment at least appreciated in value about 12 percent over 4.5 years. However, other entertainment properties, such as Paramount and Viacom, created much more value during the same period. Matsushita's "long-term vision" for hardware-software integration lasted less than five years.

Sony fared somewhat better, perhaps because it usually gives a lot of freedom to subsidiaries, whereas Matsushita prefers tight control from headquarters. However, Sony has yet to reap significant advantages from its position as a producer of both software and hardware.[9] For instance, analysts agree that the biggest consumer electronics product of the late 1990s will be compact discs with enough storage capacity to hold an entire movie. Sony and Philips (the Dutch consumer electronics giant) agreed on a standard high-density compact disc format, but in early 1995, an alliance including Matsushita, Thomson, Hitachi, Pioneer, MCA, and MGM/United Artists announced that it would instead support the digital video disc (DVD) format jointly developed by Toshiba and Time Warner. Toshiba chose in the early 1990s not to acquire a studio, instead paying $500 million for a 5.6 percent stake in Time Warner Entertainment. This investment appears to have given Toshiba at least as much strategic leverage in a standards war as Sony has, for far less capital. Sony fired the head of its U.S. entertainment operations in late 1995 and may well follow Matsushita by selling most or all of its stake in entertainment companies.

When *yokonarabi* is not a factor, the Japanese do *not* necessarily invest for the ages. Many Americans became nervous when Japanese investors began buying up high-profile American real estate in the 1980s. Because of the supposed long-term Japanese perspective, many thought that, once these famous buildings changed hands, they would never be put on the market again. Experience now suggests that these buildings were simply investments for firms and investors with a lot of money on their hands that they needed to put to work. A number of landmark properties have already been sold by their Japanese purchasers, more often than not at a loss.

Emphasis on market share

The *kaisha*'s overriding need to protect its market share also produces behavior that superficially seems to reflect a long-term orientation. Japanese companies are patient even in difficult markets because they are more concerned about protecting market position than they are about preserving profits, for reasons we discussed in the previous chapter. For instance, it is not clear that anyone will ever make much of a profit selling commodity semiconductors. However, Japanese firms remain committed to battling lower-cost rivals such as the Koreans, because they want to defend their existing market shares to preserve their power and avoid embarrassment. The Japanese model for exiting a mature, unprofitable market relies on a third party to intervene, managing the withdrawal so that all the Japanese parties preserve their reputations and status.

Resistance to changing decisions

Because expectations are solidified when decisions are made, it can be very difficult for Japanese firms to reverse commitments. To the outsider, it may appear that salarymen "stay the course" because they value long-term results over short-term ones, but insiders know that different reasons explain why they persist long after others would give up.

For example, consider the case of one Japanese company, which made a significant, highly visible investment in American real estate during the 1980s. Eventually, it became clear to everyone in the firm that the project had turned out to be a failure, due to the decline of the U.S. commercial real estate market. The company was losing money every minute it held onto the investment; a rational investor would have withdrawn. A salaryman working for this company explained in his interview why the firm hung on in the face of such adversity. "This project was initiated by the president. As long as he stays in the company, we cannot make such a proposal."

Emphasis on job security

Japanese companies can also appear to be motivated by long-term concerns when their actions are really driven by their need to maintain job security. Nippon Steel provides a good example. In the last ten years, it has diversified into such new businesses as engineering, chemicals, electronics, and biotechnology. Some Western observers wonder why American steel firms seem so stodgy and stuck on a mature business while Nippon Steel is so forward thinking and imaginative. Nippon Steel was forced to reduce its steelmaking labor force after the yen began to appreciate sharply in 1985. The company could not easily lay off employees, as this would violate social expectations, so it decided to diversify in order to create positions for the redundant steel workers. Nippon Steel is likely to persist in many of these new business areas despite economic reversals. From the outside, this may look visionary, and perhaps it will turn out to be so, but Nippon Steel's actions are not the outcome of patience and long-term sagacity.

Some salarymen in this study cited lifetime employment and training as evidence that Japanese think long term. It can be argued that these practices reflect cultural constraints. Lifetime employment is a practice initiated after the second world war by Japan's American occupiers, and it applies to the minority of the workforce employed by Japan's largest firms. It reflects the Japanese emphasis on institutional learning more than it does a national trait of long-term thinking. One of the main reasons why Japanese hesitate to lay off is that they don't want to lose the institutional learning embedded in people. Employees who have been with a bank for twenty years know their coworkers and customers well, and it is much easier for them to do business than it would be for their replacements. The same applies to blue-collar workers in the factories. They learn their companies' methods of doing business by modeling others, absorbing the accumulated experience of their seniors. In a world where learning takes place through modeling and continuity of relationships is paramount, this learning is a form of human capital that is not tossed away lightly.

Long-term planning is largely symbolic

Western management writers often argue that planning horizons reflect the characteristic long-term Japanese perspective. They score non-Japanese managers for being unable to plan past the next quarter or the next annual budgeting cycle and tell Western managers to emulate the top executives of the *kaisha,* who plan ten, twenty, even a hundred years ahead. But do Japanese companies really look that far ahead?

Companies with hundred-year plans, such as Matsushita or Softbank, have received some publicity, but in over fifty interviews for this book, no salaryman described a firm that regularly sat down and attempted to craft a vision for the next century. When we asked how they define the long term in business, most of those interviewed focused on the time horizon governing their companies' long-term planning process. The vast majority have one-year and five-year plans that they update annually, just as Western firms do. A small minority of respondents said that their firms had ten-year plans, but they added that only the five-year plans have any real operational significance. As one salaryman in consumer packaged goods said, "Our company set a ten-year plan at its twentieth anniversary. Since then, the plan has changed all the time."

Why do Japanese firms have ten- or twenty-year plans, even if the plans are largely symbolic? The primary function of these plans is to reassure customers, suppliers, and partners that the firm is committed to long-term relationships. Given the immense amount of time it takes to build solid interpersonal relationships, Japanese stakeholders appreciate constant reassurance that they will enjoy a payoff on their investment for the foreseeable future. Such encouragement is provided when salarymen speak of how the *kaisha* will serve its customers a generation from now. It is no accident that firms set ten-year plans on their ninetieth anniversary instead of their eightieth, or fifty-year plans on the occasion of the president's fiftieth year with a company. Tying such symbolic plans to anniversaries stresses what the firm has been and what it will continue to be.

Long-term goals deflect embarrassment

Long-term philosophical goals that are subject to frequent change also emerge to help Japanese companies avoid social embarrassment. If a company has a concrete, short-term goal, it quickly becomes clear whether or not it has met it. Failing to meet the goal is socially embarrassing, so long-term, general aspirations better fit a society that emphasizes process over results.

The Japanese government, too, sometimes appears to have a very long planning horizon. For example, it emphasizes long-term technology forecasts more than any other government does, but in the end these projections, too, have only symbolic value. Every five years since 1971, Japan's Science and Technology Agency (STA) has conducted a Delphi study aimed at estimating the year in which technologies with specified capabilities would be developed. In a Delphi study, experts are asked for their predictions, which are circulated among all the other experts. A second-round survey then asks the experts what they now think, having read the forecasts of their peers. The following were among 1,149 predictions from the most recent survey:[10]

- An economical method to recover materials from municipal waste will appear in 2001.

- Ceramic engines will become widespread in automobiles around 2003.

- A successful, speedy treatment for AIDS will emerge in 2006.

- Particle accelerators that can be carried by aircraft will help to restore the ozone layer, starting in 2008.

■ Researchers will identify the genes that suppress cancer in 2009.

Clearly, such forecasts are nothing more than guesses, and the track record of STA's previous Delphi forecasts has been mediocre.[11] Why does the government invest such effort—and the time of 3,000 experts—to compile them? Long-term vision has little to do with it; instead, the government is providing cover for salarymen who worry about being caught napping by a revolutionary technological advance. If ceramic engines become widespread in the automotive industry before 2003, no one can be held to blame; anyone who follows the consensus opinion of 3,000 experts can't be embarrassed over a prediction's failure to pan out.

As one American executive familiar with Japan suggests, there is no real difference between a long-term and a short-term effort, because a proper process can be designed to accomplish either kind of task equally well. The real problem may be that, in the case of long-term projects, entire tasks must be planned in advance and are difficult to change in midstream when the environment shifts. Perhaps the process by which the Japanese prepare long-term blueprints will have to adapt to accelerated rates of change.

Qualitative analysis is favored

Japanese and Western methods of planning for the future do differ in two crucial respects. First, Japanese managers rely more on qualitative analysis than do their Western counterparts. For example, today Soichiro Honda looks like a visionary because he relied on gut instinct to build in the United States, although quantitative analysis suggested Honda should locate in Europe. Japanese managers simply do not rely on the discounted cash flow analysis common in the West. Emphasizing process, salarymen make decisions based on what seems to be the right thing to do. The Japanese have infinite faith that competitive advantage stems from making one's choices work, not in making the right choices. The manager's job is not to optimize as much as it is to maintain the firm's position.

Many of the salarymen in this study had completed MBAs at American business schools. Despite being exposed to sophisticated quantitative methods, the Japanese had no intention of trying to use their newly developed financial analysis skills to help their companies. To a man, the salarymen were skeptical about quantitative forecasts. At best, they were viewed as adjuncts to the important considerations, which are qualitative. Said one respondent, "When trouble happens, American employees often use the output from a computer to try to justify their decisions. I tell them that they should doubt numbers."

The Japanese rely on numbers and measures, but they distrust *projections* based on quantitative analysis. Salarymen are meticulous and precise when it comes to numbers that describe what happened in the past. They will spend hours poring over numeric quality control data and will perform very sophisticated statistical analyses of such measures. They also trust historical cost accounting data that provide fine detail about the past. One reason why Japanese managers are good at cost reduction is that they constantly and meticulously check documented results against plans.

However, when it comes to the future, salarymen believe that one can manipulate financial projections to produce any desired outcome, given the right assumptions. One of those we surveyed does financial analysis all the time, because he is in the mergers and acquisitions department of his firm. However, he is the first to say that he doesn't believe in the numbers he has produced and that quantification doesn't work in most cases. He said that Japanese managers don't trust numbers much, because they believe that what *isn't* shown in financial analyses is more important than what is shown. The junior executive who presents financial forecasts as anything other than a *pro forma* tool soon learns that he is simply inviting senior managers to conduct a very detailed, skeptical grilling about the methodology and assumptions behind the numbers.

Japanese skepticism about the value of quantitative projections extends beyond the borders of the *kaisha*. For example, stock analysts present lots of numbers with their recommendations, but investors don't pay attention. If a leading securities firm such as Nomura recommends a stock, people care because Nomura recommended it—it is almost immaterial why Nomura is positive. At the hazy level of disclosure that prevails in Japan, there is no way to tell where listed companies are going anyway, so what matters is the story the analyst tells. Presently, certain telecommunications and consumer electronics companies are hot stocks because investors are focusing on new media. Quantitative projections of how large the market for new media will be are irrelevant; if that will be the next great growth sector, why be left behind?

Qualitative analysis can lead to disaster

The start of Japan's recession in the early 1990s perfectly illustrates the national tendency to ignore projections rooted in data. The Japanese government collects and publishes a series of leading economic indicators each month. In the spring of 1991, the leading indicator remained below 50 percent, indicating that the economy was going to turn down. On Wall Street, such a report would almost surely have sparked a reaction, but in Tokyo, most economists and businesspeople dismissed the report as an aberration, because they intuitively felt the economy wouldn't turn down. To them, the Japanese economy still seemed healthy, even though stock prices had fallen for fourteen months. Many experts suggested that stock prices simply were not reflecting the real economy, and a number of different theories that explained what was wrong with the market gained credence. It turned out, of course, that the stock market was right and the experts were wrong.

In hindsight, the leading economic indicators almost perfectly captured what proved to be the turning point for the economy. Yet, when the indicator signaled a downturn, bureaucrats in the Economic Planning Agency (which releases the leading indicators) stated publicly that something had to be wrong with the forecasting measure, not with the Japanese economy.

Throughout Japan the present economic slowdown took analysts and corporate executives by surprise. Why believe a bunch of economic statistics when, with proper spirit, we can keep the economy moving forward?

Qualitative analyses sometimes lead to notable Japanese triumphs, such as Honda's push into America or Sony's faith in a Walkman that market research couldn't justify. They can also lead to notable failures. For example, Westerners are often quite puzzled at the diversification moves of Japanese firms. Knowing that steel is a mature industry, Nippon Steel has unsuccessfully diversified into silicon wafer production and the operation of a theme park called "Space World," neither of which built on any discernible core competencies.[12] Similarly threatened by a maturing core business, Iino Kaiun, a leading Japanese shipper, decided to diversify into convenience stores, building maintenance, and sports clubs.[13] In both cases, strategic logic and quantitative analysis had nothing to do with the decisions, which were driven by the need to keep workers employed to maintain human relationships and the company's position in Japanese society.

Growth assumptions generate "vision"

A second major difference between Japanese and Western planning techniques is that Japanese plans have for decades been built on assumptions of constant growth. Entire businesses are structured assuming that the growth rate will be high enough to justify an investment that is not subjected to rate-of-return hurdles. Should the Japanese economy continue growing at a 2 to 3 percent rate, the world will witness a major change in Japanese attitudes toward capital investment and building market share. Many American companies are configured to profit with a GNP growth rate in this range, but Japanese firms structured themselves to depend on higher growth. For instance Nissan suffered an operating loss when its sales sank by a mere 5 percent, an undramatic contraction by Western standards. Many salarymen are questioning whether a corporation should be structured to withstand such fluctuations.

The robotics industry exemplifies the way different growth

assumptions have led to the appearance that the Japanese are much more visionary than Westerners. Much has been made in the West of Japan's rate of investment in industrial robots. More than half of all the robots in the world are located on the islands of Japan, which has been viewed as evidence of Japan's futuristic orientation. Between 1978 and 1991, Japanese robot production grew from 25 billion yen to more than 600 billion yen.[14] Projecting this trend into the future, some Westerners were frightened at the prospect of a Japan, Inc., that built robots to boost efficiency to produce profits, allowing it to invest in more robots in a self-reinforcing cycle.

Such outlays made qualitative sense when firms were flush with capital, assumed they would enjoy a high growth rate, and faced a predicted labor shortage. When the recession of the 1990s took hold, however, firms didn't have enough money to sustain such investments and began questioning whether at low growth rates the predicted labor shortage will materialize. Matsushita shocked Japan by saying it expected zero sales growth over a five-year period. Matsushita's response was hardly long term or visionary—faced with different growth assumptions, it simply cut costs, although not by cutting people except through attrition. It also turned out that Japanese investments in robots plummeted back to 400 billion yen by 1993, once different growth assumptions took hold.

Risk taking and caution also reflect context

Intertwined with the long-term versus short-term thinking puzzle is another riddle. From an outsider's perspective, Japanese managers gamble wildly on some occasions but show extreme caution on others.

There is a boldness to much Japanese business conduct that many Westerners admire, a willingness to pursue a vision in the face of criticism and doubt. Because Japanese managers emphasize qualitative factors that would not figure into a discounted cash flow analysis, they often approve projects that should be rejected on quantitative grounds. Again and again the Japanese have undertaken large-scale projects that would have been too chancy for others. From creating the bullet train to digging the world's longest tunnel (connecting Honshu and Hokkaido islands) to placing a giant bet on nuclear energy after the 1973 oil shock, when the Japanese perceive something is the right thing to do, they do not fear to tread where angels dare not go.

On the other hand, Japanese managers are risk avoidant in the sense that they do not initiate discontinuous change. Were they to do so, they would have no precedent, no model to follow, creating the potential for serious social embarrassment. Why do risky and cautious behaviors coexist within the *kaisha*? Salarymen don't really think of risk in terms of the distribution of expected returns, as Western analysts do. They are more concerned about the risk of being left behind or of embarrassing the company.

As usual, one must be careful not to run afoul of the fundamental attribution error. No one should assume that risk-taking behavior flows from a bold streak in the national character or in individual psyches. In a careful cross-national study of national attitudes, including those having to do with risk, the Dutch scholar Geert Hofstede's psychometric measures placed the Japanese on the risk-averse end of the global distribution.[15] Fully four-fifths of the salarymen surveyed in this study said that they felt risk averse as individuals. Just as a crowd will take chances that might make individuals quail, Japanese are collectively willing to assume risks that other nationalities would not.

Some pressures favor boldness

The salaryman's occasional boldness flows from the same source as long-term vision: the fear of being left behind. Under the capital asset pricing model so prevalent in the West, risk is viewed as the variance of returns to an investment. Risk is not negative in itself; one may lose, but one may also win. In Japan, managers are much more conscious of the potential for the firm to be left out or exposed as inferior. When a firm undertakes a project as a hedge against the possibility of missing a great chance, it can disregard a negative expected value. To cut the risks of a great defeat, managers plunged into American commercial real estate, speculated in Japanese equities, and rushed to explore cold fusion and superconductors.

Another reason why *kaisha* take risks that Western firms would not hazard is because, as we noted above, quantitative projections carry little weight in Japan. American business schools focus on teaching MBAs a rigorous quantitative approach to project analysis. The Japanese MBAs in our sample learned these techniques while they were in school and promptly forgot them; if they were used at all, they were to be used to support a decision that was justified in other ways. Japanese managers simply don't believe numeric forecasts unless they believe in the concept. They don't think in terms of expected value. Senior executives believe outcomes can occur in hundreds of unforesee-able ways, so results can be left to heaven. Salarymen don't analyze a project to find out if it is good or bad or to justify an investment; financial analysis is meant to produce numbers that support what top management wants to do on strategic grounds.

In many cases, companies undertake a project to fulfill the president's dream. Vision is not just an abstract concept; it is the CEO's behavioral model for right strategic conduct and his way of galvanizing the firm to action. It isn't terribly important whether the vision is correct or strategically sound. For example, the CEO of Teijin, a textile company, dreamed of building an oil business within the company, so he sunk its profits into Middle Eastern wells. No one was prepared to tell the president that a textile firm had no business looking for oil. It was doubly difficult to argue against his vision because he couched it in terms of Japan's national needs. Naturally, Teijin wasted huge amounts of money and never became a significant oil producer.

During the 1980s, Japanese risk taking was magnified by the nation's very profitability. Japanese firms had a lot of free cash flow, which encouraged bold thinking. The same was charac-teristic of America's postwar heyday in the 1950s and 1960s; when the money was there, Americans also took risks no one else would shoulder. During the period of great growth, mistakes seemed permissible because a properly run *kaisha* would more than make up for them. In an era of slow growth, Japanese firms are not undertaking the huge, risky capital investments they underwrote in better times.

Other forces limit risk taking

The same forces that lead to behavior that seems oriented toward the long term also encourage conservatism, not boldness. Japanese managers avoid actions that might damage their relationships or cost market share, feel compelled to match certain competitors, tend not to change established decisions, and scrupulously maintain employment security. Japanese firms strive for consistency lest they fail to meet social expectations, and, as a result, really novel departures from past practice are rare.

Additionally, salarymen do not want to stand out from the group. Japanese decision making is often slow because people do not initiate action or take responsibility, lest they appear to be trying to distinguish themselves from the group. Things get done when someone successfully frames the context in the opposite direction—what are the consequences of not acting? For example, how would an astute organizational politician spur an electric company to make large capital investments? He would make the case that the firm would fail to meet its social responsibility if it didn't build electrical generation capacity.

From the insider's perspective, the Japanese decision-making process encourages conservatism. But when a bold move is properly framed, especially by a powerful figure, Japanese can adopt it rapidly, unencumbered by the need to prepare an elaborate financial justification. This chapter's analysis of risk taking and caution closely parallels the earlier contrast of long-term and short-term orientations. Understanding the fundamental asymmetry in the salaryman's definition of risk helps untangle both puzzles. *Kaisha* can carry out extraordinarily daring moves as long as they can be justified as a hedge against being left behind by competitors.

A report on Japanese politics before the 1993 elections

summarized the Japanese attitude nicely: "Japanese Cite Need for Bold Change, But Not at the Expense of Stability."[16] Said its authors, Michael Williams and Yumiko Ono, the characteristic Japanese cultural trait is "wait and see, and then go with the group." Sociologist Akira Fujitake was quoted in this article as saying that Japan faces very strong barriers to real change. The country's agrarian origins and village mentality bias Japanese toward playing it safe, argued Fujitake. The next month, of course, Japan took the boldest step of its postwar political history, ousting the long-ruling Liberal Democratic party. Both risk taking and conservatism are programmed into Japanese behavioral models, and neither groupthink nor the supposed agrarian mentality of Japan can stop a sea change whose time has come.

Japan's technology vision is a mirage

When asked for examples of unique long-term views of business in Japan, the respondents in this study were unable to come up with any examples that were significantly different from Western practice. This was not surprising, because a survey of books and articles about Japan suggests that it only came into vogue about fifteen years ago to say that long-term vision is characteristically Japanese. Japanese-written management books are virtually devoid of definitions or examples of long-term thinking.

Some salarymen did suggest that Japan's investment in research and development reflects a characteristic long-term view, but it is not at all clear that Japanese research programs or projects have a longer-term focus than Western ones. Certainly, Japanese R&D yen are not directed primarily toward forward-thinking projects.[17] Several studies of the difference between U.S. and Japanese R&D strategies found that, compared to their Western rivals, *kaisha* invest in applied as opposed to basic research, preexisting products and technologies developed by other firms as opposed to new technologies, and imitation as opposed to first-mover innovation.[18] Japanese firms have a large number of engineers, and Japanese models suggest that all of them must be kept busy. One wonders whether technical employment drives research investment or whether it is the other way around. Comments an American executive employed by the U.S.-based research subsidiary of a Japanese firm:

> On a practical basis, new, distinct topics get funding, and the R&D organization will tend to introduce many topics in deference to many middle managers supporting many engineers who are commanded to generate "new ideas." Applied research is about researchers learning a new topic, but not researching it in great depth or in any large numbers. In middle-down management and in the presence of nebulous top-down direction, the R&D budgeting process tends to produce breadth, but not depth.

If we accept the premise that Japanese R&D spending is predicated on a long-term point of view, it is difficult to explain Japan's lack of investment in building its scientific infrastructure. Japan's R&D spending is focused on applied engineering much more than it is on science, and the nation produces thousands of PhDs who are unable to find work that builds on their scientific training.[19] This phenomenon is referred to in Japan as "over-doctoring." Newly minted Japanese PhDs often work without pay in their thesis adviser's laboratory, while their mentors try to help them find places in a competitive academic labor market. Japanese firms hire comparatively few of Japan's PhDs, partly because they look with suspicion on the professional socialization of scientists, and partly because they do not have a model for taking in new employees approaching the age of thirty.

MITI's track record is unenviable

Outside the private sector, outsiders have made much of the Ministry of International Trade and Industry's (MITI) willingness to fund long-term, visionary research, suggesting that the Japanese undertake projects that impatient Westerners ignore. For example, MITI had under way in the mid-1990s two eight-year programs to develop a propulsion system and materials for a hypersonic transport that would fly five times the speed of sound. In April 1992, an offshoot of MITI, the Agency of Industrial Science and Technology, announced a ten-year plan to develop micromachines, tiny robots that can travel in spaces as small as a human artery. Other MITI programs sought to establish Japan as the world leader in such futuristic technologies as optical computing, artificial intelligence, and virtual reality.

Is MITI pursuing a fantastic vision for the twenty-first century? Experience suggests that this is unlikely, and the modest funding MITI is supplying ($330 million for advanced aircraft, $195 million for micromachines) simply cannot revolutionize industrial society. MITI's greatest successes have been short-term, focused programs aimed at catching up with the world leader in a particular technology. It is now clear that MITI's "visionary" high-definition television effort is a spectacular failure because the Japanese simply did not aim high enough.

Why is MITI willing to fund projects with such long-term payoffs at all? Again, the context, not some group of visionary thinkers, drives MITI's actions. MITI's basic job is to meet the social expectations Japanese have for "a ministry like ours." There is a general feeling in Japan that a resource-poor island nation must depend on advanced technology to secure its future, leveraging Japan's greatest asset, the minds of Japanese. Furthermore, MITI's job is to ensure that Japan does not fall behind the West. Every area that MITI has funded, from micromachines to neural networks, is the subject of considerable Western research activity. MITI's mission is to ensure that, if Japan cannot define the leading edge, it can at least stay abreast of it and maintain the capacity to follow up breakthroughs that others make. Unfortunately, MITI's efforts since the fabulously successful VLSI project have largely foundered because it has no effective model for how to develop technology that no one else has yet.

The same factors that let MITI invest for the long term also make it very difficult for the ministry to let go of clear failures. There are few better examples than the good ship *Mutsu,* once Japan's vision of the "ship of the future."[20] In the late 1960s, the Japanese government announced its intention to revolutionize merchant shipping by constructing a fleet of nuclear-powered vessels. Initially the government looked prescient; the 1973 oil shock sent merchant marine fuel bills soaring, and Japan appeared ready to extend its emergent dominance in ship construction. Unfortunately, no one else had built a practical nuclear-powered freighter for the Japanese to improve. On its maiden voyage in 1974, the *Mutsu's* reactor began to leak, sending the ship back for repairs. Over the next 20 years, the ship logged a little less than a year of actual operation. The rest of the time was spent repairing and improving the vessel, and coping with strong antinuclear opposition in Japan. Only recently, the Ministry of Transportation decided to pull the plug on the *Mutsu,* turning it into a conventionally powered research ship. Nonetheless, the nuclear freighter of the future remains an officially active project on the ministry's books.

One might argue that the Japanese government can expect hits and misses like anyone else, but this is beside the point. It is simply wrong to assume that Japanese ministries have a clearer long-term vision than anyone else has. Futuristic projects are approved and are difficult to kill because society expects the government to ensure that Japan does not fall behind anyone else. In essence, the twenty-five-year story of the *Mutsu* is driven by the same motive that turns over hundreds of models of coffee-pots every three months in Akihabara. It is far easier for a ministry to throw billions of yen at a failing project than to risk the possibility that someone, somewhere will develop a nuclear merchant ship for which there is no Japanese counterpart. For the same reason, Japan has poured far more money into "cold fusion" than has any other country. The scientific basis for cold fusion (supposedly a way to generate energy by fusing hydrogen at room temperatures) is still extremely shaky. Yet Japan continues to invest in research and to hold international conferences on the topic as a hedge against the possibility that there might be something to it after all.

National projects may cripple innovativeness

One might regard Japan's various national science projects as extravagant nuisances, but they may actually cripple the nation's innovation capacity in subtle ways. The success stories have been highly focused catchup efforts, which were at least as much engineering driven as they were science driven. Prominent examples include the VLSI effort that gave Japan world-class semiconductor-making capabilities, or the joint project that launched the Japanese fiber optic industry by reverse-engineering Corning's breakthrough invention. Most of Japan's other projects, such as the *Mutsu,* have simply been expensive mistakes.

The way national projects are structured is positively damaging to Japanese science, in at least two ways. First, a good deal of energy is consumed in interagency wrangling and maneuvering. Of course, U.S. federal funding for science is byzantine, but at least it flows to universities whose mission is not to uphold the glory of the funding agency. In the case of superconductivity, for example, Japan's Science and Technology Agency, the Ministry of Education, MITI, the Ministry of Transport, and the Ministry of Posts and Telecommunications all have their own funding programs. Researchers in each program tend to define themselves as a reference group. As one might predict, they are principally motivated not to appear inferior to the other groups. Wrangling between different government ministries, each backing a different network protocol, is also a major reason why Japan's Internet infrastructure and usage badly trailed the West's through the mid-1990s.[21]

Second, Japan's government agencies have a track record of backing the wrong horse, spending millions of dollars to push Japanese science into isolated backwaters. This has happened because bureaucrats have preferred following established models to risking social embarrassment by backing investments in genuinely radical technologies.

A sterling example is the twenty-year Hi-Vision project spearheaded by Japan's national television network. In the late 1980s, a number of Western experts sounded the alarm, warning that the Japanese were close to developing commercial high-definition television (HDTV). Since an HDTV set contains dozens of semiconductors, the experts argued that, if the West let Japan assume leadership in this arena, Japanese chipmakers would overwhelm their foreign rivals by exploiting economies of scale, flowing from Japan's command of television set production. Once mobilized by the federal government, American R&D consortia produced not one but three different designs for high-definition television based on digital technology.

Again, the Japanese had spent their time and money perfecting an outdated technology. In Japan and the United States, television signals are transmitted as analogue waves, painting 525 lines onto a television screen. The Japanese proposed a system that would create 1,125 lines on a bigger screen, taking existing technology and perfecting it. The American approach was completely different. Using sophisticated compression algorithms, the American HDTV system will transmit television images as a series of $^0/_1$ bits, as if they were voice transmissions or computer data. The digital approach is undoubtedly superior, because there is no theoretical limit to how much information can be included in the picture. As processors get faster and compression algorithms improve, the limits of digital TV resolution will be pushed further and further. In contrast, the Japanese system can never produce a sharper resolution than 1,125 lines per screen. Furthermore, because the American television images are digital, they can be manipulated by the viewer. For example, someone watching a football game on a digital HDTV could view the entire football field and zoom in on any part of it, to any resolution desired. A viewer who taped the Super Bowl could watch it later from the perspective of the quarterback, a linebacker, the Goodyear blimp, or any other angle he wanted.

Don't write off Japanese innovation

Might the Japanese use their long time horizons and attitudes toward risk to seize global technological leadership? Movies such as *Rising Sun* tap into a deep fear that Japan will leapfrog American technology. Paradoxically, Westerners use the "Japanese threat," to justify more private and governmental investment in research, yet many believe the Japanese are incapable of fundamental innovation.

Innovation is inherently risky, and Japanese attitudes toward risk and innovation are intertwined. There *are* Japanese models for radical innovation, but structural barriers in Japanese society have crippled most national projects, such as the *Mutsu,* which aim for major technological breakthroughs. One can argue that it is more useful to understand how the models of salarymen both encourage and curb innovation than it is to debate how individually creative Japanese managers and scientists are.

Models encourage certain types of innovation

Salarymen disagree when asked whether Japanese are creative; the split hinges on different definitions of creativity. The panel of salarymen in this study was asked how it defined creativity, and two roughly equal sets of opinions emerged. One camp adopted a more Western view, stating that creativity means starting something new, doing something other people do not do. The second camp argued that creativity means making improvements that add value.

Those who hold to the first view say they do not think Japanese are creative. This is in part because the educational system does not encourage students to create new things; rather, students are urged to perfect their command of what is already known. Instead, they argued, the strength of Japan lies in synthesizing things that already exist. For example, a typically Japanese innovation is a coffeemaker with a grinder and timer built in. At a preset time, it can grind coffee beans and then brew the roast. Cordless telephones with answering machines are very popular in Japan but are difficult to find in the United States. Such products as a combination microwave and electric oven, a watch with a video game, and a watch with an English dictionary build on Japanese notions of innovation. Summarized one engineer, "Americans start with a big picture and craft it according to the needs of customers. Japanese start with pieces and add something new according to the needs of customers."

The Japanese government believes the nation is distinctively gifted at synthetic creativity, the kind that combines existing technologies into a new hybrid, and it is attempting to build on this perceived strength. In 1986 MITI's Industrial Structure Deliberation Council issued a white paper describing twenty-first-century society. In this paper, MITI published what it called an "interindustry technology fusion index," a four-by-four matrix showing how four industry clusters—electrical, machinery, metal, and chemical—were investing in research that might overlap. MITI announced that it would fund "fusion" projects, and in 1988 the Fusion Law was passed, allowing MITI to create an entire national infrastructure of centers and grants to promote fusion.

A second group of salarymen thinks that Japanese are very creative, not just because they can synthesize what already exists. They told us that application or process innovation is as important as a basic idea. They believe the process of transforming a concept into a product is important, and they also think it is creative to change the way products are sold. Because things change continuously, modification, refinement, continuous improvement, and the development of variations on an idea are all creative. A focus on process, improvement, development, evolution, and continuity characterize the inventive Japanese mind because this is the way the Japanese perceive reality. It is the same focus that influences time orientation, as we illustrated earlier in our discussion of picture scrolls.

Radical action is legitimate in a crisis

The characteristic trajectory of advance in Japan is the pursuit of perfection in the direction of a model. Haiku, flower arrangements, and the tea ceremony exemplify this quest; those who study them aim to achieve perfect conformity in spirit and practice with a prototype. Yet we think it would be a mistake to conclude that Japanese innovation will always be limited to synthesis and continuous improvement. There is a socially acceptable model that permits radical departure from existing practices. By understanding it, we can assess the conditions under which *kaisha* might exploit fundamental technical breakthroughs to pioneer new industries.

Truly original action is not only possible but is socially

accepted *in response to a crisis.* For example, a widely studied period in Japanese history is the period of warring states *(Sengoku),* which spanned the later sixteenth and early seventeenth centuries. One of the most famous generals of this time, a man who barely failed in his quest to unify Japan, was Nobunaga. Nobunaga had the thoroughly original idea of killing a superior ally, a person whose status qualified him to command Nobunaga. Such an action is normally unthinkable, but enmeshed in the crisis of one of Japan's bloodiest eras, Nobunaga was able to step completely outside the bounds of accepted behavior. Nobunaga is one model Japanese employ when they decide to "just go for it."

As another example, Americans are amazed that, at the end of the second world war, the Japanese people accepted a revolution in their religion. The emperor of Japan declared himself human instead of divine. How could the Japanese accept such a radical turn of events? What model did they use? They managed because everyone knows the rules are different during a crisis.

Will the Japanese fasten on a behavioral model that legitimates radical technical innovation? We believe that a latent model exists: in times of crisis, imaginative and radical action is permissible. If the society reaches a consensus that Japan is in crisis, salarymen will search the historical past for models that show them how to depart from existing practices.

Japan has dozens of magazines aimed at salarymen, from novices to CEOs, which contain long articles about famous events in Japanese history. Salarymen don't read them to learn how to behave in specific situations. Instead, they try to absorb the *attitude* of the stories' main characters. Incidents are not served up as models but as a way to convey a philosophy. In reading these magazines, salarymen are trying to learn how decision makers or bosses should *behave* in a certain context.

To illustrate, one such magazine is *President,* which has been around for approximately thirty years and is aimed at an older generation of managers. The topic of one typical issue of *President* during the depths of the recession was "Fighting Spirit."

The theme: Because times are tough, the manager needs a fighting spirit to survive, so what can we learn from the past about the kind of fighting spirit a salaryman should cultivate? The main article in this issue profiled the conduct of Nobunaga, his successor Hideyoshi, and Kenshin Ueasugi, another warlord. The author referred to the battle of Okehazama, a turning point in Nobunaga's career in which he defeated two more powerful warlords. The writer didn't describe the terrain or the tactics Nobunaga used to win; instead, he focused on conveying the essence of Nobunaga's fighting spirit. Readers don't expect to learn anything from Nobunaga's specific path to victory. Instead, they want to learn how to model the hero's spirit.

Astute salarymen learn from experience how to shape the way a group interprets its context. A good organizational politician can reach into the historical past and find many well-known models of unorthodox behavior in response to a crisis. Given the right context, salarymen will try to emulate the spirit of forebears who produced genuinely radical innovations. Westerners who are concerned about losing competitive battles to superior Japanese technology that is developed by patient, intelligent risk taking will find it useful to take Japan's visionary national science projects with a grain of salt. Instead, it is more profitable to ask whether salarymen think they are in a crisis situation and, if so, what behavioral models they are searching for to help them choose an appropriate response.

If Japanese behavior encompasses both long-term and short-term thinking, both caution and risk taking, what kinds of goals and controls should one expect? Another puzzle of Japanese business behavior is the coexistence of vague goals with quite stringent controls. As this conundrum is unraveled in chapter 7, it will become plain that different kinds of goals—some vague and some very concrete—coexist, just as different kinds of time horizons are employed depending on the situation.

CHAPTER SEVEN

Ambiguous Goals Are Control Mechanisms

Western writers accept indirection, subtlety, and ambiguity as characteristic of Japanese culture. As a consequence, it is often suggested that Japanese companies do not have clear goals and that their actions emerge as responses to an evolving situation (see, for example, Richard Pascale's revelation of the "real story" behind Honda's success in the United States[1]). The Japanese in this study felt that indirection is quite Japanese, but they are surprised to find that Western management texts suggest the firm's goals are only implicit and internalized. In their experience, few things are more unambiguous than the goals of the *kaisha*. Indeed, Western writers sometimes acknowledge this—for example, by urging Western firms to emulate Komatsu's simple, clear goal of "beating Caterpillar."

Goals lie at the center of a classic conflict between Japanese managers and Western employees. Westerners often complain that they don't know what their Japanese superiors expect of them. Their managers in turn complain that it is necessary to be explicit about every little thing; they wonder why Westerners don't know the right thing to do as a matter of course, the way Japanese do. The confusion stems from the fact that most Japanese firms have three kinds of goals: one deliberately ambiguous, one very explicit, and one taken for granted.

One important source of perplexity should be familiar by now. Japanese firms set goals and care about them but emphasize the process of doing business more than they emphasize results. Western employees want to know what they should do as employees to help the *kaisha* reach its goals, whereas Japanese managers tend to focus on how the employees do their jobs. On top of this, Westerners who suffer from the illusion that decision making is bottom up in a *kaisha* may well become frustrated when they don't see their suggestions or ideas passed up to the top. To help resolve some of the quandaries surrounding goals in the *kaisha*, this chapter describes the three different types of goals that exist, explores how decisions are made in Japanese organizations, and discusses how salarymen receive direction, illuminating why Japanese firms are much less democratic than they might appear from the outside. By lifting the veil surrounding Japanese organizational politics, we hope to show that, behind a facade of delegation, senior managers actually exercise a great deal of social control to accomplish their ends. We also illustrate common political tactics used to get things done.

Firms have three different kinds of goals

Clear goals and ambiguous ones coexist within Japanese firms. Salarymen accept this, seeing no contradictions between clarity and ambiguity within the *kaisha*, because different types of goals are supposed to be more or less fuzzy. This section distinguishes which are ambiguous, which are explicit, and which are taken for granted.

Ambiguous slogans extract effort

As briefly discussed in chapter 6, Japanese firms frequently publicize slogans whose meaning is open to interpretation. For example, the leading cosmetic firm Shiseido employs the motto "For beautiful human life," which is supposed to provide employees with spiritual direction. To communicate its corporate culture, Shiseido gives employees four seminars so that they can think introspectively about what Shiseido means. One covers Time and Space; the second, Expression and Language; the third, Body and Soul; and the fourth, Beauty and Truth.[2] From these seminars a culture is supposed to emerge which helps employees internalize how to set and achieve the right performance goals. Similarly, Hakuyosha, a dry cleaning and uniform concern, unveiled a new slogan in 1991: "Clean Living." Four management targets were established in conjunction with the new identity: an attractive workplace, the customer first, a challenging spirit, and harmony with nature.[3] Americans, used to concrete objectives without such spiritual content, hardly know what to make of such slogans and "goals."

Why do so many Japanese firms carefully craft and disseminate such vague, top-down goals and slogans? They aim to set in motion a *process* of exploring what the mottoes might mean. Top management frequently establishes very vague themes, such as "Cost reduction," or "Do something new," or "Contribute to society." The point of these ambiguous visions is partly to stimulate communication and partly to extract more effort from workers. With goals such as these, the hidden message is "Do whatever it takes." Salarymen do not worry much about whether they have unraveled the "correct" meaning of a slogan, because they understand the function of slogans. They know that it's difficult in a Japanese company to ask each individual, "What do you think our goal should be this year?" Faced with such a direct question, a Japanese person does not know how to behave without risking giving offense and appearing to be a fool. It is far easier for him to answer the question "What do we mean by the slogan 'do something new'?" Under the guise of discussing Truth and Beauty or Clean Living, an employee can indirectly surface ideas for the group to take up. If his suggestions don't strike a responsive chord, he can disavow them as mere attempts to explore the subtleties of a phrase that might have many meanings.

Performance targets are explicit

At the same time, the bottom-up process in the *kaisha* generates very concrete target profits and target sales for groups, not individuals. Of the two, the sales target has clear priority over the profit target. At the start of the budget season, each section propagates both sales and profit forecasts upward. Top management picks an overall target for the company as a whole and allocates numerical objectives to each division. It would be rare for a division to assign specific targets to specific subunits or individuals. Individual workers (except salesmen) seldom have quantitative goals, but even if they do, they will not be penalized for missing individual goals as long as the group reaches its goal. A crisis results when a group fails to make its goal, regardless of what individuals may have achieved.

Although targets like these are usually crystal clear, what remains ambiguous is the process by which they are reached. For example, a trading company executive told us there was no mystery to his firm's goals: "The target is 110 percent of last year's record, no matter what business conditions are this year." Yet Americans in his firm still considered the goal to be ambiguous, because they wanted someone to explain to them *why* the goal was invariably a 10 percent improvement. The salaryman does not expect a rational, logical justification for a firm's targets, so often, ambiguity over the purpose of explicit goals opens a gulf between Japanese managers and their Western counterparts.

Invisible goals also exist, which are explicit but are usually unspoken. One is to provide secure employment. A second is to match competitors and stay in the top circle, which usually includes the five or ten largest firms in the domestic industry. Another is to maintain the social standing of the company. Japanese managers are not forced to step down because of bad results, only because of socially unacceptable events, such as a scandal.

Attitudinal goals are taken for granted

The third type of goal is the most important, and the one that outsiders usually overlook. An emphasis on attitude reflects the characteristic Japanese preference for process over results. One salaryman volunteered that, when he evaluates his American subordinates, he does not evaluate what the subordinate has done. He takes for granted that the employee met his formal goals; that's what is expected of everyone. Instead, he evaluates the employee's attitude toward the job and how much effort the employee put into his work beyond what was needed to reach his goals. An employee who fails to meet his targets will be criticized, but his attitude toward the work is more important. For example, how much communication did the subordinate have with his boss? If he produces good results but doesn't communicate enough with superiors, he can expect a poor rating.

This emphasis on process is not merely a cultural quirk. In the West, employees are usually compensated on results, either via promotion or pay. Consequently, noise in the bottom line is important. Superiors have to examine why an employee produced good results—was he lucky or skilled? Japanese evaluators worry less about such questions, because the bottom line is important, but not decisive. The *kaisha* cannot punish an employee for one bad year or five bad years if it expects the person to be part of the organization for three decades. On the other hand, the *kaisha* doesn't want to reward someone for great success in one year because it doesn't know whether he will be successful over twenty-five years. This is why the Japanese place more emphasis on process or attitude and less on results.

This insight helps explain why Westerners sometimes feel Japanese goals are not clear. Japanese companies assign divisions very clear, quantified performance targets, but outsiders quickly observe that employees are not focused on achieving them. Making one's numbers simply isn't as important at a Japanese firm as it is in a Western organization. People *are* working to receive a favorable evaluation of their attitudes and conduct; meeting targets is supposedly a by-product of correct behavior, nothing more. (Chapter 8 will discuss in detail how salarymen's job performance is measured and judged.)

Top-down ambiguity confers power

As noted earlier, Westerners often complain that they don't know what their Japanese superiors expect of them. Western executives, particularly American ones, often propagate very concrete goals down an organization's chain of command. This approach often seems brutal to the Japanese. One respondent in this study stated that, to him, the American approach seems to be "This is the objective, and here is the incentive, and if you miss the target several years in a row, good-bye." In contrast, the goals that come down from the top in Japanese organizations are usually philosophical and vague.

Top-down goals are ambiguous in the *kaisha* partly because the shareholders of Japanese companies don't hold top management responsible for achieving concrete goals. If, for example, top management has to achieve a 20 percent return on equity, that is what subordinates will be asked to accomplish. Another reason why top-down goals are vague is that very senior Japanese managers do not understand the details of the businesses they run, so they tend to trust their subordinates to figure out how to achieve their targets. They monitor whether their subordinates are trustworthy, are the kind of people who will meet expectations, instead of monitoring what subordinates are actually doing to meet their goals. For example, one salaryman commented during an interview that he had never had a proposal turned down by his boss. He was very proud that his boss only briefly glanced at his proposals, because this showed how much he was trusted. It is quite common in a *kaisha* for a new boss to take charge of a business without having any sector-specific experience, because his job is to create the right atmosphere and know who to rely on, not to apply superior knowhow to the task at hand.

Many of the respondents told us that they tried to make decisions and take actions by adopting their boss's perspective and figuring out what he would do if he understood the details. Through daily communication with their superiors, they understand both the group's objectives and what they have to do as individuals. Because the *kaisha* promotes managers from within, subordinates expect someday to assume the role their bosses now occupy. As a result, they learn to empathize with the man in charge, which lets teams move quickly and efficiently as long as all members understand what the leader wants to do.

Decision making is not bottom up

It would be a mistake, however, to infer that decision making in the *kaisha* is bottom up because salarymen need only conform to vague expectations. Westerners who work for Japanese companies may believe that decision making flows from the bottom up because most proposals appear to originate from below, but this is an illusion that *kaisha* create in order to motivate employees. It assures salarymen that they will be "in the know" when a decision is made, and it commits them to supporting it, but it is not bottom-up decision making at all.

Formally, decisions are made and ratified within the *kaisha* by circulating a *ringi-sho,* a consensus-building formal document that must be stamped by each recipient to signify his assent. *Ringi-sho* usually start from the lowest-working-level salarymen affected by the proposal and work their way upward. Typically, a proposal circulates among three to ten people, each of whom must approve it before it can be executed. However, in many cases, suggested courses of action that appear to flow up from below actually originate with a division manager. Knowing what his boss wants, a salaryman will formally write up the *ringi-sho* and begin circulating it from the bottom up. Then other managers may be forced to stamp it, whether or not they agree, either because they know it is what their boss wants or because they have been maneuvered into situations in which failing to assent would violate expectations. Sometimes, this "bottom-up" process approaches comedy. One manager we interviewed, for example, spoke of the time he wrote a proposal based on something he heard his supervisor say in a small voice. It turned out that his boss had simply been muttering to himself, and the work put into the proposal was a complete waste of time.

Because Japanese managers are power oriented, they seldom delegate final authorization of a proposal, even if they don't understand its details. Generally, lower-level salarymen prepare several alternatives from which their superiors can choose.

Trusted subordinates can influence the choice substantially. For example, one salaryman described to us how his boss chose among several research and development themes his company might undertake. The senior manager preferred option A, whereas the junior wanted the company to take up option B. Eventually, the senior manager directed the subordinate to undertake option A. As the junior pursued this research theme, he also pursued option B by himself and eventually persuaded his boss that B was valuable. The junior researcher was able to influence the selection because he had successfully earned his boss's trust. Of course, what the boss trusted was the junior manager's way of doing business, not necessarily his judgment that B was a worthwhile R&D project. Thus goals and decisions ultimately flow down from above within a *kaisha*'s hierarchy, but politically astute subordinates can influence them, just as they can in the West.

Salarymen survive by anticipating contingencies

Why are Japanese managers frustrated when Western employees complain that they don't understand what to do because the goals are ambiguous? The salarymen feel that they have to spell out with every request exactly what is expected, as one would with a child. With an American, the Japanese manager feels he must say, for example, "I have a meeting with my boss Wednesday at 10 o'clock; could you prepare A, B, C, and D for me by then?" With a Japanese subordinate, the boss need only say, "I have a meeting with my boss Wednesday, could you prepare information for me by then?" The boss is implying he needs A, B, C, and D plus anything else the salaryman can think of. Through modeling, the employee is supposed to know what A, B, C, and D are. In fact, if the salaryman is capable enough, he prepares A, B, C, D, and also E, F, G, and H. The boss's response is usually just to ensure that A, B, C, and D are there, telling the subordinate that he doesn't need E, F, G, and H. The time the salaryman invested in preparing E through H may not pay off directly, but the fact that he readied these extra items stamps him as a reliable person. Such unspoken expectations are described by a well-known Japanese saying: a good subordinate "knows ten by hearing one."

Japanese managers operate this way because they usually have less expertise in a division's day-to-day business than their subordinates do. It is the manager's job to maintain harmony, not to be a technical expert. Consequently, a senior manager doesn't necessarily realize that E, F, G, and H are important to know. He gives ambiguous directions to his subordinates so they can use their superior expertise to go beyond A, B, C, and D. One salaryman explained it this way: "When my boss asks me to write a report, I infer what he wants to know and what he needs to know without being told what he wants." Another interviewee added that subordinates who receive high performance evaluations are those who know what the boss wants without needing to be told. What frustrates Japanese managers about non-Japanese employees is the feeling that, if they tell such a person they want A through D, they will never extract E through H; instead, they'll get exactly what they asked for. Inferring what the boss would have wanted had he only known to ask is a tough game, but it is the one salarymen must play.

Because the salaryman doesn't know whether the boss will need E, F, G, and H, he spends an inordinate amount of time anticipating what his superior will want to know. Overpreparation is one of the major reasons why Japanese work such long hours. Government bureaucrats set the example by preparing expected questions and answers for statesmen who intend to address the Diet (parliament). Overheads are prepared for the statesmen to cover every conceivable contingency. (Interestingly, the same practice was so ingrained at IBM, where managers spent huge amounts of time preparing ten backup overheads for every one actually scheduled to be presented, that CEO Lou Gerstner banned overheads for a time, to get IBM managers back to work.)

Fortunately, inside the *kaisha,* a salaryman has to focus only on questions pertinent to his boss's reference group. Japanese managers make a point of knowing everything about their firm, its competitors, and its governmental regulators, but keeping up with current events outside these areas is not so important. Understanding the latest trends in business is. For example, a very popular American book on business process reengineering[4] was recently translated into Japanese, and it rapidly climbed the best-seller lists, selling more than 210,000 copies in six months.[5] This misled a number of Western observers, who concluded that reengineering must be gaining momentum in Japan as it has elsewhere. Actually, very few reengineering efforts are under way; some experts estimate that Japan is at least five years behind the West in this area. Who, then, is buying the book? Virtually every salaryman is—not because reengineering is sweeping Japan, but because a good salaryman wants to be thoroughly prepared in case his boss asks him what reengineering is all about!

A salaryman never knows when his boss will want to know something. That's why it is unthinkable for a salaryman to go home in the evening before his superior does; he must be on hand in case he is asked a question. Salarymen put in very long hours on the job, but in many offices, little real work gets done after 5 o'clock. Stories abound of salarymen sitting around their offices at night reading *manga* (comic books) or playing hand-held video games on a Game Boy. One salaryman told us that, after 6 o'clock, it was common in his section for employees to drink beer and other alcoholic beverages while they worked. In such situations, productivity is clearly not of paramount importance. Of course, in some offices, serious work goes on until late in the evening, especially when an important project is under way. But most salarymen stay at the office late for the same reason firemen hang around a "ready room" even if nothing more than a card game is in progress—they must be available in case they are needed.

A Westerner might try to reduce the amount of wasted preparation time simply by asking his Japanese boss what his intentions are. If he does, he'll never get a clear answer, because a Japanese superior doesn't want to make a commitment to what he says. It is always advantageous for him to avoid commitments until the last moment to retain flexibility in decision making. For the same reason, there is no point trying to drive at what the boss wants by preparing a series of drafts for his approval. An employee won't get much feedback on a draft, because the boss wants to keep his options open. Plans are made at the bottom, whereas decisions are made at the top, because managers usually can't make plans that are detailed enough to execute but don't want to sacrifice the source of their power.

Senior managers issue ambiguous directions for good organizational reasons: to extract the best from subordinates and to increase the amount of information they acquire. The subordinate who understands that the boss requires A, B, C, and D may include G and H in the material he gives his superior as a test, to gauge the boss's intentions. The boss may reply that G is not the way we are headed, or H is not what the president is thinking about—and the employee gains valuable information.

Staying informed is the key to power

A very common complaint of American employees is that their Japanese colleagues keep them in the dark. Seldom is this intentional; the Japanese, for their part, usually feel frustrated that Americans don't reach for information that is clearly available to them. Japanese bosses don't keep their Japanese subordinates informed either, because their juniors are supposed to know ten by hearing one. How do Japanese managers stay informed, absent a flow of information from the boss (whose primary job is to keep communication flowing from the bottom up, not the top down)?

Most Westerners working in Japanese firms are familiar with the *ringi-sho*. Far fewer know about *kairan*, literally "notices running around in a circle" (*kai* means "circle," and *ran* means "read"). Unlike *ringi-sho*, a *kairan* is more a "for your information" document that requires no decision. A typical *kairan* contains a lot of information about the company that is not directly pertinent to the reader's department. Salarymen we interviewed reported that their American colleagues often ignore *kairan*, tossing them aside as not relevant to their tasks. Salarymen read each *kairan* carefully because they understand how important it is to know what is going on in other departments.

One doesn't read *kairan* simply to stay on top of things. To the salaryman, information is the source of power. Consequently, if a salaryman withholds information from a peer, the other person feels intentionally excluded from power and will retaliate. To avoid this consequence, the salaryman shares information with as many people as possible within a reference group (again, the level of information that is shared depends on the reference group). Someone who is not in the loop would feel excluded, which is shameful. Furthermore, other salarymen would think that someone who ignored *kairan* is not only strange but also foolish.

Japanese frustration over the perceived failure of Americans to seek out information extends to the training realm as well. In their book about Mazda's Flat Rock plant cited earlier, Suzy and Joseph Fucini noted that American employees frequently felt that the Japanese promised them lots of training opportunities but did not deliver.[6] The catch was that workers had to seek out these opportunities on their own initiative. Said one Detroit veteran, "Mazda had the best literature and documentation on equipment of any place I worked . . . workers could have pulled a book out, but they wanted people to tell them what to do; they didn't put their own initiative into training . . . guys viewed it like, 'Hey, they said they were going to train me, so I should be in a classroom eight hours a day.' "

To summarize, there is a certain degree of ambiguity in the tasks that senior Japanese managers assign to their subordinates. From the salaryman's point of view, there are perfectly good reasons why this is so, and the appropriate response is both to gather and to exchange as much information as possible. This may not be an efficient practice, but it helps Japanese managers feel assured that they can rely on their subordinates to cover up their seniors' lack of job-specific expertise. "Knowing ten from hearing one" is the salaryman's way of life. It may seem that this creates an environment where subordinates have considerable freedom to shape decisions. However, more subtle controls sub-stitute for overt commands.

Social control substitutes for authority

Some outsiders have painted an almost-idyllic picture of the *kaisha* as the embodiment of modern participative management. Some have argued that the only way for Westerners to compete with Japanese organizations is to create a democratic workplace in the Japanese mold. Such critics of Western organizations fasten on the outward signs of what appears to be a free environment. In a Japanese firm, bosses rarely give direct orders, goals seem to come from the bottom up, decisions require consensus so that no one's opinion can be ignored, and employees are relied on to do the right thing without being told.

Japanese firms are actually much more command driven than they appear. Three forms of control substitute for the exer-cise of overt authority. The first is social control, where group pressure is applied to achieve a desired outcome, although nobody is ordered to comply. The second form of control involves working through the system to win the cooperation of others. The third form of control plays out through the exercise of power. Very fierce power struggles take place beneath the firm's surface of harmony. To understand what a *kaisha* will do, one must learn not only the way managers exercise control, but the way the Japanese power game is played out inside the firm.

Control systems in a Japanese company are hard to observe from the outside because those in power try to hide their power. Japanese organizational politics revolves around manipulating the way others frame the context of a situation. Tactics include using appropriate intermediaries to present requests, using apho-risms or famous stories (akin to Aesop's fables) to define the context, and positioning consultations *(nemawashi)* to make it impossible for others to reject requests.

Once a particular interpretation of context is accepted as

a social fact, the Japanese can rely on one another to follow the appropriate model for this context. Managers can covertly exercise power if they have relationships with the right people, know what contextual interpretation is needed to support what they want to do, and have the ability to influence how the context is defined. Because Japanese behavior is guided by conforming to a prototype, Japanese businessmen are easily governed, though it appears to the outsider that those in authority never impose their will on others. Salarymen feel safe and stable as long as they are directed by authority or follow precedents, which is one reason why the Japanese government plays such a large role in various industries. Paradoxically, within a structure that seems remarkably free, conformity is absolute. Japanese subordinates may appear to enjoy considerable latitude, but their behavior is controlled quite tightly by the process through which the context of a situation is socially defined.

Expectations, not orders

It is not surprising that outsiders think salarymen can operate without formal control because they are socialized to want to do the right thing. Japanese businessmen do what they imagine to be socially expected. Consequently, their seniors do not need to give them direct orders, nor must they ensure that salarymen internalize proper values so they do the right thing naturally. Instead, senior managers try to convey clearly via context what the social expectations are for a given situation.

For example, salarymen are known for extraordinarily long work hours. One way the Japanese employee shows his dedication to the firm is by spending the vast majority of his time in the workplace, even at the expense of family and personal interests. Outsiders might think that this occurs because the salaryman has internalized a sort of samurai spirit, an internal work ethic long lost in the West. In fact, many Japanese believe a superior spiritual attitude toward work is the cornerstone of Japan's economic success.

However, salarymen put in long hours only when they perceive that this is what is socially expected of them. Once a

Japanese businessman senses that the environment no longer demands that he work standard Japanese hours, he responds to the shift in context by cutting back his labor dramatically. The American author Clyde Prestowitz relates an experience that illustrates the point.[7] When he took over management of a group of Japanese salesmen, he decided that, because his subordinates were hard-working people, he wouldn't ask them to come into the office at a particular time and wouldn't monitor the times when people arrived for work. Once his salesmen figured out that they weren't violating their boss's expectations, they began keeping loose hours and working short weeks. Relying on people to work hard because they are Japanese doesn't succeed. It is the context that forces people to work hard, and they do so only when they perceive that they are socially expected to put in long hours.

One person interviewed during this study is an ex-*kaisha* manager working for a Western firm in Tokyo. He works the same hours that he kept when he worked in a Japanese organization, often going home at 1 or 2 o'clock in the morning. Others in his bank just will not work this hard. They still work until perhaps 7 o'clock or even 10 o'clock in the evening, but not past midnight every day. Our friend is frustrated, for he believes there is a lot of work to do and that it's important to work as late as he does. Others ignore his frustration because they assume that they can manage their own time regardless of how late other people work, because they are working for a non-Japanese firm. The peers of our "samurai" just cannot understand why he has to work so late. At his previous Japanese employer, managers clearly communicated to everyone that a person who doesn't work past midnight isn't working hard enough. This is an expectation the Western firm never conveyed, perhaps because it hired people from so many different countries. Our acquaintance simply has no tool in his present context to force others to maintain pace with his hours.

In fact, it's not clear that a Western firm could enforce such an expectation if it wanted to. One of our respondents, a veteran of a well-known Western consulting firm, observed that European companies entering Japan expect their Japanese workers to labor as hard as they would for Japanese companies. However, one reason why Japanese join a foreign company in the first place is that they assume they will not have to work so late. That assumption is part of their social expectations for a European employer. Consequently, if a European company tries to crack down and enforce Japanese-style hours, a minirevolt will ensue. Those who call the Japanese "economic animals" fail to understand that the killing work pace of the salaryman is a product of herd behavior, not a national predisposition toward workaholism.

Social pressure produces the desired behavior

If managers are not handing out directives and giving commands in a *kaisha,* how do people know what to do day to day? Education and training provide a partial answer; one learns what to do from others. But especially for junior employees, the context communicates direction. The art of Japanese management lies in setting up a series of social pressures that guides workers to do what management wants them to do.

For example, Fucini and Fucini's description of Mazda's Flat Rock plant[8] provides deep insight into the subtle ways that social control substitutes for direct command in the Japanese enterprise. As a result of their intensive selection process, most of the Americans hired by Mazda believed they were joining a highly participative organization. "We hired your minds, not just your bodies," they were told. The plant was organized into teams of six to ten members, headed by a team leader who was an hourly employee and a union member. All members of the team were told they would be cross-trained in each other's positions, so that the team could divide its labor among members and rotate jobs if desired. The rigorous selection process and twelve weeks of training heavily emphasized teamwork and group problem solving, conveying to the workers the idea that teams were meant to identify and tackle problems themselves, not expect supervisors to tell them what to do. The workers were taught *kaizen* (continuous improvement) techniques, told that their suggestions were most welcome, and encouraged to find ways to improve their own efficiency and that of the plant. Each employee was specifically empowered to pull a cord to stop the assembly line if a defect came along that he or she could not fix—in such cases, unit leaders were supposed to come running to fix the problem.

Through extensive training, team members were taught how to arrive at consensus decisions. No Mazda manager made unilateral decisions, said top management, and even majority rule was too polarizing—teams were to learn how to produce harmonious solutions that brought together the inputs of all members. Only if a group could not come to a clear consensus would top managers intervene to make decisions.

During the plant's start-up phase, every unit of two, three, or four teams had a Japanese trainer, who made it clear that his role was that of coach, not boss. Although the trainers, veterans of Mazda's main Hofu plant in Japan, were enormously skilled, they didn't tell the American trainees how to solve problems. Instead, their approach was to encourage teams to figure out their own solutions; only after two or three trials would the trainer show the team the "right" solution.

As the training period drew to a close and the plant was put into production, morale was sky high. Mazda was egalitarian, flexible, democratic, and, above all, committed to bringing the best out of each worker. As production increased, however, and performance pressure began to mount, the workers discovered what their Japanese counterparts took for granted—there is no need to order a workforce around when managers can use social pressure to achieve the results they desire.

Social pressure tactics at Flat Rock

Flat Rock was run as a lean, just-in-time operation. There were no buffers or slack resources—when problems arose, workers had to find ways to surmount them. If a team member were sick or had a family emergency, no temporary help would be sent to replace him or her; the team would have to find a way to pick up the extra load. Consequently, social pressures discouraging absenteeism were intense. The Americans soon found out why Japanese blue-collar employees work despite aches and pains, colds and flu, and why they seldom take all the vacation to which they are entitled: when one's closest coworkers have to pick up the slack in your absence, you simply have to show up for work every day.

Teams were invited to suggest changes in the plant but found that all alterations, however minor, could not be put in place until they had been thoroughly studied and documented. Given the intense pace of just-in-time production, few employees had the time or motivation to carry out such studies on their own. Even when teams achieved consensus on a proposed change, consensus meant that any Japanese manager could reject an idea without having to supply a reason. As a result, the work proceeded according to programmed worksheets, designed by Japanese industrial engineers, which spelled out every job in minute detail.

Because just-in-time so closely synchronized operations, teams that fell behind prevented other teams from getting their work done. Social pressure was immediately brought to bear on teams that were having difficulty keeping up. This was accentuated by the *kaizen* process. A team that increased its output through a continuous improvement effort unbalanced the line until other units found ways to catch up. The system thus contained a ratchet: any one group's progress meant that others would be strained until they, too, *kaizen*ed their way to greater productivity.

The lowest level of manager in the shop, the unit leader, was given latitude to interpret work rules and issue reprimands (five reprimands were grounds for dismissal). Some unit leaders adopted authoritarian styles, but others learned that they didn't have to, because their ability to interpret rules loosely or stringently, to be lenient or strict in handing out reprimands, meant that it was in the workers' interest to curry their favor and comply with their wishes.

Added social pressure was imposed by the division of the workforce into two classes with antagonistic interests. The permanent workforce was supplemented by a flood of "support member pool" (SMP) workers, temporary employees who wore different uniforms, received less pay, and could be fired at any time without explanation. Because the SMPs were competing for permanent jobs, they had every incentive to support the unit leader in consensus meetings and to maintain an intense pace that put pressure on the regular workers to keep up.

The point here is not that Mazda lied to the Flat Rock workforce or is a heartless employer. Like every Japanese automobile maker, Mazda is all business. Its brand of participative management uses control mechanisms designed to extract as much effort as possible from workers; in return, it offers them pay, security, and a sense of identity. Mazda simply doesn't need overt direction when the application of social control produces better results.

Subtle controls eventually take over

Eventually, the type of overt social pressure one observes at Flat Rock gives way to more subtle forms of social control. Social pressure provides a mechanism to ensure that employees do jobs that are not specifically assigned to any one person. Employees do not take on such tasks out of ingrained Japanese altruism. For example, at one American investment bank in Tokyo, there is a telephone in the company lunchroom. Often, it is left ringing for a long time—even in a room full of Japanese who know there might be a customer on the other end—because it is nobody's job to answer it. In a *kaisha,* clear social expectations dictate who should take responsibility in such cases. Section members make these decisions based on whose job is equivalent to the task at hand, while ensuring that the burden of extra tasks is equalized across the section.

Sometimes it is not clear from the context what to do when a problem arises. For example, if a division is assigned a new task, its salarymen will have no trouble figuring out who should do it. However, if the job falls between organizational subunits, the context doesn't tell the salaryman what to do. This is one of the situations often cited by the salarymen we interviewed as a source of conflict. Frequently, each of the jointly responsible groups tries to force the job on the other. Occasionally the two groups might cooperate to get the job done, but in general harmony disappears because no precedent or model tells the salarymen what to do. If they can't follow a model, they fear that they might incur social embarrassment in the event they fail. Consequently, salarymen avoid responsibility for unfamiliar tasks unless the context dictates that they have no choice.

This is simply one illustration of the principle that managers use social pressures to channel the behavior of their subordinates in the desired direction. Senior managers deliberately create situations in which their subordinates do not know what is expected, because they increase their ability to control a situation by giving ambiguous directions. The junior managers cannot resolve the ambiguity by asking their supervisor what he wants, because salarymen are socially expected to know ten by hearing one. Furthermore, a leader often doesn't know where he is going or what he wants. If he has to articulate his position, it becomes public and therefore is difficult to change without embarrassment, but if his desires remain ambiguous, he can make up his mind at the last moment and retain flexibility.

Westerners who work in Japanese firms are often surprised at how seldom social expectations are conveyed in writing. A number of salarymen told us that their bosses "imply" what each member of a team should do, never putting directives in writing. This is because written memoranda take away a manager's flexibility. Occasionally, salarymen are given detailed written procedures to follow, but this only happens in back offices that are responsible for formalizing things (such as documenting securities trades in order to settle them). Outside a back office, managers are reluctant to constrain an employee by writing down what he should do. As long as nothing is in writing, the manager can ask the subordinate to do anything. Unfortunately, this works only if subordinates understand the nature of context and the importance of meeting expectations. One manager in a *kaisha's* U.S. subsidiary told us he had learned that he needed to communicate directions, information, and everything else to his American subordinate in writing. With a Japanese subordinate, one or two general conversations would suffice. If a manager feels he has to commit his directives to writing, it is a sure sign of a desperate situation.

Only politicians get things done

Ordinary business gets done in a *kaisha* because salarymen are expert at divining from unwritten, vague directions just what their daily "to-do" list should be. Sometimes, however, things get more complicated. When it is necessary for a salaryman to work through other people, he must exercise political skill.

In Western organizations, effective managers usually strive to attain specific positions in the organizational structure that let them get work done through the structure. In contrast, the way to get things done in a *kaisha* is to establish an appropriate process and atmosphere for gaining cooperation. Organizational structure is modified through process. You can't understand how things get done in a Japanese firm just by looking at the organization chart. Japanese and Western firms have similar corporate structures, but in practice, the processes by which things get done are quite different.

A *kaisha* is a top-down organization, however else it may appear to outsiders. Any time a subordinate wants to do something that requires cooperation from others, he needs a favor from his boss or from top management. Lower-level managers have implementation responsibility, but this does not give them freedom to act, because they can't do anything without the approval of superiors. Consequently, salarymen can function only if they learn to work through the system. The Japanese way is for the bottom of the organization to understand the details of the business while the top retains the power of authorization. These two factors come together through the *ringi-sho* process, and good salarymen get things done by maneuvering the context within which these action proposals circulate.

Those managers who have the authority to make a decision very seldom do the homework they would need to do to make the right choice. Usually, a project starts when a manager receives a somewhat ambiguous goal from his superior and throws this objective to his subordinates. They in turn think about what the vague goal might mean and translate their tasking into a plan that can be carried out. Usually, the plan becomes the subject of negotiations with other departments whose cooperation is needed. But the salarymen who craft the plan cannot conduct these negotiations directly; they must talk to their boss first, get introduced to people in other departments, and then begin to win their support. A subordinate's job is to keep communicating with his boss, elaborating on a plan and coordinating everything so that his superior is satisfied and gives his approval.

When tasks require cooperation from outside the section, salarymen have to secure the voluntary cooperation of their counterparts in other departments. They cannot get a project authorized just by persuading the manager who has approval authority, because the person who finally approves a project almost never touches it; others carry out the planning and execution. Salarymen must therefore coordinate with those who actually do the work in other departments, as well as those who approve project proposals.

One way to obtain the required cooperation is to set up reciprocal transactions involving exchanges of favors with people from other units. Another way is to use the hierarchy to create a situation in which subordinate managers are *forced* to cooperate. If a salaryman in unit A needs cooperation from a salaryman in unit B, he will usually ask the supervisor of unit A to ask the supervisor of unit B to communicate to B's salarymen that he expects them to cooperate with A's salarymen.

However, groundwork must be laid before a salaryman can make such a request of his manager. Suppose, for example, that someone in middle management wants to do something new. He would first talk to everyone in the organization, playing up how beneficial his project would be for the organization. The subordinate knows that his boss will have to consult with other departments to evaluate the proposal, so he strives in advance to create an atmosphere in which those the boss consults will say, "I heard that plan, and I think it's good." Only then would he talk to his boss, because the idea might be rejected outright if the boss is the first one to hear it, and the salaryman knows that, if that happens, his idea is finished. Only a change in context (such as the discovery that other companies are adopting the proposed innovation) could reverse such a turn-down once the boss has committed himself.

Shaping the atmosphere

The way to work through the system in a *kaisha* is to shape an atmosphere in which momentum builds behind an idea. Such an atmosphere is created through logrolling, persuasion, and an exchange of favors, not an appeal to authority. For example, an American might try to build support for something he wants to do by saying that his proposal fits the company's strategic thrust or implements what top management wants to do. A Japanese manager would not try to persuade people to back his idea because "it is what top management wants." Sooner or later, a salaryman has to persuade his superiors to go along with the idea, and he can't put his superiors in the awkward position of being told by a junior manager what top management wants.

In shaping the right atmosphere, a salaryman must be very careful to touch bases in the appropriate order. Japanese managers fiercely defend their domains of authority, whether those domains are formally specified by the organization or whether they exist because of an informal consensus among employees. Violating what someone regards as his territorial rights would be a huge political mistake, so salarymen have to work through others in a way that preserves the accepted pattern of ties. For example, an astute salaryman would never approach the manager of another division directly, for it is the role of his division manager to handle approaches to his counterparts.

This sort of low-level persuasion process, operating through appropriate channels, is the way salarymen ordinarily win the cooperation of others. It reminds us more of the way things are done in legislatures than the way they are done in hierarchies. Yet this is not all there is to the art of Japanese organizational politics. It also consists of framing the context, manipulating interpretations and social expectations so that opposing a proposal becomes practically impossible. Cooperation is often obtained through subtle but very powerful coercion, not simply through persuasion.

Framing a context

The word *kankyo* means "environment," and *seibi* means "shaping up." *Kankyo-seibi,* the essence of exercising political control inside the firm, is the art of manipulating the environment to channel decisions in a certain direction. *Kankyo-seibi* means setting up the way people interpret a situation so that what you want done is the only thing that others can do to meet social expectations.

Framing the context in this way is more complicated than simple networking. For instance, many Westerners have learned that the surest way to gain entree in Japan is to be introduced by a suitable go-between. However, it is often difficult to know who the key person or power figure is in a given context. Furthermore, networking is necessary but not sufficient. Although those who do not establish contact with key decision makers usually fail, those who talk to the key person don't necessarily succeed. Even if it is clear that a proposed deal is profitable and involves no risk, the key person can say that the company is not ready for it yet, so locating the key person you need to persuade is only half the battle. The other half is creating a context that virtually forces this person to accept the deal you propose. There are quite a few ways to do this, and, if you understand them, you will greatly improve your chances of gaining a salaryman's cooperation.

One way to frame the context is to exploit the key person's fear that he is not matching his competitors. If one can show that a firm's competitor is planning to adopt something similar to what he is proposing, he will very likely receive a favorable hearing. One persuades by creating a context within which direction is exerted without overt control. For example, a junior bank officer may wish to persuade his seniors to do business with a particular borrower. If the junior knows and points out that the prospective borrower is doing business with another bank, the loan is quite likely to be approved. The junior need not know why the customer is dealing with another bank; his firm's need to match the other bank creates a context within which a certain action is virtually mandatory.

Another tactic might be to take advantage of the Japanese unwillingness to appear inferior or unworthy. For example, suppose someone wants to implement an organizational innovation. If he can persuade a group that a client demands this innovation to assure the quality of service he expects, his proposal will almost surely be approved.

A third way to gain an objective quickly would be to persuade a top manager to back it at the outset. (As pointed out before, this is a risky tactic, because it will be very difficult to reverse a negative decision.) If someone receives a *ringi-sho* and notices that a very senior executive's chop is already on the proposal, he will feel obligated to sign off on it. That would be *tatemae,* regardless what *honne* he might feel toward the idea. This tactic usually won't work, because a senior manager who used it often would be considered oppressive, but, if a sufficiently senior manager is in a hurry, consultation and consensus building via *ringi* can be reduced to a simple formality.

A similar principle can be used to kill an idea one opposes. As has been pointed out, once a boss rejects a plan, it will not be brought up for reconsideration unless the context changes dramatically. Therefore, the surest way to forestall someone else's proposal is to get a superior to consider it prematurely. Once a senior manager expresses clear disapproval, the originator of the proposal must accept defeat.

Another common way to carry the day, alluded to earlier in this book, is to make it publicly clear that a majority of the group needed to form a consensus favors your proposal. Japanese behavioral models discourage a salaryman from pressing a point if he realizes he is in a minority. Once a majority clearly emerges, unanimity quickly follows. Perhaps the most common political game within the *kaisha* is knowing which ten people will be at a meeting, getting six to agree publicly to something, then letting the four remaining members know they are in a minority. A sixty-forty split would cause considerable social embarrassment, signaling a serious organizational problem, so the four would not resist. The *kaisha* may appear to outsiders to be a grassroots democracy, but in fact minorities simply do not hold out against majorities. The best a member of a minority can do is propose an amendment, which, if it is reasonable, may be supported to assuage the feelings of the minority.

Blame is nearly irrelevant

One common power tactic in the West that does not work in Japan is shifting responsibility and blame for failure onto an opponent. Generally speaking, individuals do not shoulder responsibility for plans that do not work out well, though, as we have seen before, departments may jockey to assign the blame to other departments when projects fail. One reason is that, under the system of lifetime employment and internal promotion, it is difficult to replace people simply because they make mistakes. Another reason why it is difficult to blame individuals for failures stems from the separation of approval and execution we have discussed. Most projects are approved by very senior people, and criticizing them can be politically difficult.

Some of the salarymen we interviewed are quite frustrated by this situation. One told us, "We had a manager who planned and strongly promoted a project which ended up disastrously. Although everybody knew why we failed, this manager never admitted a mistake, and he kept on being promoted on the first track." The salaryman we spoke with was angered and believed the manager should have been blamed for what he did. But, in a *kaisha*, people accept that the right attitude is more important than the right results, and many managers rise despite having signal failures on their track records.

Japanese organizations appear to provide middle managers with wide scope for action. Instead, they actually provide middle managers with wide scope for *political* action. In a similar vein,

Japanese organizations appear to be egalitarian by Western standards, but in fact have extraordinarily strong hierarchies. This easily leads to status anxiety, which is kept at bay once again by means of ambiguity. Gaining an understanding of ambiguity and politics within the *kaisha* from this chapter is a necessary foundation for understanding how ambiguous performance evaluations fit into the Japanese system of business behavior.

CHAPTER EIGHT

Status Anxiety Leads to Egalitarian Hierarchy

The Japanese corporation strikes outsiders as being among the most egalitarian in the world. Ideas seem to percolate up to the top from the bottom and middle of the hierarchy. Worker suggestions are almost always implemented. Class distinctions—ornate offices, special parking spots, executive cafeterias—are rare. The gap between the highest- and lowest-paid employees is far narrower than in Western firms. The dignity of the worker and the need to engage his or her brain is constantly emphasized.

At the same time, there are few more rigidly structured hierarchies than the Japanese *kaisha*. The system is designed so that everyone is slightly inferior or slightly superior to virtually everyone else by position, seniority, or prestige of college. The Japanese rank everything—companies, universities, government ministries, baseball teams. Between companies, the famous business card exchange ritual depends on the fact that job titles are standardized. Each person immediately knows whose rank is higher or lower or, in case of a tie, which represents the larger and more prestigious company (a major reason why Japanese firms emphasize market share over profitability). As has been illustrated, salarymen can't even use the Japanese language with each other unless both share the same view about their relative status. Why, then, does the *kaisha* seem so egalitarian, when rank and status are ubiquitous within it?

A number of themes have already emerged which would lead to the conclusion that Japanese organizations can hardly be egalitarian. The competitive nature of Japanese social structures, the insider-outsider distinction, and the importance of power to Japanese managers all contribute to pervasive and important status distinctions. In this chapter, these themes will be woven together with an extended discussion of Japanese evaluation systems and internal competition for promotion, to illuminate the distinctively Japanese way in which hierarchy and equality intermingle.

Appearing inferior is unbearably embarrassing

Overt status distinctions that constantly remind employees who is on top are rare in Japan. Does this reflect a national conviction, a basic cultural value that says people should be treated equally? A sounder conclusion would be that a more basic social mechanism underlies what appear to egalitarian cultural values. As previous chapters have shown in many different contexts, avoiding social embarrassment is a primary motive behind much Japanese behavior. People feel socially embarrassed when they appear inferior to others. Thus Japanese people go to great lengths not to seem inferior and not to make others appear inferior. Status distinctions play out in ways that protect everyone from feeling inadequate or making others feel inadequate, creating an illusion of egalitarianism.

It may appear to outsiders that strict social equality is a must for a society whose members fear appearing inferior. On the contrary, it is far easier for Japanese society to cope with this fear by establishing a finely nuanced hierarchy. Why? The behavioral model that governs interactions between superiors and inferiors prevents either party from becoming embarrassed. Each has the comfort of knowing how to behave toward the other, as the relationship between superiors and inferiors is well understood. Furthermore, because superiority is usually a function of age and experience, today's inferiors expect that, in good time, their turn will come to assume the superior's role.

Suppose, for example, that a junior executive is served tea while meeting with his boss and a client. Everyone understands the protocol governing this situation: the client drinks first, then the boss, then the junior salaryman. The rule is impersonal; there is no need for the younger man to feel inferior because he is the most junior person present. When he is the client, he drinks first. When he is with a subordinate, he drinks second, and he does not dawdle, because he knows his thirsty employee has to wait for him to take a sip before he can take one. In some ways, drinking tea with an equal is a trickier situation. It isn't easy to drink first, because a person doesn't want to convey the impression that he thinks he is superior, but on the other hand, if both parties reason this way, neither will get to drink any tea at all. This is why the Japanese prefer to know who is superior and who is inferior in a given situation. The existence of a pecking order allows them to act in accordance with a model, without worrying that they might give offense by seeming arrogant. It also curbs competition, because if A is superior to B, B is not expected to try to outperform A, whether A and B are individuals or companies.

The Japanese emphasis on avoiding the appearance of inferiority affects the *kaisha* in many ways. For example, it motivates salarymen to work hard. As one five-year veteran salaryman told us, "In my company, 80 percent of each *doki* (year group) will be promoted to *kacho* (section manager) after we've been here fifteen years. It would be embarrassing if I fail to make it." Thus, for the next decade, he and his colleagues will expend every effort to prove to their company that they have the right attitude, whether or not their pay or working conditions are good.

If the drive to avoid inferiority is so important, why aren't salarymen the ultimate careerists? It might seem to an outsider that the *kaisha* would degenerate into a war of all against all, each struggling to get ahead. The reason this does not happen is that status and prestige depend far less on individual accomplishments in Japan than they do in the West.

Status derives from group membership

The ultimate source of social standing in Japan is group membership. The decisive status competition in Japan is not for individual glory but for the opportunity to enter a particular group. So, for instance, being a graduate of a famous university confers personal prestige, but only as a function of the group's prestige. The ultimate status symbol for the salaryman is admission to Tokyo University *(Todai)*. Once a person gets into *Todai,* his major, class standing, awards, and so on count for nothing. What matters is that he is affiliated with Japan's most prestigious university.

Japanese behavioral models proscribe lording one's position over others so that they feel inferior. Powerful people are obligated to act humbly. It is accepted that they are socially successful because they are members of prestigious groups, not because they are more individually accomplished than others. Therefore, Japanese try to become superior by joining a group with social power and a strong reputation, not by emphasizing their personal accomplishments. One consequence we have observed is that Japanese attending business schools often have great difficulty crafting résumés. The sort of self-promotion that is standard fare on Western résumés is anathema to the salaryman.

When Japanese introduce themselves, they refer to a group to which they belong, saying, for example, "I am working for X Company." Only later, if at all, might they say they are working in personnel or finance, because their job is not important; only their company is. The group frame they use governs their social status; their individual attributes are a secondary matter. Invoking the name of a prestigious reference group is just like using a go-between: it provides entree by conferring an important identity on the member. Without a group identity, an individual wouldn't know where he stands. This is one reason why salarymen are often uncomfortable around foreigners; without an accepted model telling both parties who is inferior and who is superior, the salaryman fears that his status will not be accepted.

Social status is a major source of power

Social recognition is a more pervasive form of power in Japan than is authority. Japanese are socially recognized for their companies, education (especially colleges), occupations, and sometimes family. A salaryman gains status if he is working for a firm listed on the Tokyo Stock Exchange, regardless of what job he holds in the company. He gains status by graduating from a prestigious college, regardless of what he actually learned at school. A person who enjoys powerful membership affiliations will be looked up to and trusted in society. People with good membership credentials enjoy a smoother social life and are able to establish useful ties through which they can exercise power. From an economic standpoint, studying hard to get into Tokyo University and then working for a government agency doesn't make a lot of sense, because many salarymen earn more than government bureaucrats do. But this career path is highly respected in society, and Japanese people generally want respect more than they want money. For the same reason, salarymen are hesitant to work for non-Japanese companies even if they pay well, because these companies are not well recognized in society.

Within the *kaisha*, employees strive to be identified with the most prestigious sections. In many companies, certain departments are well known as paths to the top. For instance, in some companies, a salesperson will never get to the top, however much money he makes for the firm, because the path to higher management must run through engineering or planning or personnel. One reason why government service attracts the very best university students is that bureaucrats commonly "descend from heaven" into senior positions within Japan's most prestigious firms after they leave their ministerial posts. It hardly matters that bureaucrats work long hours for low pay; the ultimate payoff they enjoy in terms of prestige and power is greater than most salarymen can hope to achieve through climbing the *kaisha* ladder.

One secret of Japan's economic success is that, in almost all circumstances, customers as a group are accorded high prestige and deference. Noted one American presently working in Japan, "What counts in Japanese business is willingness to do whatever it takes to satisfy customers." For instance, one salaryman said during his interview, "When we play golf to entertain our customers, we play badly to make them look good." Salarymen are surprised when they read Western management books that exhort firms to devote themselves passionately to customers, because it would make as much sense to them if a consultant exhorted a firm to use real money instead of counterfeit currency. How could it be any other way? The customer comes first in Japan, not as a matter of smart business but as a matter of ingrained attitudes toward status conferred by group membership.

The *kaisha* places its customer on a pedestal, and its devotion to customers goes far beyond economic rationality. Customers can ask for almost anything, and Japanese firms will attempt to oblige. This stems not so much from a desire to provide superior customer service as from the need to show customers the appropriate spirit and attitude. For example, Japan has many small convenience stores, similar to 7-Elevens in the United States (in fact, many Japanese stores belong to the 7-Eleven chain). Such stores think nothing of ordering their distribution company to provide two bottles of shampoo at 3:00 P.M. today, or of placing such an order twice a day. The *kaisha's* almost-slavish devotion to the customer helps explain why consumer products companies come out with so many varieties and new models of the same product. If a customer asks for something, it is just not acceptable for the firm to say "Sorry, we don't make that." Response time and product line breadth are the two key dimensions of customer service on which Japanese firms compete.

To Western eyes, going this far may seem fantastically uneconomical. It is irrational, and the cost is passed through to Japanese consumers, who are forced to pay a surcharge because too much service is embedded in the average product. (After all, the consumer gets no benefit from buying a bottle of shampoo delivered to the store in lots of two during midday traffic.) But economic rationality is beside the point. Companies provide this type of service for the same reason their executives subtly try to lose to their customers when playing golf; namely that, other things being equal, customers have higher status in Japan than do their suppliers.

What makes a company prestigious?

Every year, the Nikkei news service polls college students to find out which companies are the most popular among them. These rankings appear in the widely read newspaper *Nihon Keizei Shinbun,*[1] so everyone knows which companies are considered the most desirable for new graduates. Furthermore, Japanese people know much more than their Western counterparts usually do about which firms are the largest and most prestigious in an industry. Although there is no formal guide to this information, ordinary Japanese are well aware of which firms belong to the top group for any important industry. One might think, therefore, that recruiting would be a simple matter for college seniors: simply pick the most prestigious firm one can find. Things are not so straightforward, because several elements complicate the choice.

First, geographic region matters. For example, in banking, two of the six main banks (Sumitomo and Sanwa) are "western" institutions, headquartered in the Kansai region located near Osaka and Kyoto. Like Kansai industrial firms, both can be expected to make a special effort to attract the top graduates from the elite Kansai universities. The top firms from the Kanto region around Tokyo will also hire graduates from Kansai institutions such as Kyoto University or Osaka University but will not make as much of a point of recruiting their top graduates as their Kansai competitors would.

Second, institutional history matters. For example, the Industrial Bank of Japan is a public company that used to be a main source of financing for all Japanese companies and is still part of the industrial policy machinery. Social expectations would place considerable pressure on the top graduate of *Todai* who goes into banking to choose IBJ. One would think that the most prestigious graduates of the finest universities would have their pick of employers, but others might wonder what is wrong with such a person if he did not pick IBJ.

Third, it would not be intelligent for everyone to work for the top company in an industry. For example, Japan's largest firm in an industry should have no difficulty attracting top graduates from, say, Tokyo University and Kyoto University. But everyone knows that only a few in each *doki* will make top management in a given company. Accordingly, it would make much more sense for, say, the tenth-ranked graduate of Tokyo University to join a smaller steelmaker, as long as it is one of the industry leaders. Decades later, the graduate will be better off as a member of the elite circle at a smaller firm than he would as a lesser manager at the industry leader, as long as his employer remains one of the inner circle in the industry. As we have seen in other contexts, the risk of failing is much greater than the gain from winning, so the best graduates in a given year group tend to spread themselves around Japan's largest companies.

Government ministries, which are even more prestigious than Japan's top corporations, recruit in a somewhat different manner. College seniors aspiring to become government bureaucrats take a single nationwide test, so the agencies have a uniform benchmark they use to measure the graduates of different schools. From the top ten scorers on the test, the Ministry of Finance is likely to attract the majority, the Ministry of International Trade and Industry will recruit some of the others, and the remainder will go to different, less prestigious ministries out of personal preference. Because ministries cannot be ranked on size as companies can, it is extremely important to the ministries that they attract the highest-scoring students they can. One reason why the Ministry of Finance is more prestigious than MITI is that more of the top scorers on the examination go to the Ministry of Finance than join MITI.

Know your rank, in any setting

Despite the formal egalitarianism and meritocratic values of Japan, virtually every aspect of society is subject to ranking. Others are almost always slightly superior or slightly inferior, never precisely equal. Because Japanese identity is relational, one's perception of other people tends to be based on his relation with respect to them. This relation is perceived in terms of superiority or inferiority, so ranking things is deeply embedded in Japanese patterns of perception.

One reason why Japanese must know their positions relative to other people is that they have to use a form of the Japanese language appropriate to the relationship. There is a polite form, a respectful form (which shows one's respect by bringing up others), a humble form (which shows one's respect by putting oneself down), and a plain form (without any polite expression). When people are equal, they will use either a polite form or a plain form depending on the psychological distance and the context. If people are close, they use a plain form, and, if they are distant, they use a polite form. However, some companies don't allow their employees to use a plain form among themselves in front of customers, no matter what the relationship may be. A salaryman who uses language inappropriately will certainly suffer social embarrassment and may hurt others' feelings.

An exchange of name cards is one indispensable way Japanese businessmen avoid social damage. The Japanese writer Chie Nakane points out:

> —[name cards'] more important function is to make clear the title, the position, and the institution of the person who

> dispenses them. . . . By exchanging cards, both parties
> can gauge the relationships between them in terms of rela-
> tive rank, locating each other within the known order of
> their society.[2]

If two individuals from companies in the same industry meet, each knows from the other's job title which person holds the higher rank, and if they hold comparable positions, deference is accorded the employee of the larger firm. If the firms have a customer relationship, the employee of the customer firm has the higher status. Comparisons are not made across industries, as long as both firms are in the top group of their industries—for example, no one would try to make the fine determination of whether the securities firm Nomura is more prestigious than Nippon Telephone and Telegraph (NTT). However, government ministries are accorded more status than companies are. If the prestige of two employers is unequal, deference is accorded the person with the senior title, which usually means the older of the two. If two persons hold the same title, the older of the two has the higher status.

To an outsider, it seems as if each Japanese must gauge his position with respect to every other occupant of Japan. In practice, most human interactions are structured enough that the context clearly communicates who is slightly inferior or superior. For example, a *kacho* at NTT and a *kacho* at Toyota are unlikely to meet in an impromptu situation. Social contacts take place within a context where each person knows enough about the other party to clarify their relative positions. People who are quite senior or junior to each other seldom have much social interaction unless they have a *senpai-kohai* mentoring relationship. One of the individuals interviewed in this study clearly recalled such an awkward situation precisely because it is so unusual. A junior salesman at a bank, he found that a prospective customer was planning a merger, and his boss suggested that he call a particular contact in the bank's mergers and acquisitions unit. The contact, who was considerably senior to the salesman, fielded his first call but, on the second, insisted on talking to the salesman's boss. It did not matter that the salesman was responsible for the deal; the merger specialist simply felt that he needed to talk to someone of comparable rank.

Unstructured situations create anxiety

Because knowing one's relative rank is so important, it is virtually unthinkable that a Japanese manager would go to a party without knowing in advance who would be present. At something like a wedding ceremony, where there may be many people from different companies, great attention is paid to seating arrangements. A guest list shows the exact seating, each guest's company affiliation, and each guest's title. Getting the titles precisely right cannot be overemphasized. It would be a major faux pas to put a *bucho* from one company with a *kacho* from another, lest the *bucho* take offense. Salarymen abhor unstructured social situations, particularly when foreigners are involved, because it is difficult to gauge a foreigner's relative status. Japanese managers spend most of their lives in controlled social situations where they interact with people near their own age and rank, because the potential for embarrassment is so great otherwise.

Japanese employ one of two basic behavioral patterns according to their relative position: an up-faced orientation to superiors and down-faced orientation to inferiors.[3] A salaryman will get into considerable trouble if he accidentally uses a down-faced orientation toward a superior after mistaking the other person's status. He cannot know which model to use unless he always accurately assesses who is superior in a given situation and who is inferior. Although he knows he must be inferior or superior to virtually everyone else, he faces social sanctions if he inappropriately acts superior, because this destroys group harmony by making others feel inferior. Groups exclude such offenders to punish their arrogance.

Hierarchy stifles competition

Hierarchy within a group serves a very useful social function: it regulates competition among the group members. Japanese people compete with those they perceive to be their equals to avoid appearing inferior when inferiority is not socially expected. Without the hierarchy provided by a group, Japanese managers would break harmony by competing furiously to keep up at least with their equals.

Because age and seniority count so heavily in a *kaisha*, genuine equality can exist only within a salaryman's year group *(doki)*, and it is within a person's *doki* that competition is most intense. Intracohort rivalry is curbed by the fact that cooperation enters heavily into performance evaluations. Still, intra-*doki* rivalry lasts for many years as peers strive to keep up with one another. It slacks off only when it becomes clear who is emerging on top. This has caused firms to change certain personnel policies to curb competition. For example, in one bank, being assigned to headquarters used to be considered an infallible sign of favor. Consequently, salarymen who were assigned to bank branches became discouraged, so this bank now places all new entries in its branches, without exception, to maintain morale and effort. Similarly, it was formerly the case at one ministry that the elite of each year group would be assigned to one specific section. This ministry now randomly assigns new salarymen to their first jobs, to curb competition. However, from the second assignment on, it still becomes clear over time who is at the top of each year group.

As a result, the well-understood hierarchy of age and seniority breaks down somewhat as the salaryman reaches the middle stage of his career. After fifteen or twenty years of service, a salaryman may find that younger men are promoted ahead of him. When this happens, longstanding social relationships may have to change, because inferiority and superiority are so ingrained in Japanese language and culture. For example, a senior manager told us the following story:

> I was assigned to be the deputy branch manager in London, where the branch manager was one year younger than I. The branch manager had been promoted at the top of his *doki* while I was two years behind the top of our *doki*, so I was his deputy although I had joined the company a year

earlier than he had. Our families had known each other for a long time, and when my wife happened to meet his wife on the street in London, my wife started to talk to her as she always had. The wife of the branch manager replied, "In our company, does seniority prevail over positions?"

The nature of the Japanese language forced this unpleasant scene. In most Western countries, two people in this situation could conduct a conversation without choosing whether to address each other as equals, but in Japanese, such a choice cannot be avoided. A wife's social status depends on her husband's position in his company, and in some firms this is reinforced because the wives of employees assigned to a foreign branch are expected to pay courtesy calls on all the wives of senior people in the branch. Like it or not, a Japanese person who knows he or she is superior in a given context insists on using a form of language that makes public who is superior to whom. Indeed, a person who allowed his inferior to speak to him as an equal would violate accepted models of Japanese behavior and suffer embarrassment.

Within a firm, different divisions may have higher or lower status. This can cause tension because the Japanese language forces those who think they are superior to assert their higher status. For example, one salaryman who works for a bank told us this story:

> When I was in the capital markets division, I worked with a colleague who is one year younger than I am. After a while, he was transferred to the planning department. This department controls the whole operations of the bank, and is considered one of the most prestigious divisions in the company. My former colleague was assigned some planning responsibilities for our operation, and one day, he came to us and ordered us to give him some information, behaving as if he were senior to us. Everyone in our department was surprised to see him change so drastically. Later, we found out that the manager of the planning department told him

to behave that way because his department is controlling everything.

When the prestige of different departments is different and employees fasten on this difference instead of seniority, interdivisional conflict is almost sure to erupt inside the *kaisha*.

Sometimes Japanese people will compete fiercely to avoid appearing inferior, but sometimes they will not. To understand when a salaryman will exert himself to avoid inferiority, you need to understand the context and the models that govern that context. Where there is no accepted model to follow, competition is not a problem. For example, many salarymen are sent by their companies to the United States to earn MBA degrees, and one might think these students would work harder than most, out of fear of dishonoring themselves and their companies if they earn poorer marks than other Japanese. In fact, this does not happen. Japanese MBA students work no harder than any others, and one salaryman attending a U.S. business school commented to us that it was refreshing for him to meet so many Japanese outside his company because he didn't have to worry about competing with them. Why?

No social expectations govern salarymen abroad at school, and no one knows how well or poorly they perform academically. Most salarymen told us that their chief goals were to make contacts, improve their English, and deepen their understanding of Western business methods—not to earn high marks. One may suspect that, if business schools made individual student rankings public, tremendous competition would ensue.

Ambiguous evaluation induces maximum effort

Whether a college graduate joins a *kaisha* or a ministry, once recruitment is over, he spends the rest of his life striving within an evaluation system that takes maximum advantage of his need to avoid the appearance of inferiority. Most Westerners know that pay and promotion in Japanese firms are based much more on seniority than is the case in Europe or North America. Consequently, it often appears to outsiders that Japanese performance evaluation systems promote egalitarianism by playing down individual distinctions. Yet, beneath the surface, salarymen compete fiercely with one another for advancement, out of fear that they will fall behind their peers as the years pass. To complete his grasp of the way hierarchy and equality intermingle within the *kaisha,* a person must understand how salarymen are evaluated and what the evaluation system motivates them to do.

Despite the Japanese emphasis on team spirit and group evaluation, it would be naive to think that individuals are not judged and ranked. Individual evaluations lead initially to power and eventually to high position. However, it is quite common for the Japanese salaryman to work for many years getting only subtle signs indicating what superiors think of him. Assignment to a sought-after position, for instance, may signify that he is progressing well, but pay and promotion offer few clear-cut signals until late in his career. Tension and anxiety result, but the system also makes it difficult for him to quit the firm.

In our interviews, salarymen were asked how their companies' evaluation systems work; it turns out that there is surprisingly little variation across *kaisha.* One salaryman cogently described to us how it works:

> In my company, there is an annual performance review. I write down my achievements of the past year along with a self-assessment. I pass this to my boss, who adds his evaluation of my performance and sends the review to the personnel department. I don't get any feedback. I think evaluation is continuous as well as qualitative, because I have never had a quantitative goal. The personnel department then collects information about my performance from other departments to reach a final evaluation. I think the company avoids giving us feedback to create an illusion that they are not evaluating employees severely, in order to avoid discouraging us. In reality, however, employees are severely

ranked and it shows in various ways, like very small differences in salary or assignments to certain sections.

The criteria by which performance is evaluated are deliberately kept obscure. A senior manager of a large Japanese manufacturer told us, "In a Japanese company, you will never know how your boss evaluates you, no matter how high you move up in the organization." Very few salarymen told us that they get feedback on their annual evaluations or know how their evaluations turned out. There are a number of reasons why this is so.

First, large Japanese corporations are not expected to lay off their employees. Given this context, the last thing the *kaisha* wants to do is discourage employees. Second, senior managers want to avoid giving the impression that they are putting employees down or making them feel inferior. Third, jobs in the *kaisha* are somewhat vague, and responsibility is diffused, so negative evaluations are difficult to rationalize. Finally, and most importantly, obscure evaluations give the *kaisha* a way to extract the maximum effort from salarymen for many years. The next section provides a detailed discussion of this point, but before the motivational impact of the evaluation system is examined, let's clarify further what the bases of appraisal are.

Appraisals are general and secret

In Japanese companies, each employee is evaluated in detail by several superiors, who use concrete scales (grades of A through F), not just qualitative judgments. However, these concrete ratings evaluate "soft" criteria, such as cooperation, creativity, communication ability, and planning ability. An employee has no objective function to maximize, no "numbers to make." The best he can do is meet or exceed the expectations of those who evaluate him. Each salaryman knows who his evaluators are, so his task is to keep on guessing what he should do to meet their expectations.

Some firms employ several evaluators who reach independent judgments, whereas in other companies, only one evaluator has a real impact. For instance, a salaryman in a financial services organization told us that, in his company, an employee's immediate superior fills in the rating form, then forwards it for comment to other evaluators. The other evaluators take a risk if they disagree with the judgment of the first, because they know that, as long as they follow the precedent established by the first rater, their ability as evaluators will not be challenged.

The salarymen in this study were asked how they thought they were evaluated. Most pointed to their reputation within the company. One senior manager, for instance, told us that he makes a special point of asking female clerical workers about junior subordinates because they provide him with the most honest and unbiased opinions. A good reputation flows from the way a person manages his relationship with his boss, exceeding expectations, showing conformity, handling problems, displaying obedience, and working long hours. Most managers told us that, regardless of what the formal evaluation scales measure, the real determinants of performance evaluation are the factors that contribute to a person's reputation. There may be no formal scale measuring obedience, for example, but it counts.

Western performance evaluations also are influenced by personal characteristics, though perhaps different ones are emphasized. The major difference between Western and Japanese practice is that no one who evaluates a salaryman discusses his observations with the employee. It is very rare for a salaryman to receive annual performance feedback. In some cases, a person's boss might hint that the employee is all right, but a salaryman's boss won't tell him he has a problem unless the two share a very strong human relationship. Westerners get feedback on whether they met their objectives, but Japanese are not told, for instance, "improve your cooperation assessment."

Motivating the low performers

The evaluation system characteristic of the *kaisha* helps the firm curb self-interested behavior. For example, if a salaryman knew he was being evaluated on sales performance, his competitive nature would surface, and he would strive to maximize sales at all costs. Because he does not know what is being evaluated, however, his only choice is to work hard, conduct himself in an exemplary fashion, and do the right thing for the company. Western firms that have explicit appraisal criteria frequently have to find ways to monitor and eliminate suboptimal behavior. For example, if a Westerner's bonus is tied to new customer sales, he might be expected to pursue this end to the detriment of others, such as handling customer inquiries and maintaining existing accounts. The Japanese firm need not worry that its incentive system is distorting its employees' behaviors in any one direction, because there is no incentive to do anything other than meet the expectations of one's boss, one's peers, and one's customers.

One personnel department manager told us that the true objective of the Japanese evaluation system is to motivate those who are in the lower layers of the organization. He believes that those who are very good at business will do well under any evaluation system. No one needs to worry about these people; instead, the *kaisha* worries about those who are not as good as the top performers. They cannot be fired for being mediocre, so they have to be motivated some other way to ensure that they work hard. One tactic the *kaisha* uses is to let many years pass before it becomes clear who is ahead and who is behind. If an employee's relative standing became clear after just a few years, some lower performers might leave the company, taking with them their institutional learning. Thus, to a large extent, the efficiency of the total system depends on motivating those whose performance is average or below average by delaying as long as possible their dawning realization that they are not destined to reach high positions.

Consequently, the *kaisha*'s promotion system is characterized by its slowness. In most large corporations, members of the same *doki* won't diverge in rank until they have been with the firm for ten or even twenty years. Most salarymen within a *doki* will be promoted to the first two managerial ranks *(kakaricho* and *kacho)* at the same time. Even in a company that starts to differentiate people from the same *doki* relatively early—say, after a decade—50 to 80 percent of a *doki*'s members will be promoted together at this milestone. We weren't able to identify any large Japanese corporations in which the top 5 percent of a year group, the ones who ultimately will reach the firm's highest ranks, are promoted to a higher rank than most of their peers within their first five or ten years of service.

Through slow promotion, the *kaisha* spares most salarymen who keep up with their year group the embarrassment of working with younger bosses or older subordinates. In many *kaisha,* those in the top layer of a *doki* will not be passed by members of more recent year groups until the very late stages of their careers. As we have seen, a salaryman feels inferior when someone who was once beneath him on the basis of seniority becomes his direct superior. A salaryman can put up with having a boss from his *doki* if he feels the superior is a very good manager, but it is very difficult for him to have a younger boss, because older subordinates who are not treated considerately may lose face and experience social embarrassment. Such situations are also awkward for younger bosses, because the context runs against the familiar models of behavior within the *kaisha.*

The system depends on growth

Because two-thirds of people in a *doki* know that they won't make it to the top, what keeps them motivated? This is becoming a difficult question for Japanese companies to answer. A generation ago, salarymen in the lower echelon of their year group knew they would make it to the level just below top management because the organization was growing. In those days, a Japanese bank with three hundred domestic branches might hire only twenty or thirty college graduates, so everyone had a good chance of making branch manager, a position one rung below top management. Times have changed, and a bank that size might have hired three hundred salarymen in each *doki* during the late 1970s and through the 1980s. How many of them will ever make branch manager?

Today's salarymen understand this demographic imperative, but few quit their initial employers anyway; after seven, eight, or nine years, they have too much to lose. Most have children and are happy to be working for one of the best companies in Japan. Those who are not promoted readjust their hopes and wait for the chance to get promoted later. A salaryman in this position might think, "I may not make president, but I can still make *bucho*," or "I may not make *bucho*, but I can still make *kacho* or *kakaricho*." By the time the salaryman's fate starts to become clear, he has little choice but to shift his career expectations and keep working to make the next rung on the ladder. As we have seen, his whole training has made him organizationally competent but not technically competent, and he finds that his skills and reputation would be difficult to transfer elsewhere even if another *kaisha* would hire him.

Slow growth and the diminished chances of promotion that accompany it are causing severe problems for Japanese companies, because salarymen value job titles a great deal. Everyone in Japanese society knows what rank a person of a certain age "ought" to hold if he has been promoted according to expectations, so it will be difficult for salarymen to accommodate themselves to a diminished set of career opportunities. Turnover isn't the problem; the *kaisha* knows that few salarymen will quit. The danger is that those who are not elevated according to expectations will lose their drive to work hard and will become mere chair warmers. To cope with this problem, Japanese companies have kept adding layers of hierarchical titles. Once, the progression of managerial job titles was clear throughout Japan: *kacho, bucho, shacho.* Because job titles have proliferated, a 1990s *bucho* does what a *kacho* did twenty years before, but managers who cannot leave their employers are still motivated to pursue titles that are increasingly meaningless. Some firms are also cutting down numbers; for example, the trading company Ito-Chu made headlines by slashing twenty or thirty *bucho* positions. Eventually, *kaisha* might be forced to end the no-layoff policy that has become expected of them, though they will probably disguise layoffs as transfers and early retirements.

Strains in the system

Confusing as it may be to the uninformed outsider, the combination of hierarchy and equality, clarity and ambiguity which firms have evolved perfectly suits the Japanese context. Whether they can continue to maintain such a balance in the future is an open question. Cracks in the system are appearing for two reasons. One is that, in a slow-growing economy, companies can't rely on growth to create enough *kacho* and *bucho* positions to accommodate everyone. The other is that Japanese companies are quite aware that their white-collar productivity is very low by world standards, and growth can no longer paper over this problem.

In the past, the *kaisha* needed to keep managers motivated as long as possible, because it needed people who knew how to do business within the firm so that it could cope with expected future expansion. Now, the nature of many important industries has changed from mass production to customer-specific products, and computer systems have dramatically increased the efficiency of communication. Japanese firms don't need as many middle managers as they used to, and they want to reduce their managerial ranks to boost white-collar productivity. Because they no longer need to emphasize retaining everyone, many firms are shifting their focus from motivating mediocre performers to encouraging top performers. Some companies have started basing compensation more on performance, making employees aware of who is receiving higher salaries and who isn't.

How will the *kaisha* that makes such distinctions avoid an atmosphere resembling "exam hell"? The answer is not yet clear, but it is reasonable to believe that firms will have to change the context governing the way employees compare themselves to one another. This will be challenging but not impossible; salarymen are perfectly capable of accepting inconsistent behaviors, as long as such behaviors are interpreted as occurring in different contexts. It seems unlikely that *kaisha* will emulate their Western counterparts by adopting bonus schemes based on quantitative targets, because the Japanese emphasize process over results. More likely, firms will try to manipulate expectations so that different models are applied to salarymen with different kinds of experiences. By finding some way to differentiate salarymen in incommensurable categories, tomorrow's senior managers will find a Japanese solution that rewards performance without creating social embarrassment.

Genuine equality is unstable

"The Japanese are either at your throat or at your feet," remarked an American statesman as the second world war broke out. Perhaps the most consistent image problem that Japanese have overseas is that they can appear to oscillate wildly between arrogance and obsequiousness. On the one hand, Japanese will declare that they are the inhabitants of a poor island nation, constantly at risk of disaster. On the other, at a deep level, Japanese truly do seem to think of themselves as superior to foreigners. When other nations complain about Japan's trade practices, its citizens often respond reflexively that there wouldn't be any problems if others were as tough, intelligent, industrious, and humble as the Japanese are.

This strange mixture stems from the characteristically Japanese emphasis on inferiority and superiority which we have described in this chapter. For a Japanese, a foreigner can never be truly equal, because, if genuine equality existed, it would place great strain on the Japanese to avoid slipping into inferiority. When a *gaijin* is a person of great status or a customer, Japanese models call for polite treatment. Otherwise, confusion results, because foreigners consistently fail to pay the Japanese what they regard as appropriate deference. A salaryman often doesn't know whether he is inferior or superior to a foreigner, and outsiders don't provide the cues needed to help the Japanese avoid embarrassment. As a consequence, the Japanese usually reaches one judgment or the other and exaggerates the behavior appropriate to his conclusion, to make up for the lack of signals from the foreigner showing that he understands and agrees with the Japanese assessment of their relative position.

Joint ventures: one partner is senior

The same problem occurs between firms, which helps explain why Western-Japanese ventures sometimes fall apart in ways that make Westerners feel exploited. A joint venture cannot truly be a partnership of equals. If a Japanese firm felt itself to be equal with its Western partner, it would be in a tense position in which it would have to move heaven and earth to avoid slipping behind. Consequently, Japanese companies tend to view themselves as either the junior or the senior partner in a given enterprise. If the foreign firm starts out as the senior partner and the Japanese firm eventually surpasses the partner's capabilities, the behavioral model that governed the venture would no longer apply. For the Japanese, either the model would have to be revised or the venture would become difficult to sustain.

A consequence is that many Western firms feel their Japanese partners have cooperated only as long as they thought they had anything to learn; once they had taken what they wanted to know, they lost interest in the venture. The Japanese do, of course, value long-term relationships and do not terminate partnerships lightly. However, non-Japanese organizations evaluating whether to cooperate with a *kaisha* must grasp whether the Japanese firm views itself as slightly superior or slightly inferior and whether this view is sustainable. As long as they lack true insight into the Japanese firm's behavioral model and expectations, Western companies will only continue to be bewildered by the supposed double standard of their strategic allies.

The preeminent are expected to lead

At least some of America's trade problems with Japan stem from this same distinction between American and Japanese attitudes toward equality. Americans usually believe they should treat Japan as an equal partner, because it would seem condescending to regard the Japanese as inferiors, and it would be intolerable to accept them as superiors. In contrast, the Japanese believe there can be only a single preeminent power in the world, because a permanent condominium of equals would create too much tension.

Through the Japanese lens, leaders must adhere to clear, well-understood behavioral models and social expectations. In Japan, the leading company sets the rules and provides clear signals to its smaller rivals about what will and will not be tolerated. In return, it respects the position of smaller rivals, refrains from unprovoked attacks on them, and takes care not to appear arrogant. Leaders who fail to act as leaders cause problems. For example, previous chapters have suggested that most Japanese firms will not attack the leader in their industry. The only exception to this rule applies when the leader for some inexplicable reason fails to defend its top position as fiercely as social expectations dictate. Inappropriate behavior on the part of the industry-leading firm is enormously unsettling to the Japanese. If the leading firm cannot be relied upon to discipline others, the Japanese fear that order will eventually break down and a bloody price war will ensue which might even drive some firms into bankruptcy.

This is why, for example, a firm such as NEC, the domestic leader in personal computers, simply must stanch its loss of market share rapidly and decisively. In the early 1990s, NEC lost a good deal of the market to American invaders such as Dell and Compaq, and it came under criticism in Japan for appearing to have been unready to wage a price war. Were NEC not to swiftly right itself and reverse its loss of share, confidence in its ability to lead might decline to the point where it would become socially acceptable for another PC maker to take over industry leadership. When they look at America, the Japanese find it difficult to imagine that firms such as General Motors and IBM could watch their market share dwindle for so many years. The only explanation that seems reasonable for this decline is that such firms are very deeply sick and thus deserve to be scourged.

In the international arena, many Japanese are truly puzzled that the world's leading nation seems unable to shake its trade deficit, put its budget in balance, and defend its share of world trade. In Japan, a sick industry leader is a sign of a sick industry, and were Japanese firms to sense that the leader lacked resolve and was unable to defend its position, a round of unbridled competition damaging to all would ensue. Because America has not fought to preserve its economic dominance as Japan would, some Japanese have already decided that the United States has entered an irreversible decline, that Japan is destined to assume the mantle of leadership, and that someone should start acting as if it were number one, to forestall a period of global disorder. Their contempt for America is open, and decadence is the only explanation they can find for a relative loss of economic power that Japan would never tolerate were it number one.

Recent public opinion surveys in the United States have shown a remarkable resurgence in American confidence; more Americans now say they are stronger than Japan than say that Japan is the world's leading economic power, reversing a majority opinion that dated back to the mid-1980s. Yet, in Japan, despite the nation's deep recession, most salarymen believe in their heart of hearts that Japan is superior. America's military might is still respected, and actions such as Desert Storm strike the Japanese as exactly what the world's leading nation ought to be doing, protecting smaller entities in the "industry" from destruction. But most Japanese businessmen still believe that, if America were truly the world's strongest economic power, it would impose more order on the global economy. Americans believe in "fair play," in the British, sporting sense of the word. That is a fundamentally different conception of the role the global economic leader should occupy, and it is interpreted in Japan as weakness. Faced with an economic leader that does not behave according to its expectations, Japan responds with what appears to be monumental arrogance. The huge gulf between Japanese and American egalitarianism lies at the center of economic friction between the two countries. It is a gap whose bridging may make the difference between irritation and trade war.

CHAPTER NINE

Gaishi Salaryman:
The Outsider's Perspective

Chapter 1 introduced a prototypical salaryman, Hiro, who is a composite character, his education and socialization story an amalgamation of many that emerged from the interviews in this study. Chapter 9 closes the book, not with one voice, but with many. It is possible to speak of a model salaryman's progress through the Japanese educational system and through his initial years in a *kaisha,* because the experiences of different young Japanese managers are so similar. In contrast, the experiences of salarymen who go to work for *gaishi*—foreign companies— diverge greatly. Once a salaryman sheds the control mechanisms of a *kaisha,* his path increasingly reflects his own choices and values, not those of his company. Therefore, in this chapter, a number of salarymen will tell their stories through pseudonyms. None of the respondents interviewed for this book wanted to go on record, for all are operating in Japan today and still have friends and loyalties at their former Japanese employers.

This chapter starts by examining why salarymen leave their companies. Although such an event is much more common in the 1990s than it was even a decade earlier, it is still unusual. For example, of over twenty Japanese students who earned MBAs at Cornell University in 1993, only two had left their employers by 1996. When someone socialized in a large Japanese company joins a Western firm, he often notices for the first time aspects of his company that went unnoticed before he had a standard of comparison. What are the chief differences between Western and Japanese companies that a newly transplanted salaryman notices? The last section of the chapter delves more deeply into one salaryman's story, describing how his firm successfully pioneered a new product in Japan. This section is meant to convey to readers how a Japanese manager in a non-Japanese firm thinks about approaching the Japanese market to gain a foothold. The chapter closes with a heart-to-heart message from the salarymen who contributed to this book. The respondents were asked what they would wish to say to a Western colleague about working effectively with salarymen. Their answers provide a window for outsiders on what insiders would say to those wise enough to understand.

Why do salarymen depart their *kaisha?*

Why would a salaryman leave his Japanese employer? Not one manager we interviewed moved from one major Japanese corporation to another one. It happens, but realistically, if a salaryman decides to leave his company, he has few opportunities to start over with another Japanese firm. Explained one respondent, whom we'll call "Masahiko," or "Masa," "I could, perhaps, join a well-known *kaisha* in a very specialized, technical job, but I would never become a director of the company. If you don't start with the company right out of university, you don't have a chance." He felt that his only options were to work for a foreign company, join a very small Japanese firm, or take a completely nontraditional job. In fact, he was interviewed for a job as a television newscaster but decided not to pursue the opportunity because such employees can be fired at any time.

Masa's story illustrates why salarymen leave their companies. After graduating from the University of Tokyo, he joined the consulting and research organization associated with one of Japan's most prestigious service firms. Masa's department specialized in contract socioeconomic studies for clients interested in consumer behavior, and his first four years were stimulating and challenging. He recalled:

> Interviewing famous people is a major way of doing research, so I met many well-known Japanese. If you're going to study, for example, the health care industry, it's important to talk to the major people in that industry. Usually I would call such people directly and ask to interview them. They usually agreed, both because my firm's parent company was very well known in Japan, and because I gave them information in return. The job was fun.

Projects were initiated either when a client requested a particular study, or when Masa's company proposed a study to a customer organization. When a study was commissioned, a senior project leader would be appointed to manage the engagement, and he picked his team of analysts. Because Masa was popular, he was often asked to join project teams, and soon he was regularly juggling up to ten projects at the same time.

To keep up with the demand for his services, Masa began to put in extremely long hours, even by Japanese standards. He told us:

> I regularly put in two to three hundred hours of overtime a month, on top of a standard forty-hour work week. There is a legal limit of about eighty paid overtime hours a month, and I quickly figured out that everyone reported his overtime was just below the legal limit, although in fact we were logging much more time at the office. No one told me to do that, but everyone did it. I usually went to bed at 2 o'clock in the morning, got up four hours later, and went back to work.

Masa learned to snatch sleep wherever he could. He recounted:

> We all took about ten minutes for lunch, then napped the rest of the lunch hour. Most days, I had to travel to Tokyo to talk with clients or interview sources, and I learned to sleep exactly one hour so that I would wake up at the right

station. We were instructed to use taxis in Tokyo, in order
to save time, and I would always tell the cab driver where
I was going, then instruct him to wake me up when we got
there.

Desire to make a change

After four years of this life, Masa met a woman, a fellow University
of Tokyo classmate, at a party, and they began dating. She worked
in Tokyo, and they snatched quick meals whenever he was in
her neighborhood. When they began to think about marriage,
Masa started to reconsider the demands of his job. He said:

> Most of the people in my company didn't have a personal
> life. I had a *senpai* a few years older than me whose parents-
> in-law worried because he never came home before mid-
> night. I can't think of anyone who left the company before
> midnight. But his wife's parents worried that he had a secret
> woman somewhere, and they used to call the company
> every night to ask if he was there. Of course, he really was
> in the company every day. Most of the salarymen who had
> children lived within twenty minutes' drive of the office so
> they could go home for an hour and have dinner with their
> families. That's their whole family life, and I wanted more.

A crisis of confidence

Masa was also having doubts about some of the choices he was
forced to make to meet the company's revenue demands. He
recalled:

> One of my jobs was to act as an information intermediary.
> The highest-priced projects we were asked to do always
> involved gathering intelligence on a firm's competitors in the
> Japanese market. Of course, all the big firms in an industry
> commissioned us to give them intelligence about each other,
> and they spent a lot of money on these engagements. We
> would give firm A insights into the strategy of firm B, when
> both were our clients. I'm sure firm A understood why we
> knew so much about firm B, and they knew that we were

selling firm B insights about firm A's strategy too. The clients knew we were giving away their strategies to other people, but it still bothered me. I didn't think it was ethical.

Masa also found it difficult to deal emotionally with his inability to serve all of his clients. He commented:

I had ten projects going at all times, which meant I had something due every two or three days. I was on the road almost every day talking to people and wrote at night. The only way I could keep up was to regard at least one or two of the projects as unimportant. That meant that sometimes I did a poor job for my clients. Now, who is going to be classified as less important? The company's attitude was that we were there to make as much money as possible. We might have a small company pay us $100,000 for a study. To them, that was very important money. They wanted to work with us because we were very prestigious, and they wanted the best. But large companies often paid a million dollars or more for their reports, and the value of our ongoing relationship with them was enormous. If I had only had one or two clients, I'm sure I could have done a good job for each one, but I often did work of poor quality, and I felt such regret that our smaller customers were getting shoddy research.

Masa ended up joining an American financial services company operating in one of the industries that Masa had covered for his employer. Although the pay was only half what he had earned before, he took the job because he was offered an interesting challenge. He said:

After five years, I was tired of only giving advice to clients. Usually, customers would read my reports, and tell me, "You are right, but you don't know the situation in our company. What you recommend is impossible to implement." I was so frustrated that I could not implement my ideas in a real business situation. I wanted to join an actual business, and the American company offered me a starting position as an

operations analyst, looking at business processes and trying
to improve them. They also said I could become a manager
within two or three years.

Inflexibility collides with a desire to change

Two elements of Masa's story are common to most of the experiences related in interviews with salarymen who left their firms.
One is a desire to change their work pattern. This collides with
the other: their employers' relatively inflexible human resources
practices. Often, this conflict either stems from or unearths an
underlying challenge to the salaryman's confidence in his firm.
For Masa, his inability to meet what he saw as his obligations
to clients undermined his belief in his *kaisha*'s way of doing
business. For another salaryman, "Takashi," an assignment to a
"no-win" job caused a similar crisis.

Takashi graduated from a prestigious university, though not
one of the most elite schools in Japan, and joined one of Japan's
largest, most well known banks. He enjoyed working in sales
and in a branch but after a few years was assigned to a job as
a stock and bond trader. Takashi soon felt he was heading down
a path that would trap him into being a player in a game Japanese
firms could not win.

As a bond and stock trader, he found himself competing
with counterparts in Western financial institutions who were free
to do anything, as long as they stayed within the position limits
they agreed on with their supervisors. Takashi also had a position
limit, but that didn't mean he could do whatever he wanted
subject to this one constraint. There were certain instruments
he couldn't trade for organizational reasons, because top management had authorized other departments to be responsible
for them. He had to gain informal approval from senior managers
for trades, even if they fell within his position limit, yet it proved
almost impossible for senior people to understand the latest
technology in the market, such as complex derivative securities.
Understandably, senior managers were afraid to make mistakes
that they could not explain to their superiors. In a system where
each boss has to keep his supervisor informed to avoid embar-

rassment, there is a strong tendency to turn down new trading ideas.

Furthermore, it seemed clear to Takashi that someone who spent 70 percent of his time on internal matters would always have great difficulty competing with traders who devoted almost all of their time to studying the market. After a year in capital markets, Takashi concluded that the *kaisha,* as efficient as it is in many domains, is just not structured to compete in an arena that changes as quickly as financial markets do.

This conclusion caused Takashi to feel uncertain about his future career in a *kaisha,* though he regarded his employer as an excellent bank in general. A trader who makes millions for a Japanese bank might receive several thousand dollars in bonuses, but, if he loses money for the firm, his career can be damaged. One reason why many young salarymen avoid trading if they can is that there seems to be so little upside compared to the downside. Japanese traders can't make a lot of money and retire early, as their Western counterparts often do. Takashi wondered if he would have any control over his career by the time he reached forty. It was clear to him that the way to get promoted in the bank was to become a specialist in the bank's organization, an expert in its people and its way of doing business. That seemed to be the complete opposite of what he had to do to be competitive as a trader. This would not have been such a problem had Takashi believed that the securities department would simply be one rotation in a long career, but the role models he saw were people who never left the securities department once they were transferred into it.

For a third salaryman, "Kazuo," the breaking point was his company's refusal to honor his assignment requests. Kazuo returned to his employer, a heavy manufacturing firm, from business school in the United States, armed with a CPA and a desire for either an overseas posting or a job in the treasury department. Despite his repeated requests, Kazuo was reassigned to the corporate finance department he had left when he was accepted to business school. In Kazuo's company, this was considered a fast-track department, and his *senpai* simply couldn't believe that the young salaryman really wanted another assignment. Persuaded that his company would not take advantage of his skills, and confident in his market value because of his CPA certification, Kazuo moved to the Tokyo office of a well-known American investment bank.

Different controls, different salaryman

The case of the *gaishi* salaryman illustrates clearly the extent to which Japanese behavior is the product of social controls. The salarymen we interviewed all worked at firms that were operating in Japan and were operationally managed by Japanese nationals, not Western expatriates. Nonetheless, these Western-owned, Japanese-managed enterprises do not resemble *kaisha* at all. Placed in a different environment with different expectations, many Japanese managers aren't very "Japanese." Some of the differences extend to simple matters of style. Noted Masa:

> At my old company, people wear very traditional, dark suits. Over here, you see people wearing pink shirts or suspenders or very Italian-looking suits. At my old company, we formally had twenty days of leave every year, but in five years, I took fewer than ten days of leave in total. Nobody took vacation time. Here, everyone uses up all the allowed vacation time within the fiscal year.

Sometimes, the differences have frustrated Masa. He told us:

> I am still a man of my old company inside. There is no image here of what a salaryman should be, and I was imprinted very, very strongly by my first five years. It is sometimes difficult for me to work with people who were imprinted differently. One of my strengths is that I can work twenty hours straight without losing concentration. Most people here can't work that hard, and sometimes I have become very frustrated at the working pace of others.

Most of the salarymen working in foreign firms concurred, noting that Japanese managers in American companies work fewer hours and take more vacation as a matter of course. Those outsiders who see Japanese managers as economic animals, conditioned for nothing but work, will have a difficult task explaining why the Japanese work ethic is so much more "Western," once social expectations permit it to be.

What else do salarymen notice when they first acquire a standard of comparison against their *kaisha* experience?

Socialization is almost nonexistent

None of the salarymen who moved to foreign companies reported that his firm had made a significant effort to socialize him to its ways. Most still regard themselves inside as men of their old company, whose way of doing business—from philosophy to details such as dress, hair, and presentation of business cards—remains as it was in the *kaisha*. The experience of "Shigeru" is typical. Upon joining an American bank, he went into the office, was told where to sit, and was introduced to many other people during his first week, but he received no training and no indoctrination. It seemed to him that his first assignment was simply to figure out what his job was supposed to be. In hindsight, Shigeru believes this lack of structure is a kind of test to see how capable a new hire is. His bank's theory is that a smart person will find a way to make himself useful.

A mundane translation job got Shigeru involved in a project team, and gradually, he became part of more teams and became involved in more deals. Typically, this kind of engagement starts when several people talk informally about the problems of a certain company. If a salaryman such as Shigeru comes up with a new idea, he is asked to create some marketing materials to support it and to join in the sales call on the prospect. Additionally, he expected to create opportunities for which they can be responsible. As Shigeru developed his reputation, he was asked to join more teams, but his basic job remained figuring out for himself how to initiate new transactions.

Takashi also had to learn how to manage without the kind

of *senpai-kohai* relationship that plays such a large role in teaching newcomers the ropes at *kaisha*. He was eventually promoted to vice president and was assigned to mentor a young associate, but this simply meant caring about his junior's career and development. Upon his promotion, Takashi was counseled that he wanted too much to be a good assistant and to learn from others and was told that he now had to work on his ability to drive the team in new directions, initiate things, and make decisions, not simply be an exemplary subordinate. He continued to learn valuable lessons from the senior members of his group, but emulating them as behavioral prototypes is not the way of his American firm.

Customer orientation is weaker

Many salarymen felt that the *gaishi's* attitude toward customers is a significant weakness. Commented Kazuo, who had joined an American bank:

> I always feel that I am working for a non-Japanese company, but am able to position myself on the Japanese client's side. The expatriates here work for the company and make decisions from the company's perspective. This difference becomes critical when our clients ask us to work on smaller business with smaller revenue. Japanese clients always start with a small order to see how well such an order is fulfilled, and gradually increase the size of the orders. This is how the relationship is built up; if we don't take up a small order, we won't get a big one. The expatriates have very clear standards with respect to size, and we always have to argue that small business is important from a relationship perspective. They always ask what concrete business we can expect from the client in the future, which can be difficult to judge. Expatriates also tend to believe that, if we're competitive, we'll stand on the starting line when big business appears; we argue that, without a solid relationship, our company won't know to begin with when a large opportunity appears.

Individual commitment supersedes institutional loyalty

Many of the respondents who were interviewed expressed surprise that both Japanese and American managers within a *gaishi* showed more loyalty to their superiors and subordinates than they did to the firm as a whole. As noted in chapter 4, trust in a *kaisha* resides in vertical, not horizontal bonds. Absent control mechanisms found in Japanese firms, these vertical loyalties overwhelm fidelity to the organization. Sometimes this can cause problems for customers. Noted Kazuo:

> One aspect in which Japanese companies differ from U.S. companies is that accountability or trust has to exist between institutions. This may be because we expect consistent service from a Japanese company. There is a negative feeling about decisions based on personal relationships, and in a formal meeting with clients, salarymen rarely mention a particular individual as a business partner.

The consequences can be harmful for customer relationships. Continued Kazuo:

> We have been working on a project for a Japanese company with our team in the United States. The other day, our U.S. team moved to our competitor and they tried to take this project from our company. Working-level people in a Japanese company preferred to continue working with this U.S. team no matter which institution they belong to, because the team knows the history of the project. However, such a change of partners was completely unacceptable for the management of the Japanese company. At the beginning, when the *kaisha* selected its partner, the decision (at least *tatemae*) was based on the reputation and accountability of the U.S. company. Working-level people wrote in the *ringi-sho* that "this company is well qualified to work with us on this project," even if in *honne* it was the team they really wanted to work with. In a Japanese company, you simply

cannot say in a formal proposal that you want to work with a specific person.

In Takashi's company, some Japanese employees publicly make personal commitments to their supervisors, and when a senior person leaves the firm, the bank expects to lose some of his subordinates as well. Why? For one thing, a *gaijin* company cannot be a meaningful reference group in Japanese society, so salarymen do not feel the sense of losing their membership as strongly when they leave a foreign firm as they do when they leave a *kaisha*. For another, individuals are rewarded for what they have achieved, not for membership in a particular institution. Reference groups are informal, held together by the fact that the boss protects their jobs, not by the sharing of information which won't be disclosed outside a circle of insiders. This context should make it clear that company loyalty is a function of evaluation and incentive systems, not inbred Japanese cultural traits.

From an information point of view, the distinction between insiders and outsiders is much more vague at Takashi's American employer than it is within a *kaisha*. Data are shared very widely through the company's electronic mail system and cross divisional boundaries much more readily than they would in a Japanese firm. Sometimes this causes problems. For instance, Takashi's team once found itself talking about a project with a division of a Japanese company. Another team at the bank was in contact with a different division of the same company. At Takashi's firm, business information tends to be shared, both intentionally and unintentionally, unless the client requests special confidentiality arrangements. The other team naturally learned about the project Takashi's team was discussing, and they mentioned it to their contact in the Japanese company. This person told the people working with Takashi's group that he had heard about the project from the American bank, causing a major incident because the salarymen working on the project had been trying to confine word of the undertaking within their division. After this incident, Takashi's team made a point of keeping in mind that information is not shared in *kaisha* the way it is in their *gaishi,* because the flow of information in Japanese organizations is what distinguishes insiders from outsiders.

On the other hand, the sense of trust between supervisors and their subordinates is often much stronger in Takashi's bank than it is in most Japanese companies. Within a *kaisha,* the basis of trust is meeting expectations, and to build trust, seniors and juniors must share the same behavioral models in various contexts. Such expectations can hardly be met in an American firm, because people from such diverse backgrounds work together. Instead, trust emerges when seniors and juniors respect each other's ability, when evaluation and reward systems are considered fair, and when subordinates think their bosses will protect them. For instance, when a highly respected senior person resigned from the bank, it was widely believed that one of the reasons for his resignation was his feeling that he couldn't get enough resources for his subordinates. As expected, many of those on his team joined him in his new company, because they strongly felt that he had tried to protect them. Although such loyalty may seem very Japanese, such a thing could hardly happen in a *kaisha,* because strong human relationships aren't necessarily a basis for trust. In a Japanese firm, a salaryman whose boss departs won't lose protection, but a salaryman who leaves the *kaisha* certainly will. This is why Japanese salarymen may follow a trusted superior who leaves a Western firm, but will not follow the same person who leaves a Japanese firm. Differences between Japanese and *gaijin* organizations, not between Japanese and *gaijin* national cultures, account for different behaviors.

The importance of personal loyalties extends to vertical ties only, not to customer bonds. It is widely recognized within Shigeru's bank, for instance, that a person hired as a "relationship manager" because of his connections won't really be able to exploit his past relationships with individuals in potential customer *kaisha*. In the first place, most of the bank's Japanese rivals have institutional relationships that are at least as strong as the personal ties an individual brings with him from past experience. In the second place, a critical part of a person's relationships is his membership. A person who had strong customer relationships when he worked for a Japanese bank usually finds those ties considerably weakened when he moves to a foreign institution. Salarymen are recognized by the name of their company, and their company affiliation is the principal source of their power. Because everything depends on context, it is quite natural in Japan for the nature of a person's relationships to change when he shifts from one employer to another.

Western organizations are more fluid and flat

Many salarymen remarked on the very different character of organization within a non-Japanese firm. Noted Masa:

> In my old company, the organization was very, very strong. In fact, it is virtually fixed. If you pick up an organization chart from five years ago, you probably could use it today. The people rotate, but the roles are fixed, except perhaps every five years or so, when a dramatic change occurs. On the other hand, in my American company, organizational change is an everyday event. At my old company, we'd all get a letter from the human resource department announcing *personnel* changes. Here, each manager sends a memo to all employees, telling us about a person who has just joined as a manager and what department was created for him. I get two or three memos a week like this.

The difference, said Masa, is that an American firm fits roles to people, and a Japanese organization does the reverse. He continued:

> We usually create an organization for a specific person. Maybe some department will be created for you, to utilize your ability or personality. If a post is needed for a specific person, the senior managers create a new position. In my old company, you had to join an existing organization. There was also a very clear image of what a manager was and how he behaved. So again and again, when someone was promoted to some position, he tried to change his personality to fit his new title and responsibility. In an American

firm, I noticed people didn't change their styles when they changed jobs. Furthermore, people call me by my name here. In a *kaisha,* we always called managers by their titles. Everyone would call you *kacho* or *bucho* where I used to work; here, they'd call you "Suzuki-san," or whatever your name is.

Another salaryman, whom we'll call "Ataru," who now works for a Western clothing manufacturer, concurred. He commented:

> One of the good aspects about a non-Japanese company is that decisions can be made swiftly, especially when an American manager is in charge. An American manager knows what responsibility he assumes and what risks can be taken. When a Japanese manager is in charge, the decision-making process slows down significantly, because he tries to make the U.S. headquarters responsible for the business.

Takashi, who had left his bank fearing that he could not compete with Western stock and bond traders, found himself spending far more time doing business, and far less time attending to internal organizational matters. In his old *kaisha,* Takashi often attended two or three meetings a day, reporting to the planning department and gaining his supervisor's informal approval for anything he needed to do. At his American employer, his group met once a week for thirty minutes, leaving him far more time to study the market or the needs of clients than his counterparts at Japanese banks enjoyed. Ideas were subject to legal compliance reviews and client approval, but his supervisor didn't expect to approve most of his ideas before they went forward. Because Takashi worked in a fairly small group, there were few organizational constraints on the kinds of opportunities he could take up. At a Japanese bank, when a client wanted something, the first question that arose was whether this fell in the jurisdiction of a department. At an American bank, if a team decided to pursue a new idea, nobody stopped them from pushing ahead.

Seniority is much less important

Lest one conclude that respect for seniors is a cultural trait of Japanese people, when salarymen are placed in a situation where seniority is less relevant, they adapt quickly. One of the difficulties Shigeru faced when he joined a foreign company was figuring out how to address senior people. Most salarymen in the bank addressed the branch manager, a Japanese citizen, by the polite form of his last name, just as they addressed one another ("Yoshimura-san"). Conditioned by his old norms, it took Shigeru a month before he could stop himself from addressing the branch manager by his title instead. Since people at the American firm use a frank version of a polite form of the Japanese language, it was hard for Shigeru to figure out who was senior to whom. In a *kaisha,* of course, even if two salarymen were separated by a single year of seniority, the more senior would use plain forms with the junior, who would use polite forms in reply. Being part of an American bank, Shigeru speaks with senior people much more frankly than he used to in a Japanese bank. He is almost twenty years younger than his branch manager, but the two talk openly, in a way that would be impossible in a Japanese bank.

Masa discovered this difference soon after he had joined his American employer. He recalled:

> During my first month on the job, I was jammed with some other guys in a small office packed with five or six desks. I was looking down at a paper I was writing one day, and when I happened to look up, I suddenly noticed a stranger approaching us. Somehow, I realized he was the president of the company. I whispered to the person next to me, asking him what was going on. He told me not to worry, this was an everyday event. The president simply believed in managing by walking around and saying hello to people. At my former Japanese company, I couldn't even meet the director of my department, much less the president or chairman of the company. Junior people just don't associate with managers that senior. In fact, our president sometimes complains

that very few people say hello to him. It's just not natural for most salarymen to talk to him.

Masa was in for an even greater surprise. After six months, he was asked to take charge of a department that had a really terrible reputation. The most difficult adjustment was supervising other Japanese employees who were considerably older than he was. He said, "I was the second-youngest person in the department, and I was in charge. I felt very uncomfortable as a twenty-eight-year-old directing people who were in their thirties, forties, or even fifties." However, given a responsibility he never would have had at such an age in a *kaisha,* Masa succeeded in turning the department around and discovered that he loved managing people.

Old status groups lose their meaning

Takashi, among others, noted that people pay far less attention to an employee's educational background in an American firm than they do in a Japanese organization. For instance, when Takashi joined his new employer as a very Japanese salaryman, he asked one of the senior managers which university he had attended. He was astonished to find that, until he had asked this question, most of the twenty Japanese in this manager's team had not known the answer, though they had worked together for years. In a *kaisha,* everyone would have known which managers were alumni of which colleges, because school ties are one of the keys to building relationships within the company.

In Takashi's firm, as at many others, the individual's affiliations are far less important than they are in Japanese firms. In Japanese society, memberships convey social status and power, which is why salarymen struggle to forge the most prestigious affiliations they can. In contrast, at his *gaishi,* individual ability is almost all that matters. From time to time, Takashi's group would receive a résumé from a person who had graduated from a very prestigious university and had worked in a famous Japanese bank for ten or twenty years. More often than not, the firm didn't hire such applicants, because their qualifications were so general that it wasn't clear what they could do for the company. This often upset people, because Japanese are conditioned to consider such salarymen very valuable because of their memberships and connections, and can hardly imagine that someone of such caliber could be rejected.

Japanese managers must relearn political skills

One problem noted by many salarymen is that more senior Japanese managers, who have spent their careers honing political instead of technical skills, may not be effective in a Western organization. Commented Ataru:

> We receive numerous proposals and suggestions from head-quarters, and many of them don't make sense because they disregard the market characteristics. The problem Japanese managers have in responding to those suggestions is that they are not good at logically arguing, or coming up with alternatives to dodge nonsensical ideas. Consequently, two types of Japanese managers emerge. One rejects almost everything coming from the United States. This type of manager becomes isolated from headquarters and internal politics, so when a problem arises, he loses the trust of other Japanese because he cannot control the situation. The other type blindly accepts whatever comes from America. Managers of this type are well accepted by headquarters, but Tokyo people have to waste a lot of time on ideas that make no sense in the Japanese market. I have seldom seen a Japanese manager who can handle this efficiently and properly, so I believe that having an American manager who mainly handles the business with headquarters can have a good effect on operations in Japan.

How can *gaijin* play the Japanese game?

Throughout this book, a number of different ways have been suggested for outsiders to take advantage of their status, using predictable Japanese behavior patterns to turn potential liabilities into potential assets. Because language and national identity remain key factors distinguishing insiders from outsiders in most situations, for the foreseeable future it will be difficult for *gaijin* to be treated as true insiders with respect to any Japanese reference group. However, being an insider is not the only key to success, and outsiders can play the Japanese game effectively if they develop an intuitive understanding of how the world looks from a salaryman's perspective. Rather than recapping the tips we have sprinkled throughout the book, let us instead suggest what foreigners can expect when they try to win Japanese clients and suggest how Western firms can operate successfully within the system by examining a case study of a successful new product that an American bank we'll call "Eagle" has pioneered in Japan.

Reviewing publicly available information, it became clear to some executives within Eagle that a large number of Japanese companies were facing a difficult situation. In the late 1980s, these *kaisha* wanted to issue a certain type of bond, but the Ministry of Finance wouldn't allow them to float such an instrument in the Japanese market, so they issued the debentures overseas. These bonds were very adversely affected by the drastic fall in Japanese share prices that took place in the early 1990s. By using new financial engineering techniques, Eagle was able to find a way to recover a considerable portion of the value the bonds had lost, without the bank's assuming much risk.[1] This allowed the bank to bring an idea to Japanese corporate finance operations that had never before been aired in Japan, one whose merit could clearly be explained to treasurers and which would allow quite a few Japanese companies to avoid some very large losses. Eagle believed that no Japanese banks could provide the service it was proposing.

Japanese companies will listen to a sensible message

The salaryman who told us this story, "Tatsuo," and other bankers within his firm contacted a variety of companies listed on the Tokyo Stock Exchange to pitch this idea. None of these firms had an existing relationship with Eagle, so the initial contact was made through calls to the person in charge of finance at each potential client. All these contacts were "cold calls"; the bankers didn't know these people at all, and they had to introduce themselves first, because almost nobody in Japan recognizes the name of Eagle. However, they had a slight advantage: salarymen are hesitant to treat any bank indifferently, because for a long time, banks were the only source of financing in Japan. After introducing themselves, the bankers briefly described what they were proposing and asked to make an appointment to discuss the idea further. (Japanese feel much more comfortable talking face to face than they do over the telephone.)

Most of these initial contacts said, "I don't think there is much we can do with your company, and you would be wasting your time to come here," by which they meant they didn't want to waste their own time either. Those who firmly believed that a meeting would be a waste of time invented an amazing array of excuses to avoid making appointments. Some clients simply refused to meet with Tatsuo's colleagues, who found out later that these firms had already chosen another way to solve the problem, so the idea they had been pitched made no sense to them. Most of those called, however, agreed to see the bankers; if what you say makes sense, you can get in the door at a *kaisha*. Had the Eagle executives simply tried to make an appointment out of the blue or tried to push a mediocre idea on clients, they would have gotten nowhere.

No matter how good your proposal is, though, you will never hear customers say, "That is a great idea; we would love to listen to you." A newcomer must bring a good idea to the table just to obtain a hearing, but can expect no more than that. Many businessmen seeking new Japanese clients initiate business relationships only through an introduction from an influential person. Some customers, however, don't feel comfortable with this practice, because such introductions are difficult to handle, fraught as they are with social expectations, and because they aren't necessarily made in the client's interest. So many businessmen, both Japanese and foreign, have used this well-worn tactic that Japanese customers are tiring of it. Certainly a go-between would have helped the Eagle team had one been available, but the bottom line is that, with or without an introduction, you can get to the table only by having a proposal your prospects find worthy of their attention.

Relationships start small

Tatsuo and his colleagues visited all of the companies with whom they had scheduled appointments. At the outset of the meeting, when they introduced the bank, many of the salarymen with whom they were talking said virtually nothing. Some didn't even nod, and the bankers weren't sure whether they were listening at all. However, once the team began presenting its financing idea, the clients became interested and began to ask questions. Eventually, some opened up, talking about the origin of their company, who the president was, and what their current business direction was. The bankers took such progress as an excellent sign that the clients felt comfortable with them, a necessary foundation for a business relationship.

For *gaijin* companies, offering a new product that Japanese suppliers can't provide is a necessary, but insufficient condition for starting a business relationship with a Japanese customer. A good idea is likely to help open lines of communication with a potential customer's middle managers, but winning these salarymen over is not necessarily the key factor in gaining new business, important as it may be. For *kaisha,* starting a new relationship with an unfamiliar company is quite a serious decision. The customer must ask itself whether adding a company will hurt the feelings of other suppliers. For this reason, merger and acquisition work has been a good way for banks to initiate relationships, because an acquisition opportunity is usually a one-time service that other companies can't offer. In such a context, Japanese firms aren't necessarily bound by existing relationships.

Most Japanese managers will hesitate to add a company to a *kaisha's* business circle without a very good reason. In some companies, only the president can decide to start doing business with a new bank. Initial marketing efforts can motivate middle managers to propose to senior executives the idea of doing business with a new company, but such decisions are usually made at high levels. Because middle managers have to sell their bosses on the reliability of Eagle, they need a lot of information. Eagle needed to build institutional trust with potential clients, trust that the clients already shared with the Japanese firms supplying them with financial services. Getting to know each other well is an important starting point for such a journey, but it is just the beginning of a long expedition.

It may surprise some readers that Tatsuo's colleagues chose to approach middle managers first, instead of pursuing contacts at the senior executive level. Initiating high-level discussions can be a useful strategy, but it can cause two problems. One is that some middle managers don't like to be influenced by the power of their seniors. The other is that middle managers might feel their territory has been violated, because ordinary salarymen are responsible for the conduct of day-to-day business. A bank that tried to build ties from the top down might gain entry into a customer's commercial circle but might also find itself getting minimal business because middle managers feel insulted. The best strategy is usually to build up good relationships with middle managers and maintain them until these salarymen rise to senior positions, a process that will take many years. What's really important is institutionalizing the relationship; knowing only people at the working level or only people at the senior level doesn't lead to significant new business. To come up with an idea that a *kaisha* will be interested in buying, a firm needs to establish very good communications with its client's middle managers, who are the only ones with a grasp of business details. To gain a favorable decision, a company must also earn trust from its client's senior managers. Japanese customers will do business with you only if their senior managers trust in your institution, while their middle managers trust in your expertise.

Reversing established decisions is almost impossible

In some cases, companies that Eagle called on told Tatsuo's team that they had already decided how to resolve the problem in question. In such cases, the experienced salarymen representing the American bank realized that their plan would never be adopted, even if a client's middle managers loved it. In a *kaisha,* a middle manager does research, seeks the opinions of senior executives, and formulates plans. He initiates a *ringi-sho,* which moves up toward the top, where it must be approved by as many as ten people before it can be executed.

Once a decision has been made, few middle managers would be willing to restart this process by submitting a new plan. A salaryman who did so would have to persuade all the senior managers who approved the original plan to agree on a new course of action. The downside risk of such an action is palpable; some of these senior managers (who evaluate the salaryman's performance) might well ask why he didn't propose this alternative plan in the first place. Additionally, if the middle manager had persuaded a senior executive to get other senior people behind the original plan, the senior executive might lose face should the decision be reversed.

For both organizational and individual reasons, Japanese are reluctant to reverse decisions that have been approved, so you must carefully pick the right time to make the right proposal to a prospective client. Unfortunately, it is quite difficult for outsiders to know where a firm is in its decision cycle, because Japanese companies characteristically disclose very little about themselves to anyone who isn't already a business partner. To get the kind of information that matters most, a bank has to build up good relationships and maintain constant contact with its customers' middle managers. Timing is everything; the key to winning against Japanese banks and securities houses is bringing an idea to a company just as it is ready to plan its financing needs.

To many businesspeople, the *kaisha's* lack of decision flexibility is a problem, but you can also take advantage of it. As we discussed in chapter 6, most Japanese companies have a medium-term plan that covers the next three to ten years in a fairly vague, conceptual way. If Eagle can get its theme woven into this plan (for example, as a broad statement that "our company has to build a risk management system in order to cope with volatile market conditions''), it has an excellent chance of developing a successful relationship. Of course, such plans are closely held by insiders, so it is difficult to know when the plan is being crafted and what it says, so it may sound impossible for outsiders to influence the process. However, if you carefully calculate how to approach clients, sincerely listen to middle managers when they discuss their problems, and are able to provide them with good ideas, you can go a long way toward swaying insider decisions.

Don't only create opportunities—Solve problems

Economic considerations alone will not prompt a manager to reverse a decision. Few managers have incentives to change things in order to increase profitability, because they will be excused for bad results as long as they do what the firm has done before, in the same manner as before. If, on the other hand, they adopt a new plan and end up with bad results, they can be blamed.

We have already seen that, in a variety of settings, *not losing* is more important to salarymen than winning. The risks of doing something new are usually obvious, whereas the rewards are not clear. There is little point appealing to middle managers' self-interest, because their compensation is not tied directly to economic performance measures. Even in *kaisha* that have adopted performance-based compensation systems, managerial performance is evaluated principally by such measures as cooperativeness, coordination skills, and effectiveness in educating young employees. These are easy, low-risk areas in which a salaryman can improve, so why should he take chances just to improve economic performance? Presentations that hinge on such arguments as ''You can save a lot of money if you buy from us'' or ''This product will make your firm such and such money'' don't appeal to salarymen much, because they won't be blamed for passing up such ideas.

On the other hand, you can get a salaryman's attention by identifying a problem that the *kaisha* needs to fix in order to avoid loss. You can also get his attention if you have fresh information about his competitors. Salarymen who don't know what their *kaisha's* rivals are doing risk getting left behind, which would be embarrassing. This is why being an insider and knowing what is going on within a competitive circle are so valuable.

There are unusual periods during which appeals to profit opportunities can work, because salarymen are motivated to make extra money. For example, from the late 1980s through the early 1990s, many Japanese corporations invested heavily in stocks, real estate, and other financial instruments. During this period, managers sought investment opportunities regardless of risk, because their companies directed them to do so. One of the most common questions that middle managers ask when presented with a proposal is "Who has done this before?" If a *kaisha's* competitor has purchased one of your products, you can create a context in which your proposal will be considered quite seriously.

Superior products and good marketing are crucial

Eagle initially approached ten companies with its idea, and one decided to give it a mandate for action. Given that the team had only two weeks to market the new product, this seemed to be a successful campaign. Only three firms seriously considered the idea, although most of those who heard it said the presentation was good. Predictably, some of the managers to whom Eagle pitched took the idea to Japanese financial institutions, which cobbled together an alternative plan. Although such actions hurt Eagle competitively, the team understood that they occurred because the bank had not yet built up enough trust with its prospective clients. One outstanding product isn't enough to create the necessary trust; a firm has to bring good products to the market consistently to build its reputation.

Without a superior product, you are likely to fail in competition with Japanese suppliers, but good marketing efforts are equally essential. For example, the first time Tatsuo's colleagues met with the firm that eventually adopted its proposal, the manager listening to their pitch asked them if they had worked for a Japanese company, because he felt that their presentation looked like a Japanese one. Some *gaijin* companies actually bring proposals written in English, an excellent way to doom their efforts. Others focus only on the economic benefits of their idea, ignoring the fact that decisions within *kaisha* are at root political. The most successful approach the Eagle salarymen have used is to write an offer in such a way that middle managers can make the best use of it when they write their internal proposals. To do that, a supplier has to know what business model its prospective client follows, so that it can understand what concerns must be addressed by those who promote the supplier's idea inside the client.

Some readers may not think much of an innovation that scores a 10 percent success rate. However, the path to success in Japan proceeds through such confidence-building steps, even though most efforts don't directly result in new business. Foreign companies that take the trouble to understand salarymen and their *kaisha* can penetrate Japanese markets. There are no hard-and-fast rules that can tell you how to play the game, but the Eagle experience suggests the key to winning business is having a good proposal, presenting it first to middle managers, getting the timing right so that it isn't necessary for the client to reverse an existing decision, and building a strong marketing effort around a grasp of the model the customer uses to run his company.

What do salarymen want Westerners to understand?

We asked the fifty salarymen whom we interviewed what they wanted their Western colleagues and friends to understand in order to work more effectively with Japanese people. Instead of closing this book by recapping the four themes we developed in chapter 2 and the six puzzles we took up in chapters 3 through 8, we want to conclude by presenting their suggestions. As you read this last section, imagine that you are in a bar, drinking with a salaryman who is ready to cross the threshold of intimacy we described in chapter 3. Here is what we think your new friend would have to say, once freed to speak candidly and from the heart, when asked what it takes to work closely and well with a salaryman, as customer, supplier, partner, or distributor.

Focus on the language more than the culture

It has been a struggle for us to explain in English how the *kaisha* works. It is an even harder struggle for most salarymen to convey outside the Japanese language the nuances they want to divulge. Although they work hard on their English, Japanese salarymen want their Western colleagues to gain as much fluency as possible with the Japanese language. Many of those we interviewed said that outsiders who do not speak the language will never know what is going on inside a *kaisha*. Our salarymen told us that they didn't feel more trust in outsiders who absorbed a stereotyped view of Japanese culture and behaved as if they understood Japan, because that is not what Japanese expect Westerners to know. It's far more important to understand what salarymen tell you, in their own language.

Show the right attitude

Salarymen don't expect Westerners to display a perfect command of Japanese. What counts more is attitude, how hard one tries to learn the language. Language aside, many salarymen said that Americans need to have a "desirable" (in a Japanese sense) attitude to be accepted in a *kaisha*. In practice, a desirable attitude means giving your best effort *(isshokenmei)* in business, language, or anything else. Unfortunately, many Japanese do not believe that Western workers generally give their best efforts. We don't think it's necessary to prove otherwise by blindly emulating everything the Japanese do, such as working the same hours, doing things that are not assigned, or knowing ten from hearing one. However, you must understand what salarymen mean by a desirable attitude, and you must communicate clearly what you can comply with, what you can't comply with, and why. Salarymen don't expect Westerners to behave exactly like Japanese, but they do demand respect for what the *kaisha* values, and they do value proper process above results.

Manage on a case-by-case basis

Because we have sensitized you to guidelines instead of asking you to memorize rules, we hope we haven't created a recipe for diagnosing Japanese behavior that you will only have to unlearn as you encounter exceptions. In a *kaisha,* there is no universal rule that can be applied in every circumstance, because context governs appropriate behavior. Many of those we interviewed told us that they had a hard time with Western colleagues who insisted on using the same pattern of behavior in different situations. Salarymen try not to blame outsiders for being unable to detect differences in context, but they want Westerners to understand that they apply different models in different settings and do not particularly value consistency when circumstances do not call for it. It will be challenging for anyone not brought up in a *kaisha* to interpret a given context correctly; such a skill takes time to master. However, your Japanese colleagues will be comforted by the knowledge that you are at least careful to think about the context before you interpret what you see.

Be patient

From a Japanese perspective, Westerners, especially Americans, tend to rush to fulfill objectives. Salarymen are tired of hearing what sounds to them like "Just tell me what to do to reach the goal," or "I'm doing this to achieve the goal, so what's wrong with that?" As we've seen in many different settings, in Japan, appropriate behavior counts for more than reaching a goal. A salaryman cannot let others down in order to reach a target. He has to ensure that all insiders are informed before a decision is finalized. Doing business the right way matters much more than achieving results, and most salarymen want their Western colleagues to understand that they have to be patient to let the system work.

Initiate communication with Japanese colleagues

Most Japanese have no appropriate model telling them how to communicate with non-Japanese, so they hesitate to initiate relationships, fearing social embarrassment. Said one salaryman, "Japanese tend to wait, so I want my Western colleagues to communicate with us actively." Another senior manager added, "Japanese may seem silent and indifferent, but it doesn't mean that we don't pay any attention to Western employees or that we don't understand them." A third salaryman told us that many of his peers are also puzzled about the way *kaisha* work, particularly when they lack benchmarks for comparison. He said that he found it useful when Americans asked him about the *kaisha,* though he warned that you have to choose carefully whom you ask such questions. If you take the initiative to start a discussion, you will find that salarymen are more interested in you than you might expect, and you may find that together you can unravel quite a few puzzles.

Say what you really think

Americans in particular are cited by salarymen as people who often don't say what they really think or feel. Of course, Japanese don't reveal their true feelings to outsiders, but they prefer to minimize disclosure instead of dissembling. It seems to many Japanese that Americans say the same thing to everyone, telling outsiders too much and insiders too little. The amount of information is not the distinguishing factor; what matters is differentiating between who should hear *honne* and who should hear nothing.

Tread lightly when others may feel inferior

Salarymen are driven to distraction when they perceive that someone thinks his way of doing things is the best way, indeed the only way, to operate. Said one senior manager, "It is a very difficult job even to understand one thing, because you need to have various perspectives to know what it really looks like." Japanese logic is seldom optimizing logic, and solutions presented as absolutely optimal seem suspect to salarymen. Logical arguments provide only one lens through which one may view things, even if they often lead to solutions that are technically correct. When a salaryman's point of view is not acknowledged as valid and worthy of respect, he feels inferior, and a violently emotional reaction is sure to ensue.

We leave you now with a very simple message: to work with or compete against a *kaisha,* Western firms need *not* try to *be kaisha,* for most of what they try to emulate is an outcome, not an essence. We urge you to question all those who urge Western managers and Western companies to be more like their Japanese counterparts. It seems to us that the *kaisha* has an organizational consistency all its own, so it is not practical to try to build hybrids that have both Japanese and Western characteristics. He who can see inside the *kaisha* and penetrate the enigma of Japanese business behavior, who understands how Japanese companies really function and how salarymen really think, can use his insights as a point of departure. The models that Japanese apply to *gaijin* are very different from the models they apply to themselves, which can be both frustrating and rewarding. We suggest that the road to success starts with understanding and ends with intelligent attempts to put to good use the very differences that separate Japan from the rest of the world.

NOTES

PREFACE

1. In fact, many of the Japanese managers we know who have attended Western business schools believe that one of the most valuable aspects of this experience is the unusual chance it gives them to compare notes with their contemporaries from other Japanese companies.

INTRODUCTION

1. Jonathan Rauch, *The Outnation* (Cambridge, MA: Harvard Business School Press, 1992), 86–87.

2. Ikujiro Nonaka, "Toward Middle-Up-Down Management: Accelerating Information Creation," *Sloan Management Review* (Spring 1988): 9–18.

3. For an extended, penetrating criticism of *nihonjinron*, see Ross Mouer and Yoshio Sugimoto, *Images of Japanese Society* (London: Kegan Paul International, 1986).

4. For a thorough discussion of dualism in society, see David Maybury-Lewis and Uri Almagor, *The Attraction of Opposites* (Ann Arbor: University of Michigan Press, 1990).

5. Takeo Doi, *Omote To Ura* [Front to Back] (Tokyo: Kobundo, 1985).

CHAPTER ONE

1. *Nihon Keizai Shimbun*, 22 March 1996.

CHAPTER TWO

1. Catherine Macklon, *Japanese Boss, English Worker* (Tokyo: Soshisa, 1991), 210–211.

2. S. Kato, J. Kinoshita, M. Maruyama, and S. Takeda, *Nihonbunka no Kakureta Katachi* [Archetypes of Japanese Culture] (Tokyo: Iwanamishoten, 1984), 30.

3. *Nihon Keizai Shimbun*, 8 May 1995.

4. *Nihon Keizai Shimbun*, 15 March 1993.

5. Boye DeMente, *The Kata Factor* (Phoenix, AZ: Phoenix Books, 1992).

6. S. J. Taylor, *Shadows of Rising Sun* (Tokyo: Charles E. Tuttle Company, 1983).

7. Ryoko Tsuneyoshi, *Ningenkeisei no Nichibei Hikaku* [Comparative Study Between Japan and the U.S. on Socialization Process] (Tokyo: Chuokoronsha, 1992), 73–74.

8. Y. Sakisaka, *Haji no Kohzoh* [Structure of Shame] (Tokyo: Kodansha, 1982), 183.

9. Yoshio Suzuki, "Japan Desperately Needs Accountability," *Tokyo Business Today* (May 1995): 23.

10. Although "Hiro" is a composite character, that story was related to us by the salaryman to whom the incident occurred.

11. Sakisaka, *Haji no Kohzoh*, 6.

12. For some more contemporary examples, see Mike Millard, "The Nobility of Failure," *Tokyo Business Today* (December 1995): 10–13.

13. R. Tobe, Y. Teramoto, S. Kamata, Y. Suginoo, T. Murai, and I. Nonaka, *Shippai no honshitu* [The Nature of Mistakes] (Tokyo: Diamondsha, 1984).

14. It is important to avoid the fundamental attribution error here. It would be inappropriate to conclude that failing to adjust in the face of failure is a Japanese trait. The point is to understand how a particular mechanism led to an inability in this case to perceive the need for change. Consider that the French generals of World War I also believed that "offensive spirit" was more important than any other battle element. Their monomaniacal focus on *esprit* led them to order bayonet attacks into the face of machine gun fire long after it became clear that such tactics amounted to pure murder.

CHAPTER THREE

1. Alvin Gouldner, *Wildcat Strike: A Study in Worker-Management Relationships* (New York: Harper & Row, 1954).

2. The English translation of *bu* is somewhat inexact. In large manufacturing concerns, a *bu* is a department or product area, and a division is a much larger grouping, headed by a *honbucho* (vice president). We use the term *division* for *bu* throughout.

3. George Taninecz, "Kazuo Inamori: 'Respect the Divine and Love People,' " *Industry Week* (5 June 1995): 47–51.

4. Not surprisingly, academic research rejects the hypothesis that *keiretsu* firms collude to raise profits. See David Weinstein and Yishay Yafeh, "Japan's Corporate Groups: Collusive or Competitive? An Empirical Investigation of *Keiretsu* Behavior," *Journal of Industrial Economics* (December 1995): 359–375.

5. On the other hand, an American professor who has spent considerable time in Japan notes that Japanese strangers were often very helpful to him and his family. The point is that the salaryman did not *expect* such behavior from strangers in the United States, so it struck him as extremely kind.

6. Kathleen Wiegner, "High Noon for Japan," *Upside* (May 1994): 44–56.

7. Eamonn Fingleton, "Jobs for Life: Why Japan Won't Give Them Up," *Fortune,* 20 March 1995, 119–124.

8. "To Encourage the Others," *The Economist,* 16 January 1993, 66.

9. "Dentsu vs. the Americans," *Advertising Age,* 22 March 1993, 16–20.

10. "Daiwa Reorganizes Banking, Letting Department Heads Go," *Investment Dealers Digest,* 2 November 1992, 6–8.

11. "Layoffs Pile Up as One Plant Cuts Staff, Two Others Close Facilities," *San Diego Union-Tribune,* 4 August 1992, E-1.

12. Dennis Normile, "Universities Yank Welcome Mat for Longtime Foreign Faculty," *Science,* 7 July 1994, 26–27.

13. Coming from Japan, "Frontline," originally aired 19 February 1992.

14. See, for example, Jeremiah Sullivan, *Invasion of the Salarymen: The Japanese Business Presence in America* (Westport, CT: Praeger, 1992).

CHAPTER FOUR

1. Of course, unhappy Japanese employees have few alternative employment options, compared to disgruntled Americans, which may affect these results.

2. For a recent literature review, see Terry L. Besser, "The Commitment of Japanese Workers and U.S. Workers: A Reassessment of the Literature," *American Sociological Review* 58 (1993): 873–881, and a reply by Robert Cole, Arne Kalleberg, and James Lincoln, "Assessing Commitment in the United States and Japan: A Comment on Besser," *American Sociological Review* 58 (1993): 882–885. These are the most careful surveys asking U.S. and Japanese workers the same questions. Surveys of U.S. workers alone in the mid-1990s show comparable results; for example, a June 1995 Gallup survey of 1,026 American workers found that 95 percent claimed to be very loyal or somewhat loyal to their employers, and 70 percent trusted their bosses. See "Gallup Survey Shows American Workers Loyal But Worried About Job Loss," *BNA Daily Labor Report,* 13 June 1995, A8.

3. Cf. William Ouchi, *Theory Z: How American Business Can Meet the Japanese Challenge* (Reading, MA: Addison-Wesley, 1981), or Richard Pascale and Anthony Athos, *The Art of Japanese Management: Applications for American Executives* (New York: Simon & Schuster, 1981).

4. For example, see Robert Whiting, *You Gotta Have Wa* (New York: Macmillan, 1989).

5. Joseph Fucini and Suzy Fucini, *Working for the Japanese: Inside Mazda's American Auto Plant* (New York: Free Press, 1990).

6. Nobuyoshi Namiki, *Tsusansho no Shuen* [End of MITI] (Tokyo: Diamondsha, 1989), 102–113.

7. "Nomura and MOF: After the Scandal, Separate Beds," *Tokyo Business Today* (July 1992): 18–20.

8. "The Humbling of Nomura," *Institutional Investor* (February 1992): 49–53.

9. "Nomura and MOF," 18–20.

10. "Japan: Nexus Goes Sour—Industry Resents Ruling Party's Demands," *Far Eastern Economic Review,* 24 September 1992, 30–32.

11. *Nikkei Sangyo Shimbun,* 26 March 1986.

12. "Biting the Hand," *Far Eastern Economic Review,* 25 March 1993, 70.

13. Fucini and Fucini, *Working for the Japanese.* Another interesting account of life in a Japanese-owned automobile factory in the United States is Laurie Graham, *On the Line at Subaru-Isuzu: The Japanese Model and the American Worker* (Ithaca, NY: ILR Press, 1995). The two books are quite congruent.

CHAPTER FIVE

1. T. Sengoku, M. Kobayashi, A. Takaguchi, and A. Tohyama, *Nihon no Sarariiman* [Japanese Salarymen] (Tokyo: Nihonhososhuppan-kyokai, 1982). Although this survey dates to the early 1980s, we uncovered no evidence that today's workers feel any differently.

2. Western economists have begun to suggest that firms following rational economic models may try to maximize revenues instead of profits, if they are trying to maximize employee welfare, among other things. See Alan Blinder, "A Simple Note on the Japanese Firm," *Journal of the Japanese and International Economies* 7 (1993): 238–255. We argue, in contrast, that Japanese managers are motivated by minimizing embarrassment and loss of status, not by maximizing employee welfare. We also suggest that firms strive to defend market share, not maximize revenues.

3. Recent research suggests that Japanese auto manufacturers do not follow their rivals into foreign countries; see Elizabeth Rose and Kiyohiko Ito, "Competitive Interactions: The International Investment Patterns of Japanese Automobile Manufacturers," University of Southern California Working Paper IB-95-7. Note that this differs from the Sony/Matsushita example discussed in chapter 6. *Yokonarabi* occurred in that case, not because the movie studios that each acquired are American, but because neither could risk the possibility that the other would gain advantage by owning a key source of "software."

4. "Hari-Kari," *Financial World,* 29 September 1992, 24–26.

5. Gale Eisenstodt, "Bull in the Japan Shop," *Forbes,* 31 January 1994, 41–42.

6. Emily Thornton, "Revolution in Japanese Retailing," *Fortune,* 7 February 1994, 143–146.

7. "The Yellow Flag Is Out for Mazda," *Tokyo Business Today* (March 1993): 44–45.

8. "The Luxury Mazda Just Couldn't Afford," *Business Week,* 9 November 1992, 46.

9 "Why the Road Less Traveled Suits Suzuki," *Business Week*, 15 June 1992, 126E.

10. Sengoku et al. *Nihon no Sarariiman*.

11. David E. Weinstein, "Evaluating administrative guidance and cartels in Japan (1957–1988)," *Journal of the Japanese and International Economies* 9 (1995): 200–223.

12. "Bad Boy Makes Good: Tokyo Steel Thrives by Being Different," *Far Eastern Economic Review*, 14 January 1993, 49–50. See also Ryoichi Higurashi, "Nerves of Steel: Aggressive Little Guy Shakes Up Industry," *Tokyo Business Today* (September 1994): 16–18.

CHAPTER SIX

1. Kato et al., *Nihonbunka no Kakureta Katachi*, 34–35.

2. Shuhei Aida, *The Humane Use of Human Ideas* (New York: Pergamon Press, 1983).

3. James Abegglen and George Stalk, *Kaisha, The Japanese Corporation* (New York: Basic Books, 1985).

4. Edwin Locke and Gary Latham, *A Theory of Goal-Setting and Task Performance* (Englewood Cliffs, NJ: Prentice-Hall, 1990).

5. "Shell-Shocked in Japan," *Far Eastern Economic Review*, 4 March 1993, 58.

6. Jathon Sapsford, "Sumitomo Debacle Reflects a Titanic Struggle," *Wall Street Journal*, 17 June 1996, A11.

7. "Money-Go-Round: Two Japanese Firms Suffer from Financial Games," *Far Eastern Economic Review*, 25 June 1992, 48–51.

8. Kiyoshi Yamauchi, "The 'Erosion' of the Japanese-style Management System," *Management Japan* (Spring 1995): 9.

9. However, Columbia Pictures cost Sony several hundred million dollars in losses, due principally to poor, highly-paid American managers whom Sony did not know how to supervise. See Nancy Griffin and Kim Masters, *Hit and Run: How Jon Peters and Peter Guber Took Sony for a Ride in Hollywood* (New York: Simon & Schuster, 1996), for a detailed version of the story.

10. Shota Ushio, "The Future of Hi-Tech: Forecast for the Next Decade," *Tokyo Business* (April 1993): 42–45.

11. Shlomo Maital, "Caution: Oracles at Work," *Across the Board* (June 1993): 52–53.

12. "If at First You Don't Succeed," *Forbes*, 20 January 1992, 68.

13. "Iino Kaiun Adding New Business Lines," *Japan 21st* (June 1992): 30–31.

14. Data from reports by the Japan Robot Association, printed in the *Japan Economic Almanac 1987* (157) and *1995* (103).

15. Geert Hofstede, *Culture's Consequences* (Beverly Hills, CA: Sage, 1980).

16. *Wall Street Journal*, 29 June 1993, A14.

17. Nor are these yen necessarily directed at innovation. See Masao Ogura and Michi Uchida, "Diagnosis, Company Hqs Suffering from 'Japanese Disease,' " *Tokyo Business Today* (June 1994): 36–39, for an estimate that 30 percent of a typical R&D staff is involved in office work only, not research.

18. Steven R. Johnson, "Comparing R&D Strategies of Japanese and U.S. Firms," *Sloan Management Review* (Spring 1984): 25–34. A more recent study suggests that Japanese R&D is still overwhelmingly focused on existing markets and is largely pegged to capital investment in growing industries. See Yasunori Baba, Jun-ichi Kikuchi, and Shunsuke Mori, "Japan's R&D Strategy Reconsidered: Departure from the Manageable Risks," *Technovation* 15, no. 2 (1995): 65–78.

19. Sheridan Tatsuno, *Created in Japan: From Imitators to World-Class Innovators* (Cambridge, MA: Ballinger, 1990).

20. David Hamilton, "Nuclear Ship Shows High-Tech Hubris," *Wall Street Journal,* 11 March 1994, A9.

21. Tom Abate, "The Midnight Hour," *Scientific American* (January 1996): 36–37.

CHAPTER SEVEN

1. Richard Pascale, "Perspectives on Strategy: The Real Story Behind Honda's Success," *California Management Review* (Spring 1984).

2. "Japan's Struggle to be Creative," *Fortune,* 19 April 1993, 129–134.

3. "Hakuyosha Co. Introduces New Corporate Identity," *Japan 21st* (May 1992): 42–43.

4. Michael Hammer and James Champy, *Re-engineering the Corporation* (New York: HarperCollins, 1993).

5. Allan Alter, "Japan Inc. Embraces Change," *Computerworld,* 7 March 1994, 24–25.

6. Fucini and Fucini, *Working for the Japanese,* 94.

7. Clyde Prestowitz, *Trading Places: How We Allowed Japan to Take the Lead* (New York: Basic Books, 1988).

8. Fucini and Fucini, *Working for the Japanese.*

CHAPTER EIGHT

1. Other magazines publish similar polls, whose results are usually similar.

2. Chie Nakane, *Japanese Society* (Berkeley: University of California Press, 1970), 55.

3. Takie Sugie Lebra, *Japanese Patterns of Behavior* (Honolulu: University Press of Hawaii, 1976), 55.

CHAPTER NINE

1. We wish we could be more forthcoming about the nature of this idea, but it still is proprietary to the bank where it originated.

GLOSSARY

bu	Division within a company.
bucho	Head of a division or department, the lowest-level manager with profit-and-loss responsibilities in most organizations.
doki	Year group, which starts out as a cohort of new recruits.
gaijin	Foreigner; person who is ethnically non-Japanese.
hensachi	Number normalized around a mean of 50 percent.
honbucho	*bucho* of the headquarters.
honne	What one really feels, as opposed to *tatemae,* what one is supposed to do.
isshokenmei	Giving one's best effort.
kabuki	Traditional, stylized form of Japanese theater.
kacho	Lowest-level manager who actually supervises employees.
kairan	Document circulated for informational purposes, in contrast to a *ringi-sho,* which is a policy document.
kaisha	Japanese company; usually refers to a large corporation.
kaizen	Process of continuous improvement.
kakaricho	Manager who supervises a role or function, but not a direct supervisor of employees.
Kankyo-seibi	Shaping up the environment, sometimes to influence the outcome of a decision process.
kata	A particular way to do a thing; a recipe or formula for a specific behavior.
Keidanren	Trade association of Japan's largest and most prestigious enterprises.
keiretsu	Industrial grouping of Japanese firms linked by cross-ownership, usually with a few powerful organizations at the center.
kohai	Junior person of a certain reference group who is sometimes mentored by a *senpai* (senior).
kyoku	Division within a government ministry.

madogiwazoku	Literally a "window sitter," an employee who is kept on the payroll but who has nothing to do.
manga	Illustrated novels; comic books popular with all ages.
mikoshi	Decorated wooden box that contains the essence of God, according to Shinto tradition.
nemawashi	System of informal consultation before reaching a consensus decision.
nihonjinron	Literature about Japanese culture and society.
Noh	Traditional form of Japanese theater.
omote	That which appears on the surface; opposite of *ura*.
ringi-sho	Formal policy document that must be initialed (sealed) by every member of a group before it takes effect.
samurai	Member of Japan's ancient military class; warrior.
sarariiman	Salaried employee; white-collar middle manager; salaryman.
Sengoku	Period in Japanese history during the fifteenth and sixteenth centuries in which warring nobles fought to unify Japan; concluded with the emergence of Tokugawa Ieyasu as Japan's first *shogun*, or military ruler (relegating the emperor of Japan to the role of revered figurehead, worshiped as a deity).
senpai	Senior person of a certain reference group (school, company, dormitory), who sometimes mentors a *kohai* (junior).
sensei	Teacher; master in relation to a student.
shacho	President of a *kaisha*.
shikata	Way of doing things; general form of behavior.
shinrai	Reliability, predictability.
Shinto	Japan's indigenous national religion (although many Japanese are of other faiths, predominantly Buddhism).
shinyo	Faith in another person's honorableness, his or her willingness to forgo taking advantage of another.
shitencho	Branch manager.
shukko	Relegation of a company's employee to one of the firm's subsidiaries or closely related companies (*keiretsu* companies).
sogo shosha	Large trading company.
soto	That which is outside; opposite of *uchi*.
tatemae	What one is supposed to do, as opposed to *honne*, what one really feels.
Todai	Tokyo University.
uchi	That which is inside; opposite of *soto*.

ura	That which is hidden beneath the surface; opposite of *omote*.
wa	Harmony, peace, lack of friction.
yakuza	Japanese criminal society.
yokonarabi	Matching a competitor's every move.

INDEX

ABOUT THE AUTHORS

Philip Anderson is an associate professor of business administration at the Amos Tuck School of Business at Dartmouth College, where he teaches courses in strategic management of technology, Internet strategy, and venture capital. He is also a senior editor of *Organization Science Electronic Letters,* a scholarly journal published via the Internet. Professor Anderson was previously an assistant professor of organizational behavior at the Johnson Graduate School of Management at Cornell University, an independent computer consultant, and a U.S. Army officer. Professor Anderson's research focuses on the impact of technological change on industries, the evolution of organizations, and the dynamics of the venture capital industry. He has written for journals such as the *Administrative Science Quarterly, Academy of Management Journal,* and *Research and Technology Management,* and currently serves on the editorial boards of the *Administrative Science Quarterly, Management Science,* and the *Academy of Management Review.*

Noboru Yoshimura is a vice president of the Japan Merchant Banking Group at Bankers Trust. He joined the firm after graduating from the Johnson Graduate School of Management at Cornell University. His main responsibilities include asset restructuring and risk management advisory for Japanese clients. Previously, he worked at Sumitomo Bank, Ltd., where he managed options and traded Japanese government bonds. Mr. Yoshimura wrote "Japanese Corporate Culture" for his senior thesis at International Christian University in Tokyo and the essay "The Cultural Dimensions of Baseball" as an exchange student at Guilford College in North Carolina.